RESEARCH ON ENGLISH LANGUAGE TEACHING AND LEARNING IN THE MIDDLE EAST AND NORTH AFRICA

The tenth volume in the TIRF-Routledge series, this book features research on the teaching and learning of English in the Middle East and North Africa (MENA). With chapters written by TIRF Doctoral Dissertation Grant awardees and internationally known scholars, the volume addresses contemporary challenges and considerations to teaching English in the MENA context. With empirical research covering a wide range of under-studied contexts, this book provides important insights and future directions to improve research and instruction. Offering up-to-date research at the primary, secondary, and post-secondary levels, this volume is an essential resource for language education programs and pre-service teachers.

Kathleen M. Bailey a Professor Emerita at the Middlbury Institute of International Studies at Monterey, USA and a TIRF Trustee.

David Nunan is Professor Emeritus of Applied Linguistics at the University of Hong Kong, President Emeritus and Distinguished Research Professor at Anaheim University in California, and a TIRF Trustee.

GLOBAL RESEARCH ON TEACHING AND LEARNING ENGLISH

Co-published with The International Research Foundation
for English Language Education (TIRF)
Kathleen M. Bailey & Ryan M. Damerow, Series Editors

Bailey & Damerow, Eds.
Teaching and Learning English in the Arabic-Speaking World

Christison, Christian, Duff, & Spada, Eds.
Teaching and Learning English Grammar: Research Findings and Future Directions

Crandall & Christison, Eds.
Teacher Education and Professional Development in TESOL: Global Perspectives

Carrier, Damerow, & Bailey, Eds.
Digital Language Learning and Teaching: Research, Theory, and Practice

Crandall & Bailey, Eds.
Global Perspectives on Language Education Policies

Papageorgiou & Bailey, Eds.
Global Perspectives on Language Assessment: Research, Theory, and Practice

Damerow & Bailey, Eds.
Chinese-Speaking Learners of English: Research, Theory, and Practice

Bailey & Christian, Eds.
Research on Teaching and Learning English in Under-Resourced Contexts

Christison, Crandall, & Christian, Eds.
Research on Integrating Language and Content in Diverse Contexts

For additional information on titles in the Global Research on Teaching and Learning English series visit www.routledge.com/Global-Research-on-Teaching-and-Learning-English/book-series/TIRF

RESEARCH ON ENGLISH LANGUAGE TEACHING AND LEARNING IN THE MIDDLE EAST AND NORTH AFRICA

Edited by Kathleen M. Bailey and David Nunan

A co-publication with The International Research Foundation for English Language Education (TIRF).

Cover image: © Getty Images

First published 2024
by Routledge
605 Third Avenue, New York, NY 10158

and by Routledge
4 Park Square, Milton Park, Abingdon, Oxon OX14 4RN

Routledge is an imprint of the Taylor & Francis Group, an informa business

© 2024 selection and editorial matter, Kathleen M. Bailey and David Nunan; individual chapters, the contributors

The right of Kathleen M. Bailey and David Nunan to be identified as the authors of the editorial material, and of the authors for their individual chapters, has been asserted in accordance with sections 77 and 78 of the Copyright, Designs and Patents Act 1988.

With the exception of Chapter 7, no part of this book may be reprinted or reproduced or utilised in any form or by any electronic, mechanical, or other means, now known or hereafter invented, including photocopying and recording, or in any information storage or retrieval system, without permission in writing from the publishers.

Chapter 7 of this book is available for free in PDF format as Open Access at www.taylorfrancis.com. It has been made available under a Creative Commons Attribution-NonCommercial-NoDerivs (CC BY-NC-ND) 4.0 International license.

Trademark notice: Product or corporate names may be trademarks or registered trademarks, and are used only for identification and explanation without intent to infringe.

ISBN: 978-1-032-32026-7 (hbk)
ISBN: 978-1-032-30490-8 (pbk)
ISBN: 978-1-003-31244-4 (ebk)

DOI: 10.4324/9781003312444

Typeset in Bembo
by Taylor & Francis Books

The Open Access version of Chapter 7 was funded by Fatema Al Rubai'ey.

We are pleased to dedicate this book to three education leaders in the Middle East and North Africa:

Dr. Ali Al-Sharhan, former TIRF Trustee and former Minister of Education, UAE

Professor Mohammed Dahbi, Al Akhawayn University, Morocco

Professor Abdul Gabbar Al Sharafi, Sultan Qaboos University, Oman

Dr. Al-Sharhan is a former TIRF Trustee. He was instrumental in securing the Sheikh Nahayan Fellowships, which were administered by TIRF and resulted in the support of nine young scholars, all of whom contributed to the 2014 TIRF volume, *Teaching and Learning English in the Arabic-speaking World*.

Professor Dahbi and Professor Al Sharafi both reviewed the applications for the Sheikh Nahayan Fellowships. Subsequently, Professor Dahbi provided feedback on the chapters for the volume and Professor Al Sharafi contributed a chapter to that first publication in the TIRF-Routledge series.

We are grateful for these leaders' expertise, their time, and their effort in support of TIRF and of education in the Middle East and North Africa. With this dedication, we wish to honor their many contributions to English language teaching and research.

CONTENTS

List of illustrations x
Foreword xii
Preface xv
Acknowledgments xix
List of contributors xx

1 ELT in the Middle East and North Africa: A survey of the landscape 1
  David Nunan

PART I
Teachers and teaching 21

2 English reading in primary school students in Lebanon 23
  Rana Aridi, Eva Kozma, Sara Kassab, Kara McBride, Mirvat Merhi, and Rajani Shrestha

3 Teaching and assessing speaking in the context of curricular reform: The case of Israel 36
  Orly Haim and Tziona Levi

4 Moroccan teachers' perceptions of EFL instruction in the wake of the COVID-19 pandemic: Lessons learned 49
Adil Bentahar, Mohammed Elmeski, and Mohammed Hassim

5 The communicative orientation of EFL classrooms: The Tunisian context 64
Khaled el Houche

6 Matches and mismatches between Egyptian high school EFL teachers' grammar instruction practices and beliefs 76
Noha Abdelhamied Ibrahim and Muhammad M. M. Abdel Latif

PART II
Identity and affect 89

7 EFL learner identity and L2 pragmatic choices: Evidence from the Omani EFL context 91
Fatema Al-Rubai'ey

8 Culture, motivation, and self-efficacy in the Sudanese EFL context 103
Elham Yahia and Aymen Elsheikh

9 An English language teacher candidate's tensions in the context of Turkey: What does an identity-oriented practicum course offer? 114
Özgehan Uştuk and Bedrettin Yazan

PART III
Academic writing 129

10 Metadiscourse in academic abstracts written by Algerian, Saudi, and native English researchers 131
Tarek Assassi

11 Introducing a curriculum-based tutoring model in the foundation English program at Qatar University 144
Mansoor Al-Surmi, Pakize Uludag, and Mohammad Manasreh

12 Teaching academic writing in the online environment: Challenges and benefits in the context of higher education in the UAE 158
Doaa Hamam and Christine Coombe

PART IV
Policy 171

13 Linguistic visibility in the University of Bahrain's linguistic landscape 173
Yasser Ahmed Gomaa

14 Factors influencing Iranian language education policy: An empirical investigation 185
Mahdi Dahmardeh and David Nunan

15 Language preferences in the Hashemite Kingdom of Jordan: An exploratory study 197
Fatima Esseili

16 Factors contributing to Gaza pre-service teachers' poor proficiency in English Language 209
Enas Abdullah Rajab Hammad

Index *222*

ILLUSTRATIONS

Figures

0.1	TIRF grantees who have authored a chapter in the TIRF-Routledge "Global Research" Series	xvii
4.1	Teachers' training in remote instruction and preferred instructional modes	55
4.2	Teachers' self-reported ICT proficiency and preferred instructional modes	56
4.3	PD in remote instruction and student learning online	56
4.4	Teachers' self-reported ICT proficiency and the frequency of their online instructional adjustments compared to face-to-face instruction	57
4.5	Teachers' perceptions of resources available for online instruction	58
4.6	Ranking of the online tools that teachers continued to use in face-to-face instruction	59
9.1	Nihat's digital collage	120
13.1	Examples of UoB campus signs	178
13.2	Examples of nonverbal elements in UoB campus signage	179
13.3	Examples of top-down UoB campus signage	180
13.4	Examples of bottom-up UoB campus signage	181

Tables

2.1	Students scoring at or below grade-level prerequisite cut-offs for the letter name task and letter sound task	30
2.2	Students scoring at or below grade-level prerequisite cut-offs for the sight word task and the reading comprehension tasks	31
2.3	Most common barriers to implementing QITABI 2 components in class	32
3.1	The development of the construct of LAL	38
3.2	EFL teachers' LAL: results of t-tests	41
3.3	Relationships between teachers' dimensions of LAL and their reported practices	43
4.1	Proficiency in ICT by Age Group (n = 356)	53
4.2	Proficiency in ICT by Gender (n = 356)	54
5.1	Frequency of teachers' responses to items about teaching approaches	68
5.2	Frequency of teachers' responses to items about roles	69
5.3	Percentages of time for four patterns of interaction	71
6.1	Matches and mismatches between the teachers' grammar instruction practices and beliefs	86
10.1	Hyland's taxonomy of metadiscoursal devices	133
10.2	The characteristics of the compiled corpus	136
10.3	The frequencies of interactive and interactional metadiscourse devices in abstracts written by Algerian scholars	137
10.4	The frequencies of interactive and interactional metadiscourse devices in abstracts written by Saudi scholars	138
10.5	Frequencies of interactive and interactional metadiscourse devices in abstracts written by native scholars	138
10.6	Metadiscourse markers in native (N), Saudi (S), and Algerian (A) abstracts	139
11.1	Students' stage ranking by tutoring service type	150
11.2	Students' writing aspect ranking by tutoring service type	151
11.3	Students' tutoring expectations by tutoring service type	153
13.1	Participants' perspectives on the value of languages used on campus	182
14.1	Key stages of the Iranian Educational System	186
15.1	Jordanians' language preferences by interlocutor	203
15.2	Percentages of participants' language preference use by activity/topic	204

FOREWORD

A number of years ago, I started my English language education career, teaching general English in a university continuing education program for Egyptian adults. My students back then came from all walks of life, ranging from university students to adults working in different professions. Their dream was to able to speak and write English like native speakers from the United States and the United Kingdom. Their motivation was to be able to travel or to find good work opportunities in international companies and organizations.

Since that time, the status of English in the world and in the Middle East and North African (MENA) region has changed, and the native speaker construct has diminished over the years. English is now viewed as a global lingua franca, driven mainly by education systems worldwide, including those in the MENA countries. All the countries in the region promote bilingualism, where the priority is the national language, with the teaching of English also viewed as a priority. In these countries, English is typically taught as the first foreign language starting in primary schools.

What makes this book so different from the many resources that are now available in the TESOL field is the number and breadth of research studies conducted across the MENA region. With twenty (20) countries in the MENA region, this book encompasses 70% of the region including articles from fourteen (14) different countries: Algeria, Bahrain, Egypt, Iran, Israel, Jordan, Lebanon, Morocco, Oman, Palestine, Qatar, Sudan, Tunisia, and the United Arab Emirates. The volume offers an up-to-date perspective on the state of English language education across the countries in the region. making it a valuable contribution to the field. The research reports within the book cover a range of topics, insights, and experiences, thus providing educators, researchers, and policymakers with a valuable resource for understanding the current linguistic landscape in the region. Here I will comment briefly on the diverse topics covered in this volume.

The chapter from Algeria concludes that although all Arab countries share a common language, Arabic, when it comes to writing and publishing applied linguistic research articles in English, Saudi, and Algerian researchers differ in their use of rhetorical conventions in persuasion. Moving on to the chapter based in Bahrain, the author investigates the public linguistic landscape of the University of Bahrain and concludes that while Arabic dominates the signs on campus, English does have substantial visibility.

In the chapter based on research in Egypt, the authors conclude that the grammar-translation and exam-driven approach to teaching English remains prevalent in public schools. The chapter from Israel reports on the introduction of a new nationwide, computerized English language proficiency test in Israeli grade 12 high schools. This new test motivated teachers to focus on the teaching of speaking skills in their classes.

The chapter from Iran examines the factors that influence the country's language education policy. Interestingly, Iranian school students are required to study both Arabic (viewed as the language of the Quran) and English, alongside their mother tongue, Farsi, starting from grade 6 until grade 12. The teaching of English in Iranian public schools follows a traditional approach, driven by a university entry exam that consists of discrete test items assessing grammar and vocabulary. The chapter on language preferences in Jordan reveals that Jordanians hold very positive attitudes towards Arabic, their mother tongue, but less positive attitudes towards Arabizi, the mixing of Arabic and English.

Two chapters address the impact of COVID-19. In Lebanon, young learners in grades 1–4 experienced learning loss in reading skills and overall language development in either their L1 or L2 or both. In Morocco, school teachers initially reported that teaching online was an overall negative experience. When they went back to face-to-face instruction, however, they acknowledged they had gained new skills in technology that could be applied in their classes.

The chapter from Oman focuses on university English language learners and their perception that using Arabic pragmatic norms while communicating in English reflects their culture and identity. They do not view that use as a reflection of their pragmatic competence or incompetence in English. University students are also the focus of the chapter from Palestine, which addresses the challenges faced by teachers and students in the Gaza University pre-service teachers' preparation program. The challenges include large classes and the use of traditional grammar-translation teaching methods, similar to the results of the study in Egypt on teaching English in public schools.

The chapter from Qatar focuses on the implementation of an academic writing tutorial center within the English Department of the Foundation Program at Qatar University. English students found the new program to be more effective than that offered at a central university writing center. The qualitative study conducted in Sudan explores the interrelationships among self-efficacy, motivation, and culture of five college students studying English and translation. The findings indicate that their self-efficacy, culture, and real-life experiences influenced their motivation to learn English.

The chapter from Tunisia highlights the discrepancy between public school teachers' self-reported beliefs about using communicative language teaching methods in their classes and their actual practice of traditional teacher-centered classroom approaches. The chapter from the United Arab Emirates investigates the challenges and benefits of online academic writing classes during the pandemic, as experienced by teachers in a university in the UAE. Initially, numerous challenges were reported; however, teachers discovered the advantages of online teaching and now embrace blended and hybrid methods. The authors note that with the advent of ChatGPT, more research is needed on integrating AI (artificial intelligence) into writing instruction, along with the development of robust policies to manage plagiarism and ethical considerations in AI-mediated academic writing.

These chapters provide a view of the diversity of educational concerns being studied in the MENA region. The volume should be of interest to a wide range of readers, including English teachers, teachers in training, teacher educators, researchers, and policymakers. In closing, I want to extend my deepest appreciation to the editors, who are my TESOL role models and whose books and publications have guided and inspired me throughout my career. I thank them and the contributors for putting together this insightful collection of research articles. This book offers a wealth of knowledge and shared experiences for those of us who are interested and invested in ensuring the effectiveness of English language teaching and learning in the MENA region.

Deena Boraie
Professor of Practice, Education
Provost of The Knowledge Hub Universities, Cairo, Egypt

PREFACE

It was in March 2013 that we first met with Naomi Silverman, who was a Senior Editor at Routledge at the time. We wanted to share with her an idea for a book consisting of research reports on projects funded by TIRF. Naomi liked the idea, but she took it much further than we had expected. In fact, she suggested a series of books based on TIRF-sponsored research. As we left that meeting, we felt like we had intended to ask her for a date but ended up getting engaged! That was the beginning of the series, "Global Research on Teaching and Learning English," co-published by TIRF and Routledge.

That first volume in the series was entitled *Teaching and Learning English in the Arabic-speaking World*. Published in 2014, it consisted of ten chapters reporting on original empirical studies, nine of which were written by the recipients of the Sheikh Nahayan Fellowships, adjudicated by TIRF. Those chapters provided information about research conducted in Egypt, Lebanon, Oman, Palestine, Qatar, Saudi Arabia, and the United Arab Emirates. We co-authored the introductory chapter, while the summary and concluding observations were written by our colleague, Dick Tucker, one of the founding Trustees of TIRF.

Now, after a decade of work on the series, we are pleased to provide the preface for the tenth volume, in which we focus once more on English language learning and teaching in the region. In fact, four of the authors from that first book in the series (Muhammad Abdel Latif, Mansoor Al-Surmi, Fatima Esseili, and Enas Hammad) have supported TIRF again with their time and their scholarship by contributing chapters to this book. We are grateful to them and to all the other authors in the present volume for their commitment and their hard work. We particularly appreciate their contributions because all the authors and editors in the series agree to forgo all royalties or honoraria, so that any profits from the book sales can be channeled to supporting TIRF's ongoing programs.

In recent years, several edited volumes have focused on important developments in the fields of language teaching and learning in the Middle East and North Africa. Several of these have been published by TESOL Arabia, which produces an annual collection of its conference proceedings, covering a range of teaching and research issues in the area. TESOL Arabia has also produced 24 issues of the journal, *Perspectives*.

In 2017, *English Language Education Policy in the Middle East and North Africa* (Kirkpatrick, 2017) was published by Springer. It consists of an introduction and 15 chapters, covering important language policy issues in Bahrain, Egypt, Iran, Israel, Kuwait, Lybia, Morocco, Oman, Palestine, Qatar, Saudi Arabia, Syria, Tunisia, Turkey, and the UAE.

The volume entitled *Innovation in Language Teaching and Learning: The Case of the Middle East and North Africa* (Reinders, Coombe, Littlejohn, & Tafazoli, 2019) was published by Palgrave MacMillan. The chapters covered several key innovations in the region, including task-based learning and teaching, reading for science, online teacher education, language learners' telecollaboration, and creating culturally appropriate English teaching materials.

More recently, two volumes have focused on the important issue of identity as it relates to language learning, teaching, and use in the region. *Linguistics Identities in the Arab Gulf States: Waves of Change* (Hopkyns & Zoghbor, 2022) and *Language and Identity in the Arab World* (Al Rashdi & Mehta, 2022) were both published by Routledge.

We are pleased to add the current volume to the collection of published scholarship produced in the Middle East and North Africa. Bringing this book to fruition has involved many challenges due to the pandemic. Some of the TIRF Doctoral Dissertation Grant recipients we originally approached were unable to contribute chapters, due to serious health challenges experienced by them and their family members. Some potential authors were facing closure of their schools and programs, while others' research projects had been cancelled because of COVID. For these reasons, we are particularly happy to have met (digitally speaking) several new colleagues, who worked to meet our deadlines and incorporate our feedback. We are delighted to welcome them as part of the TIRF family of teachers and researchers.

The series, now spanning a full decade, is strategically important to TIRF and its trustees, as its purpose goes beyond just a publishing activity. It allows us to draw attention to high-quality research projects, leverage partnerships and funding to support research, mentor the next generation of scholars in English language education, and add to the knowledge base of research in our field – all while working toward our mission of improving individuals' lives through language acquisition. Figure 0.1 shows stars placed in the hometowns of each of the TIRF grantees to date, who have authored a paper in at least one of the TIRF-Routledge "Global Research" series, including those in this volume. You can imagine the good work being done globally by our grantees and the many people they have influenced.

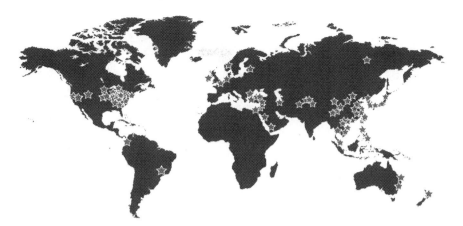

FIGURE 0.1 TIRF grantees who have authored a chapter in the TIRF-Routledge "Global Research" Series
Source: Designed by Rawpixel.com / Freepik.

The particular regional focus of the current volume was decided upon for several reasons. First, we sought to give educators a voice and a platform to highlight particular issues in their individual contexts in the MENA region. There continues to be a need for research on English language education there, and TIRF wants to do its part to address this issue. Second, we have adopted regional foci in previous volumes in the "Global Research" series in the past – Arabic-speaking nations (as mentioned above) and in China, another fascinating, rich context for researching English language teaching and learning. We aspire to continue to leverage this Series to further address English language education in particular countries and regions. Finally, the international focus of TIRF's work – addressing language education in locations beyond the borders of native English-speaking countries – is at the core of TIRF's mission.

It is our hope that this book will add to the growing body of research on English language teaching and learning being conducted in the Middle East and North Africa. After all, for newcomers to TIRF, the "R" in our acronym stands for "research." All programmatic and service-oriented activities we undertake as an organization are underpinned by research.

Kathleen M. Bailey, Monterey, California
Ryan M. Damerow, Interlochen, Michigan
May, 2023

References

Al Rashdi, F., & Mehta, S. R. (Eds.). (2022). *Language and identity in the Arab world*. Routledge.

Hopkyns, S., & Zoghbor, W. (Eds.). (2022). *Linguistic identities in the Arab Gulf states: Waves of change.* Routledge.

Kirkpatrick, R. (Ed.). (2017). *English language education policy in the Middle East and North Africa.* Springer International.

Reinders, H., Coombe, C., Littlejohn, A., & Tafazoli, D. (Eds.). (2019). *Innovation in language learning and teaching: The case of the Middle East and North Africa.* Springer International Publishing.

ACKNOWLEDGMENTS

As the editors of this volume, we wish to note the contributions of two particular individuals and a group of people who have made this volume possible.

First, we wish to acknowledge the tireless efforts and professionalism of our editorial assistant and project manager, Ms. Lydia Emory. She managed communications with the authors, solicited all the information we required from them, checked and corrected all the reference lists and intext citations, and generally kept us on track – all with clarity and good judgment. We wish her every success in her new career as a language teacher.

Second, we are very grateful to Mr. Ryan Damerow, who is the Chief Operating Officer of TIRF and also the co-series editor of the books in the TIRF-Routledge co-published series, "Global Research on Teaching and Learning English." He has been supportive, encouraging, and readily available whenever we needed his input during the year-and-a-half-long process of producing the manuscript for this volume.

Finally, we want to publicly recognize the sustained efforts and generous collegiality of the chapter authors, many of whom had never worked with either of us and some of whom were endeavoring to publish their research for the first time. These writers graciously accepted our feedback, responded to our questions, and met our deadlines, in spite of all the pressures they were experiencing due to COVID and the struggles of trying to revitalize their own educational contexts under post-pandemic conditions.

David Nunan and Kathleen Bailey, Editors

CONTRIBUTORS

Noha Abdelhamied Ibrahim is currently completing her PhD in TESOL at the Faculty of Graduate Studies of Education, Cairo University, Egypt. She works as a high school teacher in Egypt. Her research interests include language teacher education, English grammar instruction, and project-based language learning.

Muhammad M. M. Abdel Latif is an associate professor of TESOL at the Faculty of Graduate Studies of Education, Cairo University, Egypt. His research interests include L2 writing and teacher education. He received the 2008 Sheikh Nahayan Doctoral Dissertation Fellowship granted by TIRF. Muhammad has published research papers in more than 15 internationally ranked journals

Fatema Al-Rubai'ey holds a PhD in Applied Linguistics in the area of Second Language Pragmatics from the University of York, Canada. She is a full-time Assistant Professor at the Department of English Language and Literature at Sultan Qaboos University, Oman. Her research interests include pragmatics, second language pragmatics, culture, identity, and discourse analysis.

Mansoor Al-Surmi has a PhD in Applied Linguistics and is a published author in *TESOL Quarterly* and *System*. He is currently an English lecturer at Qatar University. He received a Shaikh Nahayan Doctoral Fellowship, offered by TIRF, in 2010. His research interests include investigating theoretical and practical issues in the areas of corpus linguistics, academic writing, and second language acquisition.

Rana Aridi is the English Language Coordinator at USAID-funded QITABI 2, Lebanon. Her research interests include language assessment and differentiated instruction for English as a second language. She is a very appreciated poet among literary groups. In 2021, her poem "Surrender" was selected from 300 submissions by Columbia University TC committee at the closing ceremony in the Writing Summer Institute.

Tarek Assassi is a senior lecturer of applied linguistics and a pedagogical coordinator at Biskra University, Algeria. He is also a certified assessor of aviation English using EALTS UK. His research interests are discourse analysis, ESP course design, and language assessment.

Kathleen M. Bailey is a Professor Emerita of Applied Linguistics at the Middlebury Institute of International Studies at Monterey. She served as the president of TESOL and the American Association for Applied Linguistics. From 2009 to 2022 she was the President of TIRF. Her research interests include language assessment, teacher education, diary studies, and leadership.

Adil Bentahar is an Assistant Professor of ESL at the English Language Institute with a joint appointment with the School of Education at the University of Delaware. His research interests include L2 reading, teacher professional development, and international student experience. Dr. Bentahar is the Chair-elect for TESOL's Social Responsibility Interest Section.

Christine Coombe, PhD in Foreign/Second Language Education, the Ohio State University, is currently an Associate Professor at the Higher Colleges of Technology, Dubai Men's College in the UAE. She served as President of the TESOL International Association and is a recipient of the James E. Alatis Award. Her research interests include language testing/assessment, teacher effectiveness, leadership, teacher professionalism and research methods.

Mahdi Dahmardeh is a Professor of Applied Linguistics at the University of Tehran. In 2017, he was awarded the prestigious ISEF fellowship award by the Korea Foundation for Advanced Studies. His interest particularly lies in the role of culture, gender, and politics in teaching foreign languages as well as curriculum development along with research on coursebooks/textbooks for foreign language teaching.

Khaled el Houche is a doctoral student and senior English language teacher at the Higher Institute of Arts & Crafts of Tataouine at the University of Gabes, Tunisia. His research interests include English as foreign language pedagogies, task-based language teaching, teacher education, and written corrective feedback. Currently, he is a teacher-trainer of pre-service primary school teachers.

Mohammed Elmeski is a Senior Education Advisor at the Nordic Center for Conflict Transformation in Rabat, Morocco. He served as the Co-Chair of the International Congress for School Effectiveness and Improvement in 2020. He earned his PhD in Comparative International Development Education from the University of Minnesota. His research interests include teacher leadership, social emotional learning, and inclusive education.

Aymen Elsheikh is an Instructional Assistant Professor of English at Texas A&M university at Qatar. He has a PhD in Literacy, Culture, and Language Education from Indiana University. His research interests include language teacher associations, English as an international language, and multilingualism in EMI contexts, among others. He is the co-founder and past president of Africa ELTA (English language teachers association).

Fatima Esseili is Associate Professor of English and Director of the English Language Institute at the University of Colorado Denver. She teaches various graduate and undergraduate courses in Applied linguistics. Her research interests include world Englishes, second language writing, and inter-cultural communication.

Yasser Ahmed Gomaa is an Associate Professor of Linguistics at Assiut University, Egypt. His research interests lie in the areas of language as a sociolinguistic phenomenon, cross-cultural pragmatics, genre analysis, linguistic landscape, discourse analysis, and English/Arabic translation. He has long experience in teaching English language and linguistics courses in Egypt, Saudi Arabia, and the Kingdom of Bahrain.

Orly Haim works as a pedagogical advisor at Beit Berl College where she also serves as the Vice Dean of the faculty of education. Her research areas include teacher cognition, additional (i.e., second, third, etc.) language acquisition, multilingual education, and language policy. Orly serves as the chair of the advisory committee to the Israeli national inspector of English Language Education.

Doaa Hamam is a holder of a PhD in Education-TESOL from the British University in Dubai; she is currently a lecturer at the Higher Colleges of Technology, UAE. Her main research interests are teaching and learning in higher education, teaching with technology, academic writing, linguistics, and teacher education.

Enas Abdullah Rajab Hammad is an associate professor of curriculum and instruction of English at Al-Aqsa University, Palestine. She has served as a teacher of English in United Nations Relief and Works Agency and governmental schools, Al-Quds Open University, and Al-Aqsa University for 24 years. Her research interests include English as a foreign language teaching and learning strategies.

Mohammed Hassim is a teacher trainer, ELT supervisor, and textbook writer. He served as an English Language Teaching inspector with the Moroccan ministry of education. He also served as a president of Moroccan Association of Teachers of English and participated as an editor of its publications. His fields of interest include teacher training, materials development, and ICT in education.

Sara Kassab is an English content developer at QITABI 2-World Learning. She's also working on producing OERs for Quality Holistic Learning. She is writing her master's in science education thesis, about translanguaging and conceptual change in genetics classrooms, at the American University of Beirut. Sara worked with Teach for Lebanon as a teacher and Educational Mentor.

Eva Kozma is the Senior Literacy Technical Director at the USAID-funded QITABI 2 project in Lebanon. Her research interests focus on assessment, teachers' best practices in Grades 1–6 differentiated instruction in reading and writing programs in three languages: English, Arabic, and French. She is an award-winning children's books author and loves to read to children.

Tziona Levi is the Director of the Department of Languages at Israel's Ministry-of-Education. Her interests include applying dynamic assessment (DA) and assessment-for-learning (AfL) to (EFL) learning contexts. She established 68 Teacher Learning Communities across Israel to improve professional development and English oral proficiency in schools. She led the rewriting of the Israeli EFL curriculum to align with the CEFR and oversaw its implementation.

Mohammad Manasreh has a PhD in Applied Linguistics from the University of Warwick with more than 20 years of TESOL teaching, training, and management experience. His research interests include general education, TESOL leadership, identity, and teacher training.

Kara McBride is a Senior Education Specialist at World Learning and served as technical coordinator and English lead for headquarters on the USAID-funded QITABI 2 project in Lebanon. Previously, she served on the Spanish faculty of Saint Louis University for eight years. Her research interests include teacher education and technology-enhanced learning. She received a TIRF Doctoral Dissertation Grant in 2005.

Mirvat Merhi is Monitoring, Evaluation, Learning, and Research Director at the USAID-funded QITABI 2 project in Lebanon. She holds a MSc. in Population Studies and has built her experience in research and data analysis through working at American University of Beirut, UNESCWA, UNDP, EDC, and World Learning. Her research interest is in population development, education, health, social emotional learning, and livelihood.

David Nunan is Professor Emeritus of Applied Linguistics at the University of Hong Kong, President Emeritus and Distinguished Research Professor at Anaheim University in California, and a TIRF Trustee. He has published over 100 books and articles on curriculum development, research methods, teacher education, and technology. Dr. Nunan served as TESOL President from 1999 to 2000. In 2005, he was named one of the 50 most influential Australians internationally.

Rajani Shrestha is an education and research professional with 15 years' experience leading projects in conflict and crisis contexts. Currently, she is a Senior Research Analyst with RTI International. From 2013–2022, she led the Lebanon education programming for World Learning Inc. and was the Project Director for QITABI 2. Her research interests include inclusive education, teacher motivation, and systems reform.

Pakize Uludag is the Manager of Global Learning programs at Seneca Polytechnic in Toronto, Canada. She has a PhD in Applied Linguistics from Concordia University. Her research interests include language assessment, academic writing, and corpus linguistics.

Özgehan Uştuk is a research assistant and a teacher educator at Balikesir University, Turkey. His research interests include drama in language education, practitioner inquiry, language teacher learning, identity, and emotions. He serves on the Research Professional Council (Chair, 2022–2023) of the TESOL International Association.

Elham Yahia is an Adjunct Assistant Professor of English at the City University of New York. She has a PhD in Education and Literacy Studies from St. John's University in New York, USA. Her research interests include the areas of students' motivation, language education, education equity and inequality, gender studies, community development, higher education, diversity and inclusion, and leadership and instructions, among others.

Bedrettin Yazan is an associate professor in the Department of Bicultural-Bilingual Studies at the University of Texas at San Antonio. His research focuses on language teacher learning and identity, collaboration between ESL and content teachers, language policy and planning, and world Englishes. He was awarded a TIRF Doctoral Dissertation Grant in 2013.

1
ELT IN THE MIDDLE EAST AND NORTH AFRICA

A survey of the landscape

David Nunan

The role of editor hangs low on the academic totem pole. The institutions I've worked in during a career spanning more than half a century never considered the role as carrying any credit whatsoever. The attitude seemed to be, if you can, write; if you can't, edit! During our professional careers, Kathi Bailey and I have attempted to make a decent fist of both. As editors, we see ourselves, not as gatekeepers, but as facilitators and guides and, for early career academics, as mentors. In putting this volume together, we worked *with* our contributors, advising, mentoring, and helping them shape their chapters into a volume that represents diverse interests and perspectives within a framework that provides overall coherence. The framework, or chapter template, also provides unity to the series as a whole.

My own engagement with the Middle East and North Africa (MENA – I'll use the acronym in the rest of this chapter) goes back many years. In the 1970s, while I was a graduate student in the UK, I visited Morocco, Egypt, and Turkey. These trips were for my own edification. In subsequent years, I traveled to most of the countries featured in this volume and numerous others as well. In the late 1980s to early 1990s, I served for six years as the ELT curriculum consultant and advisor to the Minister for Education in the Sultanate of Oman. My brief was to evaluate the national ELT curriculum and make recommendations for its renewal.

Despite the acronym, MENA is anything but a monolithic entity. It is as diverse as that landmass to the north-west known as Europe (Bowen, 2022). The diversity is reflected in the religions that are observed (Suni, Shia, Judaism, Christianity, etc.); the demographics (expatriates are in the majority in the United Arab Emirates and in some countries, locals constitute only about 10% of the population); and the languages that are spoken (Arabic, Persian, English, Hebrew, languages of the subcontinent, etc.). Even in countries where Arabic is the dominant language, there is considerable diversity of dialects. (An Egyptian

DOI: 10.4324/9781003312444-1

scholar of linguistics admitted to me that when visiting the UAE, he had difficulty comprehending speakers of Gulf Arabic.) The diversity of issues represented in this volume points to the complexity of language learning in the MENA region.

As you can see, we have divided the contributions to the volume into four sections. The allocation of chapters to categories is arbitrary to a degree, because of the considerable overlap in perspectives and themes. We seem incapable of getting over the 19th-Century passion for taxonomizing everything that moves, and many things that don't. Unlike plants, butterflies, and rocks, human behavior belongs simultaneously to more than one box and a Venn diagram would be a better way of representing the central concerns of these chapters. Nevertheless, I will address the four sections in sequence before making some concluding comments.

Section I: Teachers and teaching

Lebanon might be one of the smaller countries in the Middle East, but its diminutive size has not enabled its citizens to get on with their lives untouched by turmoil. Its neighbors and the homegrown militant Hezbollah have seen to that. Once civil war broke out in Syria, hundreds of thousands of refugees poured across the long border shared by both countries. The influx of refugees, followed by the COVID pandemic and a devastating explosion in Beirut in 2020, severely disrupted the education system.

The opening chapter of Part I by Aridi, Kozma, Kassab, McBride, Merhi, and Shrestha, explains that these factors led to the public school system being overwhelmed. In their study, these authors describe an innovative reading program, *Quality Instruction Towards Access and Basic Education Improvement* 2 (QITABI 2), which was designed to support initial literacy instruction in Arabic, English, and French. The study sought to identify the English reading levels of first- to sixth-grade public school students, to identify those aspects of the program that were implemented, and to find out what factors led teachers to incorporate or reject components of the approach. Developing L2 literacy skills (either English or French) at an early age is important as science and math are introduced in the second language in first grade, and the pupils' L2 reading level "has an impact on their learning outcomes across multiple subjects" (p. 24). This practice of teaching science and math in English is not uncommon in MENA (Jordan is another country that comes to mind), and may have something to do with the Arabic lexicon in certain subjects, although this seems unlikely.

Several noteworthy aspects of the program were the focus on scaffolded learning, leading learners from teacher directed to independent practice, differentiated instruction for individual and small groups, and the incorporation of a social and emotional learning (SEL) component. A SEL component is increasingly recognized as an important element in language education (Mercer, 2021; Mercer et al., 2018).

The results indicated that students' reading levels were well below grade level pre-requisites. This was hardly surprising given the amount of class time that had been lost due to COVID-19. As already mentioned, ability to perform in science and math would also be affected, given the policy that these subjects be taught in the L2. More encouraging was the observation that the SEL activities could be integrated into all school activities, and that holistic teacher training in SEL enhanced teacher wellbeing and had a positive impact on their ability to perform.

Curriculum innovation was also the motivation for the Israeli study. It was stimulated by the introduction of a computerized English proficiency test that focused on speaking and was administered at the end of year 12. The study focused on teachers' language assessment literacy (LAL) and the relationship between their LAL and their pedagogical practices. A total of 432 EFL teachers responded to an online questionnaire. Of these, 27% were primary school teachers, and 71% taught at the secondary level. Responses were analyzed using exploratory and confirmatory factor analysis. As I mentioned above, a large number of methods for the collection, analysis, and interpretation of data featured in the studies reported here, with the majority on the side of qualitative/naturalistic research. A mixed-methods research design, in which qualitative and quantitative data are used to address the research questions, was also common. While the researchers who carried out this particular study collected both quantitative and qualitative data, only the quantitative data were used for this report. This is often the case in numerous mixed-method studies, the reason given being word length limitations. Several studies in this volume also reported descriptive statistics (frequencies, percentages, and standard deviations). Of the 15 studies, the project in Israel was one of the few to use inferential statistics, so called because they are used to make generalizations from samples to populations. (In this brief introduction, there's no space to describe the logic of inferential statistics. For a detailed account, see Nunan and Bailey, 2009.)

The two statistical tools used in the study were factor analysis and t-tests. Factor analysis is a sophisticated version of correlation. Simple correlation indicates the strength of association between two variables. Factor analysis can identify multiple "clusters" of correlations in a set of data. In this study, it was used to identify which responses on the LAL questionnaire clustered together. Results identified three clusters, to which the researchers assigned to following labels, or dimensions: teaching and learning assessment cycle, assessment methodology for speaking, and the impact of assessment. While correlation indicates an association, the t-test indicates the direction of the association, that is, whether the independent variable (in this case, teacher level: primary/secondary) caused observed differences in the dependent variable (strength of endorsement of the LAL dimensions). The results indicated that, while both primary and secondary teachers endorsed the dimensions, the secondary teachers' strength of endorsement was significantly higher than that of the primary group. The researchers conclude that the findings "resonate with the qualitative data suggesting that secondary school teachers tended to view the aspect of assessing speaking to be vital for their instructional practices, as compared with primary school teachers, who focused more on classroom activities" (p. 41). This interpretation makes sense, as secondary teachers are more acutely aware of the speaking test their students will undergo in year 12.

Many readers will find research question 3 on the relationship between language awareness literacy (i.e., the teachers' theoretical knowledge) and their teaching practices particularly interesting. I certainly did: It's arguably the central of the three questions. The results indicated a close relationship between the three dimensions of LAL and their reported practices. This finding is consistent with the literature. (See, for example, the work of Simon Borg, 2003, a key researcher into language teacher cognition.) That said, I should point out that self-reports remain controversial in the field of cognitive psychology.

Perhaps the most valuable contribution of this chapter is methodological rather than substantive for researchers working within a positivist paradigm. This is the instrument developed for the study. All indications are that it is a valid and reliable tool for measuring teachers' language assessment literacy.

The Moroccan study coincided neatly with the outbreak of COVID-19. Not surprisingly, references to COVID are a motif through the collection, occurring no fewer than 40 times. The only surprise is that its appearance isn't more prevalent. However, the only chapter featuring the term in its title is the one from Morocco. In my introduction, I mentioned that my first visit was in the early 1970s. In those days, I was on the "Hippy Trail": Unless you could afford to fly (which counted me out), entry was by ferry from southern Spain, past the majestic Rock of Gibraltar to Ceuta, a Spanish enclave on the North African coast. The country has come a long way since then. In 2020, following a UNESCO report on the global disruption of COVID on all aspects of life, including education, all schools in Morocco moved exclusively to online teaching and learning.

In this study, the researchers sought to compare teachers' experience in moving from face-to-face to online instruction, to document teachers' perceptions of student engagement with online instruction, and, interestingly, to determine what practices developed during online instruction could be transferred back to the face-to-face classroom. The study shared some characteristics with the Israeli project: Both quantitative survey data and qualitative data collected through semi-structured interviews were collected. Like the Israeli study, because of the word limit, the report is largely limited to the analysis and interpretation of the quantitative data. It used chi-square to test the data for significance. In all, 356 teachers took part in the survey. Statistics are provided on participants' gender, professional development training in "remote" (online) teaching, self-reported information communication technology (ICT) proficiency, teacher estimates of amount of student learning, and preferred instructional mode.

The chi-square tests indicated the following:

1. Those trained in remote instruction had a significantly greater preference for hybrid learning, while those who had no training had a significantly greater preference for fully in-person instruction.

2. Of those who self-reported advanced ICT proficiency, half selected face-to-face, and almost the same number selected hybrid (online + face-to-face); the vast majority reporting limited ICT proficiency (87.5%) preferred face-to-face, and only 12.5% chose hybrid.
3. Those trained in remote/online teaching reported learner gains in online learning as being at least equivalent to those in face-to-face instruction while the vast majority (76%) of those who had not participated in professional development for online teaching reported that students learned less in online settings.

Some comments on these outcomes are warranted. In the first place, perceptions of learning gains seem to be based on teachers' intuition rather than on test scores or other indicators of learning outcomes. While teachers responded negatively to online instruction, those who received professional development and who reported advanced ICT proficiency present quite a different picture. Regardless of their professional development and familiarity with ICT, several viewpoints were shared across the teaching community. One was the lack of support by school administrators, who were "unavailable" or "largely unavailable". With teachers and students absent from the school, the attitude seemed to be one of "out of sight, out of mind". A related opinion was that classroom management skills could be directly transferred to online learning.

Another negative perception of online instruction was the disengagement and lack of student-to-student communication online. Shortcomings of technology as well as lack of computer literacy was another factor. These and other challenges, such as the reluctance of students to turn on their video, are noted in several contributions to the volume, as was the experience of teachers in many parts of the work. Despite these misgivings, the authors end the chapter on an optimistic note, observing that technology and blended learning are here to stay.

The focus of the Tunisian study is the implementation of communicative language teaching (CLT). The author, Khaled el Houche, begins his account by reminding us that CLT gained prominence in the research literature in the 1970s. In Tunisia, a methodological rethink led, in 2006, to the revision of the language syllabus following the principles of CLT. Some 15 years later, el Houche thought it useful to look at the extent to which the revised syllabus had been implemented in the classroom. The aim of the study was to document teachers' perceptions and beliefs about language pedagogy, and to examine the extent to which these were realized in the classroom. In other words, he wanted to examine the extent to which theory matched practice. Participants in the study were 44 teachers of English to young learners. Data for the study came from a questionnaire about the beliefs and attitudes that guided their practice. The 19 items were completed by all participants on a six-point Likert scale. Three of the participants were chosen through "convenience sampling" to have their classes observed. Lessons were recorded, transcribed, and analyzed using a modified version of the Communicative Orientation of Language Teaching (COLT) scheme.

Let me say something about COLT. From the 1960s onward, but particularly in the wake of the "communicative teaching revolution", researchers became increasingly concerned with documenting what actually goes on in language classrooms rather than assuming teachers actually implemented procedures recommended by methodologists. Various schemes were developed for documenting what went on. In his book on second language classroom research, Craig Chaudron (1988) analyzed no fewer than 23 schemes. Originally developed by Fröhlich et al. (1985), COLT was designed to evaluate language classrooms of different kinds against principles of CLT. (For a description of the scheme and its use to evaluate a variety of English and French L2 programs, see Spada, 1990.

In this chapter, el Houche's instruments, their development from the COLT, and their validation and implementation are described in detail. The results of the survey indicated that the teachers understood and had a positive orientation to a learner- rather than a teacher-centered approach. In an open-ended question, teachers were asked to nominate the roles they adopt. *Facilitator, monitor, organizer,* and *guide* were most frequently identified. The most frequently nominated role for the learner was to be an active participant.

The author then looked at patterns of classroom interaction. The three focal teachers were observed for a total of 150 minutes, and times were allocated to "teacher to student/whole class," "choral work," "individual work," and "managerial talk". Teacher-centered instruction dominated all three lessons with the teachers relying heavily on the textbook, and on a 'traditional' lock-step (i.e., non-CLT) method.

In summary, el Houche notes that there is a massive mismatch between teachers' perceptions of what happens in the classrooms and what actually happens. He suggests that the extremely limited student talking time could be addressed by developing speaking-enhancing instructional materials. Given the limited scope of this study, he recommended much more comprehensive research into the implementation of CLT in Tunisian classrooms. Indeed, the gap between what teachers imagine they do and their actual practices is well documented in the literature. For example, in the 1980s, I carried out a study looking at the implementation of CLT. Although the context and data collection methods were different, the conclusion was almost identical (Nunan, 1987).

The final study in this section also looked at the practices and beliefs of EFL teachers, although the context was in Egyptian high schools, and the focus on the teaching of grammar. In the introduction we learn that there is a debate over whether grammar should be a main focus of instruction or whether it should be eliminated entirely. The authors cite studies from disparate ESL and EFL contexts on the tension between the teaching of grammar or a focus on communication. The persistence of this false dichotomy after more than four decades of research and scholarship is a concern, although there is no suggestion that the authors subscribe to the dichotomy. In keeping with the Tunisian study, their concern is on the tension between teachers' beliefs and practices.

The authors justify their study on the paucity of research into English grammar teaching in Egypt. The only relevant study cited is one carried out by the second author of the current study (Latif, 2017), who found that two-thirds of instructional time was devoted to grammar instruction, the preponderance of which consisted of deductive grammar explanations by the teacher. That research provided a point of departure for the present study, which was to investigate matches and mismatches between the beliefs and practices of Egyptian high school teachers' grammar instruction, and to identify the factors underlying them. Fifteen teachers participated in the study. Data for the investigation came from classroom observation and post-observation interviews carried out by the first author. Both authors then independently analyzed the observation notes and interview transcripts and documented the themes that emerged. They then exchanged their notes and came to a consensus on the themes.

From their interviews, the researchers identified five pedagogical beliefs. In three instances, there was a match between the observation and the subsequent belief statements. These are summarized in Table 6.1 (p. 86). For reasons of space, I'll confine my observations to the two mismatches. The first of these relates to the deductive versus inductive teaching of grammar, and the second to the use of non-communicative versus communicative grammar activities. These two issues are obviously closely related, and I'll discuss them together. In the interviews, according to the researchers, teachers believed that "English grammar should be taught inductively, to foster students' engagement and communication", and "English grammar should be taught communicatively to help students have interesting and real-life learning experiences" (p. 86). Both beliefs are reasonable enough and are part of the "received-wisdom" of CLT, although whether all 15 teachers subscribed to these views is unclear. For the record, I believe both have a place in communicative language teaching, although my bias is towards inductive teaching and communicative activities. (For a discussion of the advantages and disadvantages of induction and deduction, see Thornbury, 2000, and Nunan, 2005, pp. 15–21.)

So, what was revealed by the classroom observation? In the first instance, teachers depended "largely on deductive grammar teaching", and in the second they drew "heavily upon non-communicative grammar activities". Reasons given by the teachers for the mismatches/tension were that deductive/non-communicative grammar teaching was used to "save time", and the students' low proficiency level. The authors also speculated that students had been biased toward deductive learning and would resist inductive learning. This view, along with the other studies in this section, raises fascinating issues and brings with it clear implications for policy, practice, and future research.

Section II: Identity and affect

The focus of the Oman chapter is on the pragmatic choices that language learners make when performing speech acts in their second language. As the title of the chapter indicates, the topic is central to affect and identity. In addition to being a central construct in the three chapters that make up this section, identity is also important to three chapters in the policy section of this collection: those from Bahrain, Iran, and Jordon.

Drawing on the work of specialists in speech act theory and research, such as Cohen (1996) and Kasper (1992), Fatema Al-Rubai'ey identifies some of the problems for L2 speakers when it comes to performing speech acts such as refusing requests and invitations. One particular problem is pragmatic transfer, or the transfer of norms from one's own L1 to the L2. There are at least two problems with the concept of pragmatic transfer. The first is the assumption that there are norms that all L1 speakers of the target language share. This is not the case. Norms differ among speakers of a language because of social class, education, and so on. One norm that differs considerably is the degree of directness/indirectness (Thomas, 1995). Another complicating factor when it comes to world languages such as English is that there are far more L2-to-L2 interactions between speakers worldwide than interactions between L2 speakers and native English speakers.

Al-Rubai'ey introduces into her study yet another complicating factor. She makes the point that in examining learner perceptions, it is important to determine *why* learners make certain choices. This issue, to her, is a matter of learner identity. The focus of her study is on how learners define and construct their relationship to English when put into socially difficult and potentially highly charged situations, such as having to refuse requests and invitations. Participants in her study were 10 fourth-year English majors at Sultan Qaboos University. Data were collected through eight oral discourse completion simulations in which participants had to refuse invitations and requests. The simulations varied according to degree of imposition, social distance, and cultural distance. Two semi-structured interviews followed the simulations, and participants had the choice of responding in either Arabic or English.

In pragmatics research like this study, discourse and roles play have been criticized for their relative artificiality, the question being whether the interlocutor would make the same choices when facing similar situations in real life. Researchers using simulations and role plays point out that it is difficult to see how this information can be obtained in any other way. (The same criticism and defense have been made of introspective and retrospective data elicitation methods.)

This chapter provides interesting insights. In interviews, participants referred to the desire to maintain and express their identity as Omanis when using the excuse strategy – not a reflection of their relative pragmatic competence. Although they had the (mis)perception that native speakers of English are "succinct, direct, and straightforward in refusing," they used the excuse strategy very often when the simulation specified that they were refusing a native-speaking professor. Al-Rubai'ey reports that the use of Arabic pragmatic norms when communicating in English reflected a desire to maintain their Omani identity, and that "pragmatic choices could be seen as their enactment of their identity"

(p. 100). Her findings challenge, and suggest a revisiting of, some of the predetermined notions in "mainstream" second language acquisition research.

The title of the Sudan chapter leaves readers in no doubt of the primacy of affect within the chapter. Many Sudanese citizens are highly motivated to learn English, although the source of the motivation varies. Among these are the social and economic capital proficiency in English bestows on those who possess it, its utilitarian value to those who wish to travel, and the advantage it brings to those who want to exploit social media in communicating internationally. However, as the authors are quick to point out, scant research exists into the juxtaposition of motivation, culture, and identity. It is this gap that their study proposes to address. The chapter differs from the others in the collection in that the authors, although both Sudanese nationals, are living and working abroad. Within applied linguistics and language education, culture and motivation have been widely researched. This is not the case with self-efficacy. In this investigation, the authors explore the interrelationships among the self-efficacy, motivation, and culture of five Sudanese college students (three females and two males) who plan to become either teachers or translators.

The five participants in the study were described as coming from low socioeconomic backgrounds, and as facing conditions adverse to study, such as a long daily commute to and from the university. Data were collected through three formal interviews conducted in Arabic by the first author. The interviews were audio-recorded and augmented with hand-written notes made during the interview. Using a grounded approach, the researchers identified and coded themes and subthemes. Four of the participants planned to become EFL teachers. The fifth, one of the males, intended to become a translator. All five saw proficiency in English as bestowing a certain cache, given its status as an international language. The aspiring translator saw the financial benefits and possibilities of travel as bringing additional value.

The first insight relevant to the research questions was that participants' motivation was enhanced by their real-life experiences, self-efficacy, and culture. In discussing the results, cultural factors are mentioned three times. The first is related to the fact that all five interviewees were the eldest in the family, and in Sudanese culture, the first-born bears heavy responsibility for family wellbeing. The second is that in Sudanese culture, people look up to those with good English. This was a significant motivating factor. The third linked religion and culture. The Prophet Muhammad was revered a great teacher. Because of this, teaching is highly valued. In terms of self-efficacy, Participant B exhibited "remarkable resilience" and this, according to the researchers, may have been an indicator of self-efficacy and success in learning English. Participant C had a "strong and determined personality" and this may have contributed to her sense of self-efficacy. So did Participant E, whose family saw education as the only way to achieve prosperity and advancement. For participant E, memorizing the alphabet through song is cited as an example of self-efficacy. Participant D's self-efficacy was inspired by his educated parents. Distinctly unmotivating were the old-fashioned teaching methods. Participant D rebelled against these methods, which were rooted in the teaching of the previous century. His generation and the students he would teach are well-versed in technology, so he intends to incorporate into his teaching digital photos, stories, drama, and music.

While there are common threads running through this collection, each chapter has unique features. Methodologically, one of the things that makes the contribution from Turkey noteworthy is the fact that it is a case study of a single teacher-in-preparation. In keeping with the Omani and Sudanese chapters, identity is a central motif in the Turkish chapter. When I received an early draft of the chapter, I was intrigued by the subtitle. What was an identity-oriented practicum, and what are the tensions that it creates? In their introduction, the authors describe tensions as "teachers' feeling of in-betweenness and the internal struggles of being pulled in different directions" (p. 115). In this study, the authors describe the redesign of an existing practicum course so that all activities had identity work as an explicit focus.

The research takes the form of a qualitative case study of an EFL teacher candidate whose pseudonym is Nihat. In designing the identity-oriented activities, the authors intended the activities "to foster dialogic engagement as a group, as well as collaborative and individual reflection on language learning and teacher identities" (p. 115). I was intrigued by the requirement for participants to create art-based activities such as collages, memes, paintings, and sculptures. These were intended to stimulate beliefs, values, and priorities concerned with language learning and teaching. While on the surface, these seemingly have little to do with the business of language teaching, according to the authors, they encourage participants to think laterally and "pedagogize".

Nihat's motivation to improve his English and become a language teacher was stimulated by a visit to a U.S.-based relative during his high school years. His own formal language learning experiences were dehumanizing and delivered by remote, disengaged teachers. At the end of the course, he participated in semi-structured interviews. In engaging in his identity work, Nihat began to critique the professional discourse and developed a discourse of his own. He also came to view various practicum activities, such as observing other teachers and engaging in practice teaching, through the lens of ongoing identity work.

Much of the analysis is based on a self-description of a digital collage Nihat created to represent his ideal study space for language learning. Through the internet and digital media, he was able to exploit real-life resources for learning and using language in an engaging, playful way. "For him, it was important to use English as a part of his everyday life" (p. 121). This is an important point, and yet this is one of the few chapters to link classroom learning with opportunities for activation beyond the classroom (Nunan & Choi, 2018; Nunan & Richards, 2015).

The "tension" in the title of the chapter reflects Nihat's frustration with his teaching practicum classes. As these classes were simply "on loan" to him, he had to follow the lesson plans of the regular class teacher. Those lesson plans were identical to the decontextualized, traditional classes he had disliked as a student and was anxious not to incorporate as a part of his teacher identity. In one interview, he explained that he had pulled back from using the practicum lessons as an opportunity to try out his teaching philosophy because he wasn't ready to get out of his comfort zone, but he did want his students to have fun in his classroom. The researchers conclude with reconceptualizing the practicum as praxicum, that is "a practicum that is based on *praxis*: action and reflection ... for identity-oriented teacher education" (p. 125).

Section III: Academic writing

The three chapters in this section examine different aspects of academic writing. To the uninitiated, the title of the contribution by Algerian scholar, Tarek Assassi, may seem off-putting. However, beneath the title is an issue of considerable importance to the thousands of academics around the world who are required to publish in English-medium journals despite the fact that English is not their first language. The issue is whether perceived lack of proficiency in academic English is one of the criteria used by academic gatekeepers (principally editors, reviewers, and publishers) to reject articles submitted by non-native English-speaking academics. Assassi doesn't foreground this issue at the beginning of the study. Motivation for investigating metadiscourse markers by native and nonnative writers is given as to "help us understand the writing processes of these different discourse communities" (p. 133). The focus on metadiscourse markers in academic articles is justified on the grounds that (A) abstracts are the public face of an article and are accorded "immense importance" by gatekeepers, and (B) using metadiscourse markers helps writers to organize their text and to signal that organization to their readers.

The database for the study consisted of 60 abstracts – 20 from each of the designated groups. Care was taken to match word length, type of journal (peer-reviewed, international), and field (applied linguistics). The abstracts were read and metadiscourse markers were highlighted and classified according to Hyland's (2005) system. The system divides markers into interactive resources, which help guide the reader through the text, and interactional resources, which involve the reader in the argument. Chi-square analysis was used to check for significant differences between the three groups of writers. (Differences between the interactive and interactional markers among the three groups of abstracts were not significant.)

In terms of results, with few exceptions, patterns of metadiscoursal use by the Algerian authors were much closer to the native English users than to the Saudis. While this information satisfies the imperative to answer the questions that the study was carried out to answer (and it is surprising how frequently this imperative is overlooked or ignored in published research), the really interesting discussion, to me, at least, comes at the end of the last section of the chapter. This concerns the possible bias against NNS writers by the custodians of academic writing standards. Here, the author admits to a concern at the relative paucity the of articles published by Algerian authors in high-indexed journals. The author reiterates the finding that in contrast with the Saudis, Algerian scholars use rhetorical conventions similar to those used by the native speakers. From this finding, he correctly infers that the lower number of Algerian publications can't be attributed to the presence/absence of metadiscoursal markers. Assassi quickly and correctly points out that the lower number of published articles might reflect the fact that fewer articles are submitted to refereed journals. He concludes by supporting Flowerdew's (2019) argument that L2 writers have problems that are different from L1 writers, and that they suffer linguistic disadvantage.

The purpose of the Qatar chapter is to evaluate the introduction of a curriculum-based tutoring model in the Foundation English Program at Qatar University. The chapter begins with a discussion of writing centers, which are described as offering one-to-one feedback to students by tutors. Several other models of writing centers are described. The authors describe one model, which presumably depicts the model followed at Qatar University: "Traditionally, writing center tutorials are offered through an on-campus center, which collaborates with departments that offer composition courses. The departments that offer the writing courses typically run the tutorials in writing centers" (p. 146). The growth of online centers as an alternative to on-campus writing centers is also described. The popularity of such centers continued post-COVID, despite challenges such as equity of access to technology, and the need to train tutors to teach online, factors which have been mentioned in other contributions to the volume.

At Qatar University, the English Department offers two academic writing courses, within their Foundation Program: the first on essay writing, critical thinking, etc., and the second on summarizing, critical reading, and short response papers. Students are offered one-to-one tutorial support through a writing center. Due to pressure of numbers, and the "limited capacity of the university writing center," the department designed an "in house tutoring service". English Department lecturers served as tutors on the course. While it's unclear who manages the writing center, it's clearly not the English Department. (It's not uncommon for such academic writing skills units to be part of larger cross-faculty academic skills center.) The in-house Student Tutoring Scheme is described as a "unique" new approach to teaching academic writing. The major differentiating feature is that it is a curriculum-based alternative to the one-to-one support service offered by the writing center. By *curriculum-based*, the authors mean that it is closely linked to the two Foundation Program writing courses. Another differentiating feature is that it is offered online.

There seems to be a degree of tension between the writing center and the department. At one point, the authors note that "writing center tutorials are offered through an on-campus center, which collaborated with the department". However, at another point, the comment is made that "Lack of collaboration between writing center tutors and writing course instructors makes it difficult for tutors to tailor their practices and fulfill the needs of L2 writers" (p. 147). It seems this was another factor in the decision by the department to develop their in-house alternative.

The aim of the study was to collect data on students' perceptions of the two tutorial support models employed at the university. Data for the study came from a survey which was administered to 272 undergraduate students enrolled in the English-medium courses across a range of undergraduate degree programs. The survey was administered at the end of a three-semester program. Students were asked at what stage of the writing process they sought tutorial assistance, what aspects of the process they needed help with, and, crucially, which model they preferred – tutoring by the department course teachers or the writing center teachers. From the third question, I assumed that students were able to avail themselves of both options. If they had only experienced one option, how would they be able to make an informed judgment on one over the other?

Results showed that, while the majority of students preferred the in-house option to the writing center, this view was by no means universal. The major advantage of the in-house support was that the tutors, who also taught the writing courses, had a clearer idea of what was expected in assignments. The major disadvantages of the writing center was the need to book in advance, and a 30-minute time limit for consultations. In the in-house mode, a tutor was always available, and students could "drop-in" at any time.

The United Arab Emirates (UAE) is a collection of city states that amalgamated into a federation in the 1970s. The best known of these are Abu Dhabi, the capital, and Dubai. The latter has promoted itself as an international center of education. The UAE is unique in several ways. Expatriates and immigrants (mostly from the subcontinent) vastly outnumber the locals. It has a handful of public universities, and dozens of private educational institutions as well as campuses of foreign universities. The vast majority of these institutions use English as a medium of instruction.

The study reported by Hamam and Coombe investigated the challenges and benefits of teaching academic writing online. Like many of the studies reported in this collection, the data were collected through an online questionnaire containing seven open-ended questions. This questionnaire was distributed to writing teachers in seven public and private institutions of higher education in the Emirates. (Input had been solicited from here 40 teachers of whom 12 responded. All were experienced in teaching face-to-face and online.) In keeping with thousands of educational institutions from elementary through tertiary education, when the seriousness of the pandemic became evident in 2020, institutions were instructed to move from face-to-face to online teaching. In the case of the UAE, this shift had to happen in the space of less than two weeks.

The researchers focused on seven aspects of instruction: resources used, feedback to students, supporting entities (such as a library), peer collaboration, professional development needed by teachers, ethical issues (such as plagiarism), and technological issues. Once questionnaire responses had been returned, they were analyzed thematically.

Not surprisingly, at the beginning of the online teaching process, most teachers encountered challenges. One highly experienced teacher reported feeling just as lost as they had been as a beginning teacher 40 years before. What the researchers did find novel was that teachers were able to find solutions to problems as they arose and reported teaching online to be a positive experience. In summarizing the outcomes of the study, the researchers concluded that critical to the success of online instruction is the collaboration of teachers, students, and institutional administrators. Also crucial is training for teachers (and, I would add, students) in the use of online academic writing programs. High speed WIFI and an appropriate learning space are also important but often difficult to obtain.

Two final issues raised by the UAE researchers concern plagiarism and the effectiveness or otherwise different modes of instruction. Both of these issues have emerged in several other studies in the volume. This is the only chapter to deal with the impact of AI in general and ChatGPT in particular, on learning and teaching, but this issue is becoming a major concern in the academic literature as well as in popular media. For many years, Laurel Richardson (cited in this chapter) has argued the case in favor of writing, not only as a tool for communicating, but also as a powerful method of inquiry. Quick-fix AI apps not only facilitate plagiarism, but also subvert the fundamental educational benefits of writing as a thinking process (Richardson, 2001).

Section IV: Policy and ideology

As a field of study, investigating linguistic landscapes has been around for quite a while, but has only recently begun to gain traction. Yasser Ahmed Gomaa's investigation of the linguistic landscape at the University of Bahrain (UoB) is a welcome addition to this volume as, indeed, it is to the literature on linguistic landscapes. To Gomaa's knowledge, this is the first study to be published on university linguistic landscapes in the Arabian Gulf. In addition to documenting campus signage, it also canvasses UoB students' perceptions of the languages employed on the signs. The study documents five aspects of linguistic landscapes: the languages that are present, the position of English vis-à-vis other languages, the relative number of top-down (official) and bottom-up (unofficial) signs, student attitudes, and student preferences on the positioning of languages on signs.

Two sources of data were drawn on in the study: a photographic corpus of 409 items found on the campus, and 213 questionnaire responses from students. Not surprisingly, the vast majority of responses (92%) were from Bahrainis. The rest of the responses were from Indian, Saudi, Jordanian, Egyptian, and Pakistani nationals. Of the 409 signs, 148 were Arabic only, 122 English only, and 139 contained both Arabic and English. A small number of signs also contained non-verbal symbols for students, staff, or visitors who spoke neither Arabic nor English. Gomaa points out that the function of Arabic signs was not purely informational, but also served as a symbol of national unity. Numerous students commented on the fact that only Arabic and English appeared on the signs and expressed a desire for a greater range of languages. Gomaa believes the exclusion of languages other than Arabic and English was deliberate rather than a chance occurrence. However, he doesn't speculate as to why this might be so, and makes the point that there is no official policy or are there any guidelines governing the use of signs. That said, the prominence of English suggests to him that English is being promoted as an "official language" as well as a tool for communication. In terms of the top-down bottom-up distinction, 94% of the signs belonged to the former category and only 6% to the latter. The main policy recommendation is that there needs to be a written policy with formal rules that regulate the UoB campus linguistic landscape.

The Iranian study is the most explicit policy-oriented chapter in the book. Although I am listed as a coauthor of the study, Mahdi Dahmardeh was very much the lead author. The chapter differs from others in the book in that its database consisted of official policy documents produced by the Iranian Parliament, the Supreme Council of the Cultural Revolution, and the Ministry of Education. The overarching aim of the study was to determine the attitude of the State towards the role of foreign language within the curriculum, and the factors influencing language education policy. We sought to identify which official organizations influenced policy settings, the role of foreign languages in the curriculum, and the stance of authorities towards the teaching of foreign language in general and English in particular. Persian (Farsi) is the official language of the country. Minority languages include Kurdish, Azeri, and Arabic. Data collection involved scanning many official documents that contained information and instructions on the role of foreign languages and how they were to be taught.

Foreign language teaching and learning are popular within the school system, as well as in private language institutes in larger urban areas. Within the school system, Arabic and English are compulsory from Key Stage 3. At the next key stage, the students may continue with these subjects and have the option of studying German or French. English has been, and remains, the most popular foreign language to study.

In 2011, a supplement to the Comprehensive Scientific Plan was published. The document criticized segments of Iranian society which had gained access to Western media and popular culture through the internet. Although possession of satellite dishes for accessing Western programs was illegal, their use was widespread. According to the supplement, many children were exposed to home environments that were eroding Iranian social and cultural values. In part of the document, the teaching and learning of foreign languages was seen as fueling this trend towards Western lifestyles and values, while in another part, there is a statement supporting the learning of foreign languages in general and recommending that people improve their English language speaking skills in particular. Two years later, the National Curriculum promoted the teaching/learning of foreign languages as an opportunity to understand cultural interactions and a means for "transferring scientific achievements ... within the framework of the Islamic system" (p. 190). Foreign languages would be a tool for Iranians to engage in science and technology, and to transmit Iranian culture to those who do not speak Persian.

The chapter concludes by stating that everything in Iran is judged from a political perspective. This is particularly true of foreign languages. Despite the general popularity of English, it is seen as embodying values that are at odds with those of Iran and Islam. In dealing with the first research question, we described how, while education is nominally the preserve of the Ministry of Education, numerous other bodies have a major say in the direction it should take. In terms of language education in general, and English in particular, there is an ambivalence, and in some cases, there are contradictory criteria in documents and policy papers. Not surprisingly, the stipulation by the Supreme Council of the Cultural Revolution (SCCR) that in order to preserve Iranian cultural values foreign languages should be "localized" (a euphemism for airbrushing out the cultural norms carried by the foreign languages) has not been particularly successful. Curriculum reforms are carried out centrally and transmitted to the regions, thereby failing to meet local needs. And, as we have seen in numerous instances across MENA, national, standardized examinations focus students on passing discrete-point tests of grammar and vocabulary rather than the ability to communicate in the language.

The Jordan contribution to the volume differs from the others in this section, in that it focuses not on official policy, but on the language preferences of Jordanians. When it comes to language choice, the options are English, Jordanian Arabic (JA), and colloquial Jordanian, which exists as a number of dialects. Classical and Modern Standard Arabic are used in formal settings, for literacy practices, and in religious contexts. In addition to these languages, several minority languages are also used. English is the principal foreign language and is used as a medium of instruction for mathematics and science in some private schools.

The researcher, Fatima Esseili, looked at what determines the choice of one language over another, the interlocutor, or the activity/topic. Data were collected through a 20-item (17 closed and three open items) questionnaire. This survey was completed by 665 adult participants who had the option of completing either a standard Arabic or English version of the questionnaire. The software package Qualtrics was used to create and disseminate the questionnaire and to calculate descriptive statistics.

Results indicated that JA was the preferred option for communicating with extended family and friends, percentages varying from 97% with grandparents, to 65% with friends and 60% with domestic helpers. Just 51% used it to communicate with teachers/professors and co-workers. Eighty percent stated that standard Arabic should be used for formal instruction. The second most popular means of instruction was Arabizi, a mixture of JA and English. In relation to the second question, JA was the preferred language for most activities. The only activities in which English was the preferred option were writing emails, completing a job application, watching movies, and surfing the internet. A relationship was also noted between a preference for English and private school/ university attendance and household income. Three quarters of respondents preferred the Arabic questionnaire, which reflected "Jordanians' values and cultural and religious loyalty to Arabic" (p. 206).

The general conclusion from the study is that the strong preference for standard and colloquial Arabic reflects Jordanians' pride in their native language, strong ties to Jordan's traditions, and a sense of Arabic/Muslim identity.

The English language proficiency of Gaza pre-service teachers is the focus of the Palestine research. Motivating the study is the paucity of research examining the factors affecting Palestinians students' English language proficiency. Hammad intended to fill this gap by soliciting the views of the pre-service teachers themselves along with their EFL university instructors. Participants for the study are 30 fourth-year undergraduate English majors, and six university English teachers. Data for the study came from semi-structured interviews with five focus groups of students and individual interviews with six instructors. The interviews were audio-recorded and translated into English.

Despite the fact that some students were intrinsically motivated to learn English (Hammad doesn't say how many or how intrinsic motivation was operationalized), they failed to achieve "high levels of proficiency". Again, there is no indication of how the proficiency was measured. According to the students, the failure rested with their teachers, whose lessons were "uninteresting and dull" and teacher centered. The students were not allowed to participate actively in the lessons. In writing lessons, no feedback was provided and in reading lessons, the teachers read an English text aloud, translated every sentence into Arabic, and then discussed the answer to the comprehension questions which followed the reading passage. These would have to be memorized and regurgitated in the exams. Other shortcomings included failure to teach learning strategies, and the overuse of Arabic. The instructors' own English proficiency was also criticized.

Not surprisingly, instructors largely located the root of the problem in the students, who were variously described as having inadequate "aptitude, knowledge, intelligence, and/or the capacity required for majoring in a foreign language" (p. 216). Some teachers also accepted a portion of the blame, indicating that they lacked adequate (or even any) training in English language teaching and learning. A number had specialized in English literature and knew nothing about methods for teaching language.

In discussing the implications for policy, practice, and future research, Hammad recommended that "teachers need to replace the teacher-centered method with a more student-centered approach so that students can actively participate in the learning process and use English communicatively" (p. 217). The problem, of course, is that the instructors appear not to have received any training in how to implement a student-centered approach or, indeed, basic classroom techniques, such as giving feedback and introducing strategies for the developing the four skills. Compounding the problem is that when the teachers themselves were learning English, it is more than likely that they did so through the procedures they subsequently perpetuated in their own teaching. It is also likely that when their own students become English teachers, they will also resort to the same techniques, such as reading aloud and rote learning, and thus the cycle is perpetuated. That said, there is some evidence in the student interview data that some learners are at least aware of where the problems lie.

Last words

Some years ago, I wrote about the experience of being an expatriate in Hong Kong. I'd been an expat for most of my adult life, and thought I knew a thing or two about the subject. Using the standard definition of expatriate as "someone living in a country other than where they were born", I interviewed a wide cross-section of the community, from leaders of business to refugees. Embedded in the 70 hours of recorded interviews were 18 stories that each demanded a chapter in their own right. Each bore out Jerome Bruner's adage that we seem to have no way of describing "lived time, save in the form of a narrative" (Bruner, 2004, p. 691). In an afterword to the stories, I made the following point:

> In these days, in terms of numbers, the global flow of people is greater than at any time in history: greater than the post-World War II diaspora, we are told. The transnational flow of people who leave their birthplace, either by choice or from force of circumstance, will be one of the defining characteristics of this generation.
>
> *(Nunan, 2018, p. 281)*

The inter- and intranational flow of peoples across and between MENA countries, those that are featured in this collection and those that are not, is a theme that runs through the volume. The flood of refugees and the resulting pressure on educational systems, politics, and resources are specifically mentioned in relation to Palestine, Jordan, Lebanon, and Syria. Of these, only the Lebanon chapter deals at any length with the destabilizing influence on the educational system of the massive influx of Syrian refugees, while the Sudanese civil war is not specifically mentioned but is constantly in the headlines. While refugees are rarely welcomed anywhere, guest workers who are prepared to do the manual work that is shunned by locals are tolerated, as are Western expatriates, although for very different reasons. Also adding richness and diversity to local cultures are minority groups and the languages they bring.

Diversity is also evident in the identification of research topics, and the methods used for collecting, analyzing, and interpreting data. Methods include discourse analysis, public signs and notices, questionnaires, and surveys, interviews, classroom observation, documentary analysis, proficiency tests, coding schemes, and case studies. A grounded approach to data analysis was reported in several chapters, and descriptive statistics in a number of others. Only two studies used inferential statistics and reported levels of statistical significance.

Given the global disruption brought about by the pandemic, and the impact it had on education systems around the world, I was surprised at the paucity of references to COVID/pandemic. Only two studies made it a focus of the research (Morocco and the UAE). One (Lebanon) listed the pandemic as having a disruptive effect, and another (Qatar) gave it a brief mention in passing. The most likely explanation is that most of the studies that we accepted for further revision and ultimate publication were underway by the time the full implications of the pandemic had been brought home to the global community.

Less surprising is the extent to which technology has become an important tool for teachers, learners, and researchers in this part of the world, although, as some scholars point out, resources are not equally distributed. Most of the studies reported herein have either utilized technology for collecting data (most often through online questionnaires and surveys), for data analysis, and for managing teaching and learning through software packages such as Qualtrics. Several studies have focused on the switch from face-to-face to online learning, often at short notice thanks to the pandemic, and the challenges this posed: the sudden realization that teaching and learning online is not the same is teaching face-to-face, the disengagement of learners and the difficulty of fostering student-to-student communication. Particularly enlightening on pedagogical pros and cons are the studies carried out in Morocco, Qatar, and the UAE.

It seems fitting that this contribution to the TIRF-Routledge series on *Global Research on Teaching and Learning English* should appear a decade after the initial volume in the series (Bailey & Damerow, 2014). Both bring to a global readership key studies in one of the most dynamic and fluid regions of the world, and both demonstrate that quality research can be conducted in often challenging contexts and conditions.

References

Bailey, K. M., & Damerow, R. (Eds.). (2014). *Teaching and learning English in the Arabic-speaking world*. TIRF & Routledge.

Borg, S. (2003). Teacher cognition in language teaching: A review of research on what language teachers think, know, believe, and do. *Language Teaching*, 36(2), 81–89. https://doi.org/10.1017/S0261444803001903.

Bowen, J. (2022). *The making of the modern Middle East*. Pan Macmillan.

Bruner, J. (2004). Life as narrative. *Social Research*, 71(3), 691–711.

Chaudron, C. (1988) *Second language classrooms: Research on teaching and learning*. Cambridge University Press.

Cohen, A. (1996) Speech acts. In S. L. McKay & N. H. Hornberger (Eds.), *Sociolinguistics and language teaching* (pp. 383–420). Cambridge University Press.

Flowerdew, J. (2019). The linguistic disadvantage of scholars who write in English as an additional language. *Language Teaching*, 52(2), 249–260.

Fröhlich, M., Spada, N., & Allen, P. (1985). Differences in the communicative orientations of L2 classroom. *TESOL Quarterly*, *19*(1), 27–57.

Hyland, K. (2005). *Metadiscourse: Exploring interaction in writing*. Continuum.

Kasper, G. (1992). Pragmatic transfer. *Second Language Research*, *8*(3), 203–231.

Latif, M. M. M. (2017). Teaching grammar using inductive and communicative materials: Exploring Egyptian EFL teachers' practices and beliefs. In B. Tomlinson, M. Hitomi, & F. Mishan (Eds.), *Practice and theory for materials development in language learning* (pp. 275–289). Cambridge Scholars Publishing.

Mercer, S. (2021). An agenda for well-being in ELT: An ecological perspective. *ELT Journal*, *75*(1), 14–21. https://doi.org/10.1093/elt/ccaa062.

Mercer, S., MacIntyre, P., Gregersen, T., & Talbot, K. (2018). Positive language education: Combining positive education and language education. *Theory and Practice of Second Language Acquisition*, *4*(2), 11–31. https://www.journals.us.edu.pl/index.php/TAPSLA/article/view/7011.

Nunan, D. (1987). Communicative language teaching: Making it work. *ELT Journal*, *41*(2), 136–145.

Nunan, D. (2005). *Grammar*. McGraw-Hill.

Nunan, D. (2018). *Other voices, other eyes: Expatriate lives in Hong Kong*. Blacksmith Books.

Nunan, D., & Bailey, K. (2009). *Exploring second language classroom research*. Heinle/Cengage Learning.

Nunan, D., & Richards, J. C. (2015). *Language learning beyond the classroom*. Routledge.

Nunan, D., & Choi, J. (2018). Language learning and activation beyond the classroom. *Australian Journal of Applied Linguistics*, *1*(2), 49–63.

Richardson, L. (2001). Getting personal: Writing-stores. *International Journal of Qualitative Studies in Education*, *14*(1), 33–38.

Spada, N. (1990). Observing classroom behaviours and learning outcomes in different second language programs. In J. C. Richards & D. Nunan (Eds.), *Second language teacher education* (pp. 293–312). Cambridge University Press.

Thomas, J. (1995). *Meaning in interaction*. Longman.

Thornbury, S. (2000). *How to teach grammar*. Pearson ELT.

PART I
Teachers and teaching

2
ENGLISH READING IN PRIMARY SCHOOL STUDENTS IN LEBANON

Rana Aridi, Eva Kozma, Sara Kassab, Kara McBride, Mirvat Merhi, and Rajani Shrestha

Introduction

Issues that motivated the research

Over the last 15 years, Lebanon has faced a series of challenges that have placed enormous stress on its public education system. The influx of roughly 1.5 million Syrian refugees further destabilized an education system that was already struggling. Over 277,000 Syrian students are currently enrolled in Lebanon's public schools (Human Rights Watch, 2021) and – as the country faces cascading economic crises exacerbated by COVID-19, political instability, and the devastating 2020 Beirut port explosion – tens of thousands of Lebanese students are dropping out of private schools and enrolling in public schools.

State of Lebanese public education in recent years

Historically, the quality of public education in Lebanon has been perceived to be low. Even though almost half of the country's schools are public, 70% of the slightly more than one million Lebanese students were enrolled in private schools in 2015 (Jalbout, 2015). However, with the economic crises and the Lebanese pound losing over 90% of its value in the black market (Reuters, 2022), many families were unable to afford private schools. As a result, around 54,000 students moved from private to public schools in the 2020–2021 school year alone, thus adding more pressure on the public school system (World Bank Group, 2021). There has also been an alarming increase in dropout rates, due to the extended pandemic closures and the need for additional income among families impoverished by the crisis. "Three in 10 young people in Lebanon have stopped their

DOI: 10.4324/9781003312444-3

education, while 4 in 10 reduced spending on education to buy essential items like basic food and medicine" (UNICEF, 2022).

Most primary grade teachers in Lebanon lack a foundational understanding of pedagogy and appropriate developmental practices needed to teach reading, as most teachers lack a teaching diploma or have a background only in secondary teaching. This issue is urgent, as poor reading skills have a negative impact on students' ability to do well in other subjects (Bigozzi et al., 2017). In addition to Arabic, all children in public schools in Lebanon are taught either English or French, starting in first grade, and their math and science classes are taught in the same language. This means that children's English reading level has an impact on their learning outcomes across multiple subjects.

School disruptions

The academic year 2019–2020 in Lebanon suffered significant disruptions due to the political uprising that began in October 2019 and the COVID-19 outbreak in February 2020, resulting in more days of cancelled classes than days that school was in session. The following academic year, 2020–2021, started with a hybrid learning mode, but within a few weeks, the Minister of Education issued a decree (Circular 536/m/2020) eliminating the face-to-face learning mode due to the escalating number of COVID-19 cases. This was a major setback, as a lack of devices and poor connectivity made learning delivery and access to education a challenge, especially for the most vulnerable and marginalized students (Akar, 2021).

In-person instruction resumed with the start of the 2021–2022 academic year in September 2021. Yet in the first semester, students only received 25 days of instruction, instead of the planned 60 days, due to teachers' strikes protesting the low salaries of the education workforce. Thus, Lebanon experienced nearly two full school years of extremely disrupted education (2019–2020 and 2020–2021), plus an additional year of moderate but still highly disrupted activity in primary education (2021–2022).

Efforts to improve education at the primary level

This chapter focuses on interventions in the teaching of reading in English to children in grades 1–6 in Lebanon. The study was carried out by a project funded by the U.S. Agency for International Development (USAID). The project is called *Quality Instruction Towards Access and Basic Education Improvement 2* (QITABI 2). QITABI 2 takes the literacy model used in QITABI (2014–2019) in Arabic instruction in grades 1–4 and expands the methodology to grades 1–6 in English, French, and Arabic. Like QITABI 1, QITABI 2 works closely with the Ministry of Education and Higher Education (MEHE) and the Center for Educational Research and Development, the entity responsible for teacher training and curriculum development.

The literacy approach used in the QITABI programs is an adaptation of the Balanced Literacy Approach (Pressley & Allington, 2015). The core teaching technique in the Balanced Literacy Approach is to use an *I do – we do – you do* structure, through which the teacher (here, "I") gradually releases responsibility to learners ("you"). It culminates in independent practice time, during which the teacher can give differentiated instruction to individuals and small groups. In QITABI 2, social and emotional learning (SEL) is integrated into the lessons by following a developmentally appropriate scope and sequence of SEL skills. The SEL skill of the week (such as "Use positive self-talk to stay focused and on task") is explicitly named and practiced at least twice weekly, and opportunities for practicing it are integrated into other moments of the week's activities.

Because of the various school disruptions mentioned above, MEHE decided to reduce the national curricula, as a means of guiding instruction while instructional time was severely limited. The QITABI 2 team collaborated with the ministry on these decisions. The reduced curricula were published in September 2020 (Circular 30/m/2020). QITABI 2 continued working with MEHE and the Center for Educational Research and Development to then reorder the curriculum in the most developmentally appropriate way and ensure a systematic inclusion of the five foundational reading skills: phonemic awareness, phonics, vocabulary, reading fluency, and reading comprehension (National Reading Panel, 2000). The teams then created teaching and learning materials to guide instruction, while using as much as possible and adapting where necessary the national textbooks (last updated in 1997). The new materials include diagnostic assessments at the beginning of each unit and formative assessments for every class session. This procedure was done in order to provide teachers with the information needed to adapt English lessons to students' current level of ability, and to *differentiate* instruction – that is, tailoring instruction to meet individual needs.

Implementation begins

The first opportunity to get the new teaching and learning materials to teachers and train them on their use came with a five-week summer catch-up program, which ran in July and August 2021, after nearly two years of minimal instruction for most public schools' primary students (Akar, 2021). These summer sessions met four days a week and provided daily one hour of Arabic instruction, one hour of second language instruction (English, for the students in the present study), one hour of math instruction, and one hour exclusively devoted to SEL. The program aimed to offer students an opportunity to reengage with their peers, acquire SEL skills to regain their wellbeing, and recover some learning gaps in preparation for the academic year 2021–2022 (Circular 131/m/2021). Participating teachers received six hours of training on the QITABI 2 materials and methodology and were supported by MEHE coaches and project-specific learning facilitators. The catch-up program was conducted in 300 schools around the country, with a mixture of public and private school students. The instruction was led by public school teachers.

The summer catch-up program anecdotally received enthusiastic accolades and provided a much-needed opportunity for primary school students to receive structured in-person instruction after nearly two years without, but the circumstances in the country were such that it was often impossible to implement the program as planned. The currency crisis had engendered shortages in critical items, such as fuel and paper. More than 5% of the teachers could not attend the training due to the rising cost of transportation and scarcity of fuel. Recurrent power cuts and an inability to print documents obstructed activities involved in assessing and tracking students' performance. Other issues that were present in the summer catch-up program and continued into the following school year included a shortage in teaching staff due to a limited number of teachers, recurring teacher strikes, and challenging economic conditions necessitating many teachers to work overtime.

The next round of teacher training happened in two phases during the 2021–2022 school year, during which time teachers were trained on (1) understanding the reduced curriculum; (2) diagnostic and formative assessment tools and how to use them; (3) differentiating instruction to meet individual students' needs; (4) using the teaching and learning materials; and (5) teaching SEL and self-care. Phase 1 happened in November 2021 and represented three hours of teacher training. Phase 2 happened from April to June 2022 and comprised two five-hour days of training that furthered teachers' mastery of the topics from Phase 1.

Research questions

The research reported here presents data from a larger study that targeted 120 primary schools distributed proportionally among the eight regions in Lebanon. Of the 120 schools, 65 teach English as the first second language, as opposed to French. This study aimed to measure students' reading levels in English at the outset of QITABI 2 teacher training and teachers' uptake of teaching practices presented in QITABI 2 training. Specifically, three research questions were addressed:

1. What were the English reading levels of first through sixth graders in public schools near the end of the 2021–2022 school year?
2. Which aspects of the QITABI 2 teaching approach were grades 1–6 public school English teachers implementing in the first school year of the QITABI 2 intervention at their schools?
3. What factors do teachers identify as leading to uptake or lack of uptake of the various components of the QITABI 2 approach?

Research methods

Context

In order to inform policy and planning in primary school education, MEHE and QITABI 2 collaborated to conduct a nationwide study of learning loss in April and May, 2021. The study was conducted by trained data collectors in the 120 aforementioned public schools. The test items were taken from the early grade reading assessment (EGRA) test developed between MEHE and QITABI previously (Dubeck & Grove, 2015). The Arabic reading skills of 2,400 second and third graders were measured against national benchmarks. The study found that the overwhelming majority of second and third graders were reading at two or more levels below grade level expectations. Only 1.9% of second graders and 2.0% of third graders were reading at or above grade level expectations.

While these results are limited to the Arabic language and second and third graders, there was reason to expect similar or possibly larger learning gaps to exist in second language English classes, and in other grades. It was against this backdrop that the present study was conducted. Unlike the Arabic reading study described above, the investigation of English reading relies on data coming directly from the classroom teachers, and not from professional data collectors.

Participants

The English teachers at the 65 English-teaching schools were asked to fill out a teacher self-assessment tool and conduct a diagnostic assessment of their students' reading skills. Teacher self-assessments were collected for 191 English teachers (187 females), 144 of whom had attended Phase 1 training in November 2021. The results on the reading diagnostic test were collected for 6,613 students (3,098 females) in first through sixth grade.

Data collection procedures

Assessment of students' reading in English

For each grade 1–6, a diagnostic test was created to determine whether students have mastered the reading prerequisites for the grade they are enrolled in. For example, one learning objective in the third-grade national curriculum is, "Explain how character's actions affect other characters." The second-grade learning objective, "Describe actions and physical appearance of characters in a story" is considered a prerequisite skill (Circular 114/m/1997; Circular 30/m/2020).

The test was conducted with the full class, and each child received a copy of the test. For grades 1–4, the test started with letter name and letter sound identification tasks, in three parts: First, the child saw rows of four lowercase letters.

For each of the 15 rows, the teacher chose one of the letters and said its name out loud twice. Students needed to circle the correct letter. Next, the task was repeated with capital letters (15 rows of four letters). For the third letter identification task, the child saw rows of four lowercase letters. For each row, the teacher chose one letter and twice uttered the canonical sound associated with the letter, for the students to circle the correct letter.

These tasks were followed by a sight word identification task. *Sight words* are high frequency words whose irregular spellings require memorization (e.g., *to, the*) (Murray et al., 2019). For the sight word task, which was part of the diagnostic test for all grades 1–6, the students saw 10 rows of four words. For each row, the teacher chose one word and said it out loud twice. Students were asked to circle the word they heard. The words on the test were from the sight word lists from the previous grade's curriculum.

Finally, all grades had two reading comprehension texts. The first reading text was at the previous grade's beginning-of-the-year reading level, and the second one was at the end-of-the-year level for the previous grade. Grade 1 texts were 14 and 26 words long; grade 6 texts were both around 200 words long. For both texts, there were comprehension questions; three of the questions came directly from the text, and two of them required some level of inference. For grades 1–3, the questions were multiple-choice, with three options each. For grades 4–6, the questions were open-ended. Teachers were told to accept any answer that indicated that the student knew the correct answer; spelling and grammar were not scored.

Teachers were trained on how to administer the diagnostic test during the teacher training sessions, and instructions were available in the testing materials as well. Materials for English teachers were provided in English. Teachers were asked to administer the diagnostic test to all of their students. A follow-up, one-on-one oral exam was conducted later with students who scored 40% or below on the questions on the first reading comprehension text, to confirm results and gather more information about the students' levels.

Teachers began administering the diagnostic test to their students shortly after receiving Phase 1 training. Because teachers needed to fit this additional task into their teaching schedules, and many teachers had to conduct numerous individual follow-up tests, results came in staggered over the next few months.

Teachers' self-assessment

In February 2022, the QITABI 2 team sent a link to an online questionnaire, using Google Forms, to the school principals in the 65 selected schools. The principals shared the link with their grade 1–6 English language teachers, requesting them to complete the form. This English-language online tool consists of 17 yes/no questions which ask about the teachers' use of various components of the QITABI 2 training and materials, such as, "Do you implement a beginning-of-class greeting as part of class meeting [first five minutes of class]?", "Do you implement a warm-up SEL or language-focused activity as part of class meetings?", and "Do you implement the mini-lesson format presented in QITABI 2 trainings, focusing on only one learning objective and following the I Do – We Do – You Do structure?" Each yes/no question had a space for optional comments. At the end of the survey, an additional open-ended question asked the teachers about the most common challenges they faced in implementing the components during the 2021–2022 academic year. The self-assessment instructions and the message accompanying the link to the questionnaire emphasized to principals and teachers that the self-assessment was intended as a baseline measurement and not as an evaluation of the teachers.

Focus group discussions

The QITABI 2 team conducted qualitative data collection in the form of a focus group discussion with four teachers and phone interviews with four other teachers. Half of the eight teachers taught grades 1–3, and the other four taught grades 4–6. The teachers were selected based on their students' diagnostic scores. Four of the teachers had 70% or more of their students meeting prerequisites, as determined by the diagnostic, and half of the teachers had 70% or more of their students not meeting prerequisites.

Data analysis procedures

Analysis of student reading assessment data

Teachers recorded the assessment results on the scoring sheets provided by QITABI 2. Next, the team collected the results and entered them into an Excel form and cleaned the data of any duplicate entries. At the level of student performance, the team calculated percentages of students performing at different levels for each reading skill domain (letter name, reading comprehension, etc.). Scores were then converted into two categories to indicate whether the student met grade-level prerequisite expectations or whether their score fell below the grade-level cut-off score.

Analysis of teachers' self-assessment data

The team calculated the percentage of teachers' self-reported use of the various QITABI 2 elements when teaching students. The QITABI 2 team calculated Cronbach's alpha to estimate the internal consistency and reliability of the items in the survey. Cronbach's alpha for teacher self-assessment was found to be 0.73. For the open-ended items and comments, the teachers' responses were compiled. Similar answers were transformed into unified options under themes and then the team counted the options accordingly.

Analysis of focus group data

Qualitative data collected through the interviews and focus groups were analyzed using an ethnographic analysis, where we drew primarily on responses from the group discussion labeling them into *themes* and *illustrative quotations* (Krippendorff, 2012). The themes were based on frequently repeated words and topics, and the illustrative quotations were direct quotes from respondents that highlighted what the discussants reported within our research questions. This procedure was done while maintaining the integrity and accounting for the context of the focus group or interview.

Findings and discussion

Student reading performance

The Letter Name and Letter Sound tasks were completed only by students in grades 1–4. The results for these tasks are shown in Table 2.1.

We can see that for these first through fourth graders, mastery of the primary sound associated with a letter (letter sound task) met grade-level prerequisite expectations for the majority of students, whereas well under half of students reached grade-level prerequisite expectations in knowledge of the letters' names. Both skills contribute independently to reading ability, but letter-sound knowledge is more directly involved in reading itself, whereas letter-name knowledge is primarily important in the communication needed to talk about reading and understand reading instruction (McBride-Chang, 1999).

Table 2.2 shows the scores across all six grades for the Sight Word and Reading Comprehension tasks.

These findings indicate that the majority of the children tested were able to recognize isolated letters (letter sound task, Table 2.1) and isolated words (sight

TABLE 2.1 Students scoring at or below grade-level prerequisite cut-offs for the letter name task and letter sound task

Grade		Does Not Meet Prerequisites		Meets Grade-Level Prerequisites	
		Letter Name	Letter Sound	Letter Name	Letter Sound
1	%	78.4	38.8	21.6	61.2
	n	845	412	233	651
2	%	72.2	22.5	27.8	77.5
	n	774	241	298	830
3	%	67.5	18.5	32.5	81.5
	n	684	187	329	824
4	%	69.5	11.5	30.5	88.5
	n	759	125	333	966

word task, Table 2.2). However, they were unable to use that knowledge for the higher-level skill of reading comprehension, as, on average across all grades, only 27% of students scored high enough to reach the prerequisite knowledge for their grade level. Note that these benchmarks are only meant to indicate readiness to learn the curriculum for the grade in which the students are enrolled. The higher percentage of students below the benchmark in first grade suggests that these students received less previous English instruction than other students. The drop in the percentage of students reaching the reading comprehension benchmark between grade 3 and grade 4 is likely due in part to the fact that for grades 1–3, the questions were multiple choice, whereas in grades 4–6, students had to write out answers to open-ended questions.

Teachers' self-assessment

English teachers in the 65 primary public schools self-assessed their implementation of QITABI 2 practices inside the classroom and indicated the most common challenges they faced implementing these in the 2021–2022 academic year. For the 11 items that asked whether teachers followed the procedures they were trained on in QITABI 2, the agreement ranged between 80% to 98%. The remaining six yes/no questions asked whether the teacher was using specific resources while teaching, such as information technology, children's leveled books, and the PowerPoint presentations provided by QITABI 2. Answers to these ranged from 45% (using the PowerPoint files) to 78% ("Do you use other

TABLE 2.2 Students scoring at or below grade-level prerequisite cut-offs for the sight word task and the reading comprehension tasks

Grade		Does Not Meet Prerequisites		Meets Grade-Level Prerequisites	
		Sight Words	Reading Comprehension	Sight Words	Reading Comprehension
1	%	50.4	77.2	49.6	22.8
	n	531	794	523	235
2	%	28.0	66.8	72	33.2
	n	293	669	752	333
3	%	23.3	59.3	76.7	40.7
	n	224	550	741	378
4	%	14.2	82.6	85.8	17.4
	n	147	800	893	168
5	%	11.4	80.1	88.6	19.9
	n	130	871	1008	216
6	%	9.6	70.4	90.4	29.6
	n	104	752	973	316

tools in your classroom?"). While uptake of the teaching techniques presented in the QITABI 2 trainings does appear to be fairly high, the teachers' self-assessment is almost certainly exaggerated, based on classroom observations from MEHE coaches and project learning facilitators. This tendency might be due to teachers' misunderstanding of the questions and/or of what it means to implement each of the features they believed they were implementing. Also likely is the presence of both *acquiescence bias* – the tendency to agree to items on a survey – and *social desirability bias*, which is the tendency in survey responses to deny undesirable traits or actions (Presser, et al., 2004).

The open-ended question regarding the challenges that teachers faced that made implementing QITABI 2 practices difficult was answered by 127 teachers. Some teachers described more than one challenge in their answers. The most common challenges are listed in Table 2.3.

Most of the challenges had to do with limited resources and issues related to Lebanon's current political and economic crises.

Focus groups

The teachers were asked if the QITABI 2 training was helpful, and what was helpful.

All eight teachers agreed that the training was very important for their professional development. They expressed that it was helpful for them to know how to plan and organize their teaching in a way to help the students get back on track. In addition, they noted it was important to learning how teachers can heal themselves, after years of national crises, to be able to help students get engaged in the learning process. This latter comment is in connection to the SEL integration in the teacher training.

TABLE 2.3 Most common barriers to implementing QITABI 2 components in class

Challenge	N of Responses
The students have a weak foundation in English	35
The students are suffering from a huge gap due to the learning loss in the past two years	23
The lack of resources (office supplies and technology)	21
Students in the same class are at different levels, and it is hard to implement for different levels	17
The lack of steady electricity and internet in schools	14
The intermittent operation of schools due to continuous strikes and closures	6
The limited time the teachers have to use QITABI 2 techniques	6
The lack of parental engagement with the teachers to support the students	5
The large number of students in the classroom (around 25 on average)	3

The teachers whose students mostly tested as having met the prerequisites said that they benefitted from the guidelines on how to deal with students' behavior, using SEL techniques. These teachers used the QITABI 2 approach and resources to differentiate their instruction, by, for example, providing shorter texts for beginning readers. Teachers whose students mostly did not meet prerequisites also reported benefiting from the training, but they did not describe differentiating instruction effectively in class. Two of these teachers said they felt they needed a teaching assistant supporting students below grade level until they reach grade level and can work with their classmates.

Teachers were also asked if they administered the diagnostic assessment and how they used its results to group students. All teachers reported difficulty in administering the assessment close to midterm exams, yet they did it. The teachers stated that the diagnostic assessment results were important to them to know the level of students in order to choose appropriate reading material for them and support them at their level.

All teachers noted that the diagnostic assessment helped them specify each student's level, and the exact areas where a student needs support. One of the teachers whose students mostly met prerequisites said, "I thought of every student when I was correcting the assessment, and I was reflecting according to my knowledge about him/her."

There are some limitations to this research project. First, the data for this study were collected by the teachers themselves. There may be some variability in the way that the teachers conducted the reading study. Most but not all of the teachers had attended Phase 1 of the training, where they were trained on conducting the test. Second, the teachers are also the source of information about the implementation of the practices. This fact means that their perception of implementation might sometimes not align with what was intended by the questions. Additionally, throughout the time of data collection, strikes were ongoing. Strikes and other phenomena that arise during a time of unpredictable changes affect scheduling and the teachers' ability to plan. Paper and electricity shortages also make it difficult to plan for and carry out diagnostic assessments and self-assessments.

Implications for policy, practice, and future research

The results of the diagnostic reading test indicate that most students were performing well below grade-level expectations. Such gaps in fundamental reading skills in English will affect their ability to perform in their science and math classes as well, since the policy in Lebanese public schools is to teach these courses in the second language the children study at school. It also means that these students would be unable to keep up in English classes taught at grade-level expectations. Lags in developing fundamental skills tend to compound over time, causing gaps between student level and grade-level expectations to increase over time (National Reading Panel, 2000). It is therefore urgent to continue training and coaching teachers on how to differentiate instruction so that they are able to teach students what those children are developmentally ready to learn. Differentiated instruction also requires that teachers are competent in using diagnostic and formative testing.

Evidence needs to be collected as to what is working in educational contexts of crisis and learning loss, and these findings need to be shared and their recommendations implemented widely (see, e.g., Bailey & Christian, 2021; Erling, 2017). Coordination of efforts is of utmost importance, so as to implement systemically coherent changes, as opposed to piecemeal efforts, which tend to confuse stakeholders and diffuse the efficacy of efforts. For example, it is important to closely coordinate teacher training with the production of teaching and learning materials, and to coordinate ongoing teacher coaching with teacher training. Evidence is also vital to inform an ongoing curriculum revision process.

Finally, children's healthy development and ability to perform in school can be greatly supported through systematic and developmentally and culturally appropriate instruction in SEL. Holistic teacher training in SEL includes supporting teachers' wellbeing, which in turn supports teachers' ability to perform. The SEL activities integrated into QITABI 2 teaching and learning materials and teacher training demonstrated that SEL can be integrated into all school activities. Our findings indicate that including SEL in these activities supported English language learning.

Acknowledgments

This chapter was made possible by the generous support of the American people through the United States Agency for International Development (USAID). The contents are the responsibility of QITABI 2 and do not necessarily reflect the view of USAID or the United States Government. The authors are listed in alphabetical order, to reflect their equal levels of contribution.

References

Akar, B. (2021). *Basic education in Lebanon: Rapid education and risk analysis and social inclusion analysis (RERA+SI)*. ECCN.

Bailey, K. M., & Christian, D. (Eds). (2021). *Research on teaching and learning English in under-resourced contexts*. TIRF & Routledge.

Bigozzi, L., Tarchi, C., Vagnoli, L., Valente, E., & Pinto, G. (2017). Reading fluency as a predictor of school outcomes across grades 4–9. *Frontiers in Psychology, 8*. https://doi.org/10.3389/fpsyg.2017.00200.

Dubeck, M. M., & Grove, A. (2015). The early grade reading assessment (EGRA): Its theoretical foundation, purpose, and limitations. *International Journal of Educational Development, 40*, 315–322. https://doi.org/10.1016/j.ijedudev.2014.11.004.

Erling, E. J. (2017). *English across the fracture lines: The contribution and relevance of English to security, stability, and peace*. British Council.

Human Rights Watch. (2021, March 26). *Lebanon: Action needed on Syrian refugee education crisis.* https://www.hrw.org/news/2021/03/26/lebanon-action-needed-syrian-refugee-education-crisis.

Jalbout, M. (2015). *Reaching all children with education in Lebanon.* Theirworld. https://theirworld.org/resources/report-reaching-all-children-with-education-in-lebanon/.

Krippendorff, K. (2012). *Content analysis: An introduction to its methodology* (3rd ed.). Sage Publications Inc.

McBride-Chang, C. (1999). The ABCs of the ABCs: The development of letter-name and letter-sound knowledge. *Merrill-Palmer Quarterly, 45*(2), 285–308. https://www.jstor.org/stable/23093679.

Murray, B. A., McIlwain, M. J., Wang, C., Murray, G., & Finley, S. (2019). How do beginners learn to read irregular words as sight words? *Journal of Research in Reading, 42* (1), 123–136. https://doi.org/10.1111/1467-9817.12250.

National Reading Panel (U.S.) & National Institute of Child Health and Human Development (U.S.). (2000). *Report of the National Reading Panel: Teaching children to read: An evidence-based assessment of the scientific research literature on reading and its implications for reading instruction.* U.S. Dept. of Health and Human Services, Public Health Service, National Institutes of Health, National Institute of Child Health and Human Development.

Presser, S., Rothgeb, J. M., Couper, M. P., Lessler, J. T., Martin, E., Martin, J., & Singer, E. (2004). *Methods for testing and evaluating survey questionnaires.* John Wiley & Sons.

Pressley, M., & Allington, R. L. (2015). *Reading instruction that works: The case for balanced teaching* (4th ed.). Guilford Press.

Reuters. (2022, January 11). *Lebanon's currency plummets again amid financial crisis and political deadlock.* https://www.reuters.com/world/middle-east/lebanons-currency-plummets-again-amid-financial-crisis-political-deadlock-2022-01-11/.

UNICEF. (2022). *Searching for hope report: A grim outlook for youth as Lebanon teeters on the brink of collapse.* https://www.unicef.org/lebanon/reports/searching-hope-report.

World Bank Group. (2021). *Lebanon sinking (To the top three).* https://documents1.worldbank.org/curated/en/394741622469174252/pdf/Lebanon-Economic-Monitor-Lebanon-Sinking-to-the-Top-3.pdf.

3
TEACHING AND ASSESSING SPEAKING IN THE CONTEXT OF CURRICULAR REFORM

The case of Israel

Orly Haim and Tziona Levi

Introduction

Issues that motivated the research

The motivation for this study was a novel nationwide computerized English proficiency test administered at the end of high school (12th grade) in Israeli schools as part of the matriculation exams. The incorporation of this test has generated various changes in the EFL (English as a Foreign Language) curriculum, placing greater emphasis on speaking tasks and activities accompanied by assessment methodology. Furthermore, the Israeli Ministry of Education has initiated a comprehensive in-service teacher education program focusing on the teaching and assessment of speaking. This reform may have fundamental implications for how the construct of speaking is perceived, taught, and assessed by EFL teachers (see, e.g., Cheng & Curtis, 2004). Questions arise as to the potential impact of this reform on teachers' dimensions of professional knowledge and practices as well as the relationships between them. Finally, it is vital to explore teachers' views about implementing speaking instructional and assessment practices considering this reform.

Language Assessment Literacy (LAL) is defined as the knowledge and ability to identify aspects of assessment and engage in language assessment practices (Engelsen & Smith, 2014). This study draws on the construct of LAL, viewing it as an aspect of teachers' professional knowledge (Vogt et al., 2020), including teaching and assessing speaking.

The term LAL is generally used to refer to "a repertoire of competencies that enable an individual [i.e., various stakeholders] to understand, evaluate, and, in some cases, create language [assessment instruments] and analyze [assessment] data" (Pill & Harding, 2013, p. 382). LAL as a construct is especially pertinent for

DOI: 10.4324/9781003312444-4

language teachers, due to their involvement in both internal and external assessment in their dual role as teachers and assessors (Tsagari, 2020). Recognizing the significance of teachers' LAL has motivated the development of the construct to include a wide range of interrelated, overlapping dimensions of assessment knowledge and skills (e.g., dispositions, values, goals, ideologies, and contextual factors), as delineated in Table 3.1.

As shown in Table 3.1, the construct of LAL has evolved to be conceived as multicomponential, developmental, and contextually embedded. Indeed, interest in LAL has increased dramatically in the past two decades. Nevertheless, very few studies have thoroughly examined the construct of LAL as it relates specifically to speaking.

Recently, Harding et al. (2021) explored nine elements required for application of LAL as they particularly relate to spoken language assessment, arguing that "the assessments of different language skills will require unique applications of knowledge within each of the categories" (Harding et al., 2021, p. 374). Their analysis accentuates the features associated with the process of assessing speaking (e.g., administration, scoring, washback, pedagogical knowledge), which hence necessitates teachers and stakeholders to possess the required knowledge and skills, in order to effectively implement assessment procedures for speaking. These authors further highlight the role of technology and language modalities in language for the teaching and assessment of speaking.

Research questions

This study aims to explore the components of LAL pertaining to the teaching and assessment of speaking, and how they interact with teachers' speaking practices, situated in the Israeli context. The results may be helpful in designing teacher education programs to impact successful enhancement of instructional speaking practices. Thus, the following questions guided the study:

1. What are the major dimensions of EFL teachers' LAL which are associated with teaching and assessing speaking?
2. What are EFL teachers' practices for teaching and assessing speaking?
3. What are the predictive relationships between teachers' LAL and teaching practices? Specifically, which dimensions of LAL predict EFL teachers' reported teaching practices?

Research methods

Context of the research

The study was conducted in Israel, where large-scale tests are dominant, and 80,000 12th graders are annually tested to examine their speaking proficiency in English. The study context involves a new national curriculum focusing on

TABLE 3.1 The development of the construct of LAL

Model	Conceptualization of LAL
Davies (2008)	LAL is conceptualized as a schematic model suggesting professionalism in assessment activities based on solid knowledge and critically reflecting on current assessment practices. The model involves skills (e.g., relevant methodologies of test writing, administration, analysis, and reporting), knowledge, and principles (ethics and fair use of language tests).
Inbar-Lourie (2008)	LAL encompasses three major dimensions: (1) the purpose of assessment (why) (2) the content (what), and (3) the assessment format (how). The format reflects the testing culture, i.e., the notion of high-stakes, standardized testing with the appropriate psychometric knowledge and skills. Additionally, LAL is contingent on the socio-cultural attitude within an interpretative, constructivist approach to knowledge conceived as assessment culture.
Taylor (2009)	LAL is contextualized and linked with stakeholders' sufficient and relevant knowledge to perform their role within the assessment process.
Fulcher (2012)	LAL involves a dialectical scheme including assessment constructs along with contextual factors (e.g., historical, social, political, and philosophical). Accordingly, teachers can only "own" LAL once they understand how assessment practices and contextual factors interact.
Scarino (2013)	LAL is conceptualized to include teachers' interpretations emerging from their experiences, knowledge, understandings, beliefs, and self-awareness.
Pill & Harding (2013)	LAL is viewed as a five-stage model ranging from illiterate to literate according to different stakeholders' needs that define their necessary levels of assessment literacy (e.g., policymakers should reach the 'functional level', while teachers need 'multidimensional' or 'conceptual and procedural' literacy).
Taylor (2013)	LAL is theorized as an elaborated model referring to stakeholders' specific levels of literacy for eight key dimensions depending on context and needs. These include dimensions of knowledge, skills, and principles: language pedagogy, sociocultural values, local practices, personal beliefs/attitudes, scores, and decision-making. Additionally, five degrees of literacy are suggested.
Inbar-Lourie (2016, 2017)	LAL encompasses a dynamic merging of expertise in language assessment within a social-educational context, including general guiding principles for different assessment literacies, discerning local needs and incorporating them. In 2017, the model was expanded to address a pluralistic framework of localized LALs.
Malone (2017)	Students' perspectives in defining the construct of LAL were added, suggesting relevant assessment methodologies.
Tsagari (2017)	LAL is viewed through a constructivist lens, situated in a specific context, constituting an aspect of teachers' knowledge and beliefs.
Levi & Inbar-Lourie (2020)	LAL is regarded as contextualized and multifaceted integrating the language-learning construct and its corresponding assessment practices.
Kremmel & Harding (2020)	Obtained from large-scale research, LAL is conceptualized according to nine dimensions, representing the perspectives and contexts of language teachers and various stakeholders (rather than researchers).

speaking as an essential skill and the introduction of a computer-based version to test speaking.

This study is part of a large-scale research project incorporating mixed methods (Creswell & Clark, 2017), utilizing questionnaires and interviews. This paper reports on some of the key quantitative findings addressing the research questions. The qualitative data are used primarily to gain a better understanding of the quantitative findings and for data triangulation.

Participants

The study included 432 EFL teachers currently working in Israeli schools, of whom 53% (n = 224) were born in Israel, 32% (n = 136) were born in English-speaking countries, and 15% (n = 66) were born in non-English-speaking countries (France, Germany, etc.). Twenty-seven percent of the teachers taught in primary schools and 71% of the teachers taught in secondary schools (i.e., 7th through 12th grades). Approximately 24% of the teachers taught in high socio-economic status (SES) schools, 61% taught in medium SES schools, and 15% taught in low SES schools.

Data collection procedures

An online questionnaire consisting of closed and open items was distributed to EFL teachers currently teaching in Israeli schools. The data were collected during one school year, utilizing a convenience sampling procedure (Vogt & Johnson, 2016), which involved contacting accessible EFL teachers via the Israeli English Inspectorate site. The study followed ethical guidelines, requesting the teachers to sign a consent form for participating in the study; respondents were protected in terms of anonymity and confidentiality.

The teacher questionnaire, which was developed especially for the study, consisted of 44 items and was divided into four main parts. First, demographic and professional details were gathered with 14 closed items eliciting information about the teachers' background and school contexts. Second, teachers' LAL about teaching and assessing speaking was addressed with 20 statements adapted from Kremmel and Harding (2020) and presented in a Likert scale format, tapping the teachers' assessment literacy knowledge with regard to speaking. Third, the section on teachers' practices included seven closed questions, five of which addressed dimensions of teaching and assessing speaking (e.g., the role assigned to speaking in the syllabus, frequency of incorporating speaking activities, student engagement in the activities, etc.). Two other items elicited information concerning types of speaking activities and assessment instruments. This section also included two open-ended questions addressing teachers' perspectives regarding speaking activities (e.g., strengths and weaknesses of their speaking programs, advantages and disadvantages of using technology for speaking activities).

The development of the questionnaire included a pilot phase with 95 teachers to examine relevance and clarity of the items, instructions and scales, order of questions, estimation of time required to complete the questionnaire, and internal reliability. This phase included a focus group discussion with 20 teachers and teacher trainers who completed the questionnaire, in order to obtain qualitative feedback about the content validity of the instrument. The items on the questionnaire were closely examined according to their relevance to teaching and assessing speaking in EFL contexts (i.e., determining whether each item was essential, useful but not essential, or not necessary). Moreover, the focus group participants were asked to comment on the clarity of the items and instructions, order of questions, length of the sections, and suitability of the scales. The feedback and the item analyses required several revisions. Specifically, two Likert scale items were discarded, reducing the total number of items in this section from 22 to 20. Also, the number of questions on teacher practices was reduced from a total of 12 items to eight.

Data analysis procedures

The construct validity of the instrument was examined using exploratory and confirmatory factor analysis methods as described below. The questionnaire was examined with item analysis and reliability measures, using Cronbach's alpha, the results of which ranged from 0.95 to 0.96.

As the next step, an exploratory factor analysis (EFA) was done. Factor analysis is a statistical procedure for dimension reduction, identifying the underlying major concepts. We used oblique rotation to reduce the number of dimensions. Based on Field (2009), an item was considered to be loaded on a factor if it achieved an absolute factor loading of ≥ 0.40. The Kaiser-Meyer-Olkin measure verified the sampling adequacy for the analysis, KMO = .96 ("superb" according to Field, 2009). Bartlett's test of sphericity (x^2 = 9206.055, p < 0.001) indicated that correlations between items were sufficiently large for Principal Component Analysis (a statistical procedure for data reduction which is used to create one or more index variables from a larger set of measured variables).

A four-factor solution emerged, accounting for 84% of the variance. Factor 2 included only one statement and was, therefore, excluded from our subsequent analyses. Based on the results of the factor analyses, the reliability of the remaining three factors was calculated. Appendix A presents the factor loadings and the reliability of each factor. We interpreted the factors to represent the following dimensions of EFL teachers' LAL with respect to speaking based on the contents of the statements loaded on each factor: (1) teaching, learning, and assessment cycle (α = 0.96) (2); assessment methodology for speaking (α = 0.96); and (3) the impact of assessment on instruction and learning (α = 0.95). Based on the factor analysis results, the summary scores of each of the three factors were constructed, averaging all the items included in each. This step was taken in order to determine the three main variables representing the dimensions of LAL.

Teachers' reported practices for teaching and assessing speaking were calculated based on their content by summing the number of events indicated for each one of the practices (e.g., discussions, role plays, etc.). The means and standard deviations were calculated for the following dimensions of speaking practices and used for the subsequent analyses: (1) role of speaking in the syllabus, (2) frequency of incorporating speaking activities, (3) students' engagement in speaking activities, (4) using technology for teaching speaking, and (5) using technology for assessing speaking. Data addressing teachers' perspectives on the role of technology in teaching and assessing speaking were elicited through the open-ended question in the questionnaire and analyzed qualitatively using content analysis methods (Corbin & Strauss, 2008).

Findings and discussion

The first research question asked what major dimensions of EFL teachers' LAL were associated with teaching and assessing speaking. Means and standard deviations were calculated for each of the three summary scores of the dimensions of teachers' LAL. As shown in Table 3.2, the teachers demonstrated positive endorsement of the LAL dimensions. (Means are based on a five-point Likert scale, with standard deviations given in parentheses below the means.) Yet, independent samples t-test results indicate that secondary school teachers differ significantly from those teaching in primary schools in the strength of endorsement of the LAL dimensions. That is, secondary school teachers demonstrated a tendency to rank the LAL dimensions higher than did the primary school teachers, and those differences were all statistically significant ($p < .01$).

These findings also resonate with the qualitative data suggesting that secondary school teachers tended to view the aspect of assessing speaking to be vital for their instructional practices, as compared with primary school teachers, who focused more on classroom activities in their accounts. Specifically, the secondary school

TABLE 3.2 EFL teachers' LAL: results of t-tests

LAL dimension	School level		t	df
	Primary ($n = 112$)	Secondary ($n = 298$)		
Teaching, learning, & assessment cycle	3.30 (1.01)	3.72 (1.11)	-4.42★★	408
Assessment methodology for speaking	3.08 (1.08)	3.35 (1.02)	-2.35★★	404
The impact of assessment	3.12 (1.05)	3.50 (0.60)	-2.04★★	403

teachers contended that the use of technology motivates students to assume an active role as learners and assessors of their own speaking performance. These results highlight the central role of context in understanding teachers' LAL and practices (Vogt et al., 2020). The aspect of assessing speaking is presumably more prominent in secondary schools due to the recent reform of the speaking component in the Israeli matriculation exam and secondary school teachers' in-service programs, which may have created a washback effect, influencing teachers' beliefs and decision making.

The second research question asked, "What are EFL teachers' practices for teaching and assessing speaking?" The findings show that despite the current centrality of speaking in the Israeli English curriculum, 35% of the teachers did not receive training to teach and assess speaking in their pre-service programs. Yet, most of the teachers (83%) assigned an important role (53% of the teachers) or a very important role (30% of the teachers) to speaking in their syllabi. Over half of the respondents reported they frequently incorporated face-to-face speaking activities in their lessons (i.e., 44% every lesson and 14% twice a week). The majority of the teachers (77%) perceived their students to be engaged with their speaking classroom activities. Moreover, 75% of our participants reported they incorporated technology in speaking activities, whereas 35% of the teachers use technology for assessing the following dimensions of speaking: content, accuracy, fluency, and communicative skills.

Finally, the majority of the teachers reported using various instruments to assess speaking, such as rubrics (92%), speaking projects (67%), and checklists (65%). These results can be interpreted to imply the centrality of speaking in Israeli EFL classrooms, indicating the potentially strong impact of the national reform in the English curriculum on classroom instruction. Thus, these findings extend previous research highlighting the crucial influence of contextual factors on teaching and assessment practices as well as the teachers' LAL (e.g., Crusan et al., 2016).

The final research question asked, "What are the predictive relationships between teachers' LAL and teaching practices?" To address this question, a series of multivariate linear regression analyses was conducted. Linear regression is a statistical procedure that estimates predictive relationships between one dependent variable and one or more independent variables.

The three indices of LAL served as independent variables, while the variables "the role of speaking in the syllabus", "frequency of incorporating speaking activities in EFL classes", "perceived students' engagement in speaking activities", "using technology" for teaching speaking, and "using technology for assessing speaking" were inserted to the model as dependent variables.

Results from teachers in primary and secondary school (summarized in Table 3.3) indicate a differential pattern of prediction of the dimensions of LAL for each one of the practices (except for 'frequency of speaking activities,' which was not found related to any of the LAL dimensions). The dimension of the *teaching, learning, and assessment cycle* contributed significantly to the prediction of the variable "students'

TABLE 3.3 Relationships between teachers' dimensions of LAL and their reported practices

"The role of speaking in the syllabus"				Dimension of LAL
R^2	β	SE	B	Teaching, learning, & assessment cycle
.07	.01	.74	.01	
	.01	.07	.01	Assessment methodology for speaking
	.27**	.07	.17	The impact of assessment
"Frequency of speaking activities"				Dimension of LAL:
.02	.08	.14	.11	Teaching, learning, & assessment cycle
	-.04	.14	-.05	Assessment methodology for speaking
	.06	.14	-.08	The impact of assessment
"Perceived student engagement"				Dimension of LAL
.11	.30**	.09	.25	Teaching, learning, & assessment cycle
	-.05	.09	-.04	Assessment methodology for speaking
	.10	.09	.08	The impact of assessment
Dimension of LAL "Incorporating technology for assessing speaking"				
.06	-.47***	.04	-.06	Teaching, learning, & assessment cycle
	.13*	.05	.18	Assessment methodology for speaking
	.24	.04	-.01	The impact of assessment
Dimension of LAL "Incorporating technology for teaching speaking"				
.04	-.15	.04	-.06	Teaching, learning, & assessment cycle
	.44**	.05	.18	Assessment methodology for speaking
	.24*	.04	-.01	The impact of assessment

Note: *p < 0.05, **p < 0.001

engagement in speaking activities" (β = .29, p < .001), explaining 11% of the total variance. In Table 3.3 and the rest of this discussion, the dimensions are italicized and the practices are marked by single quotes.

The dimension *impact of assessment on instruction and learning* contributed significantly to the prediction of the 'role assigned to speaking in the syllabus' by the teachers (β = .27, p < .001), explaining 7% of the total variance. The results further indicate that the dimensions of *assessment methodology for speaking* (β = .44, p < .001), and *the impact of assessment on instruction and learning* (β = .24, p < .05) significantly contributed to the prediction of teachers' reported "use of technology for teaching speaking", explaining 5% of the variance. Moreover, the dimensions of *assessment methodology for speaking* (β = .13, p < .05) and *teaching, learning and assessment cycle* (β = -.47, p < .001), were found to contribute to the prediction of teachers' reported "use of technology for assessing speaking", explaining 6% of the overall variance. The positive standardized beta coefficients of the former variable highlight the direct link between "the use of technology for assessing speaking" by the teachers and their general belief about assessing speaking. Conversely, the negative effect of the latter variable suggests that teachers were more likely to perceive "the use of technology for assessing speaking" as inversely related to the *teaching, learning, and assessment cycle*.

The relative strength of the standardized beta coefficients of the LAL dimensions *assessment methodology for speaking* and *teaching, learning, and assessment cycle* compared to the third dimension (i.e., *the impact of assessment on instruction and learning*) highlight the relative powerful influence of these two dimensions of LAL on teachers' reported practices. Moreover, these results concur with previous research suggesting that the processes of teaching and assessing speaking are perceived as linked (Harding et al., 2021).

The qualitative data shed light on the quantitative findings, particularly in connection to the use of technology for teaching and assessing speaking. The teachers' accounts portray conflicting views concerning the incorporation of technology for teaching and assessing speaking. Specifically, the teachers perceive technology as a useful pedagogical resource, yet they simultaneously argue that it involves inherent instructional limitations. They view technology as a motivating resource affording students opportunities to develop speaking skills independently. Despite these advantages, some teachers argue that technology lacks the communicative and sensitive aspects involved in real-life conversations and hence may be insufficient for teaching and assessing speaking in and of itself. Some of these conflicting views are illustrated in the quotes below:

> Technology can be very helpful in teaching speaking since it exposes students to authentic speech with everyday situations as well as accurate and clear accent of the speaker. It is a safe environment, so the students feel comfortable speaking.
>
> *(Teacher #1)*

> I don't think using technology is efficient in teaching speaking. I think that assessment should be done by a human being. There is a lot more to communication than artificial intelligence interpretation of student language.
>
> *(Teacher #2)*

Taken together, these views can be interpreted to suggest that technology-based and face-to-face interaction activities may complement each other for effective instruction.

Implications for policy, practice, and future research

This study was initiated to examine the dimensions of EFL teachers' LAL related to the skill of speaking. Additionally, teachers' reported practices for enhancing speaking in the classroom were examined, as well as the predictive relationships between dimensions of teachers' LAL and their practices. An instrument for examining teachers' LAL specifically related to the teaching and assessing of speaking was developed and validated. Moreover, utilizing a large-scale online questionnaire, quantitative and qualitative data about teachers' instructional practices addressing speaking were collected. However, it should be acknowledged that the data were collected at one point in time (two years after the reform had been introduced) within the EFL Israeli context.

From a theoretical perspective, this study generated a valid and reliable instrument for measuring EFL teachers' LAL for teaching and assessing speaking, which is contextually embedded (Levi & Inbar-Lourie, 2020). Concurring with research in the area of teacher cognition that shows close relationships between aspects of teachers' knowledge and beliefs and their practices (e.g., Borg, 2003, 2009), our findings clearly indicate that these LAL dimensions are related to teachers' reported practices. Our findings further highlight the role of context in explaining teachers' dimensions of LAL and their practices associated with assessment of speaking (e.g., Davies, 2008; Fulcher, 2012; Harding et al., 2021). Indeed, speaking has become a vital component in the context of the Israeli matriculation examinations, and, hence, may have created a washback effect which, as a result, has motivated teachers to focus on improving the speaking skills of their students.

The results of this study have important implications for teacher education programs. Specifically, aspects of teaching and learning to speak in EFL contexts and teachers' LAL should both be thoroughly addressed in pre- and in-service teacher education programs. Teachers should acquire theoretical and practical knowledge of the multifaceted nature of the speaking pedagogy and assessment. This goal can be achieved through various reflective and research-oriented tasks.

A further contribution of the current study is that it provides a comprehensive understanding of how dimensions of LAL, specifically addressing speaking, are related to EFL teachers' practices in Israeli schools. Indeed, within the Israeli context, the English Inspectorate has initiated various in-service programs promoting speaking throughout schooling, which have strongly impacted the teachers' practices in the classroom and also contributed to their enhanced LAL. Future research should examine the adapted LAL questionnaire for assessing speaking in other contexts where English is taught as a foreign or an additional language. Finally, research should examine the factors that can potentially influence the relationships between dimensions of LAL and teachers' practices, in teaching speaking as well as other language skills.

References

Borg, S. (2003). Teacher cognition in language teaching: A review of research on what language teachers think, know, believe, and do. *Language Teaching*, *36*(2), 81–89. https://doi.org/10.1017/S0261444803001903.

Borg, S. (2009). Language teacher cognition. In A. Burns & J. C. Richards (Eds.), *The Cambridge guide to second language teacher education* (pp. 163–171). Cambridge University Press.

Cheng, L., & Curtis, A. (2004). Washback or backwash: A review of the impact of testing on teaching and learning. In L. Cheng, Y. Watanabe, & A. Curtis (Eds.), *Washback in language testing: Research contexts and methods* (pp. 3–17). Lawrence Erlbaum Associates.

Corbin, J. M., & Strauss, A. L. (2008). *Basics of qualitative research: Techniques and procedures for developing grounded theory* (3rd ed.). Sage.

Creswell, J. W., & Clark, V. L. P. (2017). *Designing and conducting mixed methods research*. Sage.

Crusan, D., Plakans, L., & Gebril, A. (2016). Writing assessment literacy: Surveying second language teachers' knowledge, beliefs, and practices. *Assessing Writing*, *28*, 43–56. doi:10.1016/j.asw.2016.03.001.

Davies, A. (2008). Textbook trends in teaching language testing. *Language Testing*, *25*(3), 327–347. https://doi.org/10.1177/0265532208090156.

Engelsen, K. S., & Smith, K. (2014). Assessment literacy. In C. Wyatt-Smith, V. Klenowski & P. Colbert (Eds.), *Designing assessment for quality learning* (pp. 91–107). Springer Netherlands.

Field, A. (2009). *Discovering statistics using SPSS*. (3rd ed.). Sage Publications Ltd.

Fulcher, G. (2012). Assessment literacy for the language classroom. *Language Assessment Quarterly*, *9*(2), 113–132. https://doi.org/10.1080/15434303.2011.642041.

Harding, L., Kremmel, B., & Eberharter, K., (2021). Language assessment literacy in second spoken language assessment contexts. In T. Haug, W. Mann, & U. Knoch (Eds.), *The handbook of language assessment across modalities* (pp. 373–382). Oxford University Press.

Inbar-Lourie, O. (2008). Constructing a language assessment knowledge base: A focus on language assessment courses. *Language Testing*, *25*(3), 385–402. https://doi.org/10.1177/0265532208090158.

Inbar-Lourie, O. (2016). Language assessment literacy. In E. Shohamy, I. Or, & S. May (Eds.), *Language testing and assessment* (pp. 257–270). Springer International Publishing.

Inbar-Lourie, O. (2017). Language assessment literacy. In E. Shohamy, S. May, & I. Or (Eds.), *Language testing and assessment* (3rd ed.), Encyclopedia of language and education (pp. 257–268). Springer.

Kremmel, B., & Harding, L. (2020). Towards a comprehensive, empirical model of language assessment literacy across stakeholder groups: Developing the language assessment literacy survey. *Language Assessment Quarterly*, *17*(1), 100–120. https://doi.org/10.1080/15434303.2019.1674855.

Levi, T., & Inbar-Lourie, O. (2020). Assessment literacy or language assessment literacy: Learning from the teachers. *Language Assessment Quarterly*, *17*(2), 168–182. https://doi.org/10.1080/15434303.2019.1692347.

Malone, M. E. (2017). *Including student perspectives in language assessment literacy* [Conference paper]. The 39th Language Testing Research Colloquium, Universidad de los Andes, Bogotá, Colombia.

Pill, J., & Harding, L. (2013). Defining the language assessment literacy gap: Evidence from a parliamentary inquiry. *Language Testing*, *30*(3), 381–402. https://doi.org/10.1177/0265532213480337.

Scarino, A. (2013). Language assessment literacy as self-awareness: Understanding the role of interpretation in assessment and teacher learning. *Language Testing*, *30*(3), 309–327. https://doi.org/10.1177/0265532213480128.
Taylor, L. (2009). Developing assessment literacy. *Annual Review of Applied Linguistics*, *29*, 21–36. https://doi.org/10.1017/S0267190509090035.
Taylor, L. (2013). Communicating the theory, practice and principles of language testing to test stakeholders: Some reflections. *Language Testing*, *30*(3), 403–412. https://doi.org/10.1177/0265532213480338.
Tsagari, D. (2017). *The importance of contextualizing language assessment literacy* [Conference paper]. The 39th Language Testing Research Colloquium, Universidad de los Andes, Bogotá, Colombia.
Tsagari, D. (2020). Language assessment literacy: Concepts, challenges, and prospects. In S. Hidri (Ed.), *Perspectives on language assessment literacy* (pp. 13–32). Routledge.
Vogt, W. P., & Johnson, R. B. (2016). *The SAGE dictionary of statistics & methodology: A nontechnical guide for the social sciences* (5th ed.). Sage.
Vogt, K., Tsagari, D., & Spanoudis, G. (2020). What do teachers think they want? A comparative study of in-service language teachers' beliefs on LAL training needs, *Language Assessment Quarterly*, *17*(4), 386–409. doi:10.1080/15434303.2020.1781128.

Appendix A

Results of factor analysis (factor loadings over .40 appear in bold).

Item	Rotated factor loadings			
How knowledgeable do EFL teachers need to be about each aspect of language teaching/assessment below?	Factor 1	*(Factor 2)	Factor 3	Factor 4
how English speaking is used in society	**1.010**	0.122	0.080	0.110
how to diagnose students strengths and weaknesses in speaking	**0.793**	0.029	−0.064	−0.063
how to motivate student learning of speaking	**0.751**	−0.117	−0.005	−0.221
how to guide learning or teaching goals of speaking	**0.715**	−0.056	−0.190	−0.080
how to use techniques to promote English speaking in the classroom	**0.676**	−0.096	−0.057	−0.278
how to develop tasks and activities to teach speaking in the EFL classroom	**0.634**	−0.051	−0.207	−0.162
how to give useful feedback on the basis of speaking assessment	**0.412**	−0.117	−0.323	−0.299
the speaking assessment traditions in Israel	0.062	**0.650**	−0.255	−0.314
the professional terminology related to the teaching and assessment of speaking	0.010	0.213	**−0.938**	0.111
how to apply the concept of validity (how well a speaking assessment instrument measures what it claims to measure)	0.022	−0.086	**−0.795**	−0.182

Item	Rotated factor loadings			
how to apply the concept of reliability in assessing students speaking ability	0.030	-0.132	**-0.743**	-0.234
how assessment of speaking can influence teaching and learning in the English classroom	0.184	-0.007	**-0.601**	-0.219
how to select appropriate rubrics for your classroom speaking activities and assessments	0.471	-0.047	**-0.528**	-0.018
how to evaluate students' progress of speaking skills	0.403	-0.123	**-0.430**	-0.207
how to make informed decisions about what aspects of speaking to teach and assess students in English lessons	-0.016	-0.022	-0.054	**-0.903**
how assessment of speaking can influence teaching and learning in the English classroom	-0.037	0.067	-0.089	**-0.851**
how to accommodate students with disabilities or other learning impairments in an oral proficiency setting speaking assessment setting	0.172	-0.131	-0.005	**-0.764**
how teachers own knowledge of teaching speaking and assessment might be further developed	0.109	-0.019	-0.109	**-0.727**
the potential advantages and disadvantages of speaking/oral exams	0.157	0.388	0.052	**-0.664**
how teachers' own beliefs/approach towards English language proficiency influence their classroom teaching	0.128	0.154	-0.087	**-0.660**
Eigenvalue	14.39	1.021	0.809	0.509
% variance	71.9	5.106	4.40	2.54
α	.96	–	.96	.95

4
MOROCCAN TEACHERS' PERCEPTIONS OF EFL INSTRUCTION IN THE WAKE OF THE COVID-19 PANDEMIC

Lessons learned

Adil Bentahar, Mohammed Elmeski, and Mohammed Hassim

Introduction

Issues that motivated the research

In 2020, UNICEF published a COVID response strategy entitled "Averting a Lost COVID Generation: A Six-point Plan to Respond, Recover, and Re-imagine a Post-pandemic World for Every Child." In 2021, UNESCO published a landmark report entitled "Reimagining Our Futures Together: A New Social Contract for Education." These two reports acknowledge COVID as a worldwide disruptor as well as a global reset opportunity for breaking with business-as-usual approaches to human development. The 2020 report is prefaced with cautionary words from the UNICEF Executive Director, noting that post-COVID reconstruction cannot be "about a return to the way things were. Children will never accept a return to 'normal' after the pandemic because 'normal' was never good enough" (UNICEF, 2020, p. 2).

COVID set back millions of people on almost all the United Nations Sustainable Development Goals (SDGs). According to Abidoye et al. (2021), the pandemic triggered a chain reaction that derailed efforts to ensure healthy lives (SDG 3), disrupted food supply chains, impeded efforts to end poverty and hunger (SDGs 1 & 2), and exacerbated inequalities due to health restrictions. It also hindered students' access to free, equitable, and quality primary and secondary education (SDG 4.1). The pandemic exposed widening economic and technological disparities evident in inequitable access to feeding programs, learning resources, psycho-social support, vaccines, and treatment.

Learner engagement was also affected by the pandemic. This construct is a measure reflecting students' attention, curiosity, motivation, interest, passion, and excitement about learning (Glossary of Education Reform, 2016). This measure, which was affected by the shift from in-person to remote learning, might also be a matter of the gender of the participants. While males are thought to have more confidence using technology, young women seem to manifest higher competence beliefs regarding learning in digital settings than their male counterparts (Perkowski, 20133).

In Morocco, the pandemic was a rough stress test of the country's disaster preparedness, especially with respect to technological resilience. Between March and June 2020, all students were moved to online learning. In the school year 2020–2021, 80% of households chose hybrid learning, which combines remote learning and face-to-face learning to ensure learning continuity and improve student experience (UNESCO, 2020), compared to only 20% who selected fully online classes (High Council for Education, Training, and Scientific Research, 2021). The 2020 school closures in Morocco resulted in "the loss of at least three months of learning for an estimated 900,000 pre-schoolers, eight million primary (elementary) and secondary (high) schoolers, and one million students in tertiary education" (The World Bank, 2020, para. 9). These losses came at a time when the educational gaps among students of different socio-economic statuses were already widening, and in the face of the disaster, one wonders how these public-school students were learning a new language amidst the pandemic. Scholars have examined such an impact on teachers and students.

In the US, Bentahar and Alalou (2022) explored the experiences of English learners during the emergency remote teaching period and reported instructors' negative perceptions of online teaching. The 44 college instructors in that study reported lower student engagement and student-student interaction. Other researchers have documented the experiences of instructors in Moroccan university language courses (e.g., Jamiai, 2021; Jebbour, 2022) and in secondary schools (e.g., Boukhari & Bekkari, 2021). While Jamiai (2021) examined graduate students' reflections on their use of technology during COVID, Jebbour (2022) explored college instructors' views on the challenges and benefits of teaching English remotely. His two research questions aimed at pinpointing the challenges and benefits of teaching English remotely during the COVID-19 lockdown. The researcher highlighted the dearth of information and communication technology infrastructure, low student engagement, and the need to create opportunities for "flexibility in the time and pace of teaching and learning and increased learner-content interaction" (p. 1). Likewise, Boukhari and Bekkari (2021) underscored the need for materials and infrastructure to facilitate distance learning accessibility and use for teachers and students.

While conducting our review, we noticed a paucity of studies researching remote learning experiences of EFL instructors and/or students in secondary schools in Morocco. One of these few studies was conducted by Sayeh and

Razkane (2021), who investigated 171 high school EFL teachers' use of Microsoft Teams. While Sayeh and Razkane's data were collected from one regional academy, the present study is based on data from the 12 regions of Morocco. By highlighting the experiences of teachers from all regions of Morocco, we hope to contribute to the emerging research on teaching EFL in the post-COVID era in the context of Morocco.

Research questions

This chapter presents the results of the quantitative phase of a mixed-method study of Moroccan EFL secondary teachers' experiences during the COVID-19 transition to online teaching. We sought to understand the lessons teachers learned from online instruction to improve their instructional resilience and learning continuity, should other disasters hit. In this study, we were interested in raising a broad overarching question: What was Moroccan EFL teachers' experience of online instruction during COVID, compared to face-to-face instruction? To investigate this issue, we posed six specific research questions:

1. What is the teachers' self-reported proficiency in information and communication technology? Does self-reported proficiency differ by teachers' ages and/or gender?
2. What were the teachers' preferred teaching modalities (face-to-face, fully online, or hybrid)?
3. What were the teachers' perceptions of student-student interaction in online environments?
4. What were the teachers' views of their online teaching experience?
5. What differences did the teachers perceive in student engagement, interaction, and learning in an online environment, compared to face-to-face settings?

Finally, we wondered how the teachers' experiences of teaching online may have influenced their subsequent teaching in face-to-face instruction. Therefore, we posed another broad question, which addresses the phrase "lessons learned" in our chapter title: "What practices (if any) adopted from the online transition have the teachers implemented in their face-to-face instruction?"

Research methods

Context

The purpose of this study is to explore Moroccan secondary education EFL instructors' perceptions of teaching during the COVID-19 pandemic and in its wake. We employed a mixed-methods sequential explanatory design using an online survey and semi-structured interviews. With a mixed-methods sequential explanatory design, quantitative data are collected and analyzed first before proceeding with the qualitative data in two consecutive phases within a single study (Creswell & Plano Clark, 2007). To carry out this plan, we collected the survey responses first before conducting semi-structured interviews. The use of quantitative and qualitative data was intended to ensure a more complete understanding of these teachers' experiences; however, due to word-limit constraints, in this chapter we present the quantitative results only.

Participants

Three hundred fifty-six secondary school EFL teachers across Morocco participated in the survey. The sample comprised EFL teachers currently teaching in preparatory secondary schools (middle) and qualification secondary (high) schools.

Sixty-one percent of the 356 survey respondents were male, and 39.1% were female. One-third of the respondents were in their thirties, one-third were in their forties, and one in every five teachers were in their twenties. Only 14.5% of the teachers were over 50. The demographic data also indicated a balanced mix of years of teaching experience, ranging from one to five years to more than 20 years. In terms of their teaching contexts, 82.4% of the respondents were working in public schools, another 13% were teaching in public and private schools, and fewer than 5% were teaching in private schools only.

Data collection procedures

The survey, which was written in English, consisted of 41 questions broken into several sections. It included Likert scale items inquiring about factors accounting for student experiences in the EFL classroom. Key factors include students' home conditions affecting learning, familiarity with technology, and student engagement. Questions 1–10 covered the consent form and the demographic information. Questions 11–16 examined teachers' experiences with information communication technology (ICT); questions 17–27 invited the teachers to reflect on their classroom experiences in terms of any resulting adjustments and accommodations (also known in Morocco as modifications). Such adjustments include reducing the amount of in-class reading, using asynchronous instruction, allowing more time for students to submit assignments, and so on and forth. Questions 28–31 asked the participants about their teaching practices after they switched from face-to-face to online instruction. Questions 32–36 inquired about teachers' perceptions of the differences between teaching online and face to face (e.g., how connected they felt toward other teachers) and the extent to which they incorporated collaboration online tools or platforms (e.g., WhatsApp, Zoom, and Kahoot) from their online experience in their physical classrooms after the lockdown ended. The final part of the survey addressed lessons learned from the experience of teaching online. The survey included reversed wording, a strategy entailing the use of words with an opposite meaning. "When I switched from face-to-face (f2f) to online instruction, I observed that student-student interaction declined (compared to f2f)" and "... my students were less engaged" are two examples of reverse wording.

The data were collected using the Qualtrics online survey platform. The link was sent to Moroccan EFL teachers through the Facebook group page of the Moroccan Association of Teachers of English. The recruitment message (translated and posted in Arabic and English) detailed the rationale and criteria for participation. Additionally, the same invitation was shared with EFL teacher supervisors, requesting them to encourage teachers in their online communities to complete the survey. One reminder post was shared two weeks after the initial invitation. No identifying information on the survey respondents' names or affiliations is known. Those teachers who expressed interest in participating were invited for the interviews.

Data analysis procedures

We conducted a variety of analytical techniques with the questionnaire data. Descriptive statistics helped capture common and group-specific characteristics, mainly pertaining to gender, age, years of experience, prior training, and familiarity with ICT. We primarily relied on chi-square as an inferential technique to report statistical significance when applicable. In the discussion below the number of responses is fewer than 356 because some teachers did not reply to all the questions.

Findings and discussion

In terms of proficiency in information and communication technology, 56% of the respondents reported average proficiency, 34.4% reported advanced levels, and 9.6% reported limited knowledge. Table 4.1 shows that younger teachers were more likely to report higher skills in ICT compared to older teachers.

Table 4.2 shows that the percentage of male and female respondents reporting average proficiency in ICT was almost identical. However, more male respondents than females reported advanced proficiency, and more female respondents reported having limited proficiency in ICT, compared to their male counterparts.

TABLE 4.1 Proficiency in ICT by Age Group (n = 356)

Age group	20–30	31–40	41–50	50+
Limited	7.1%	9.5%	10.1%	12.5%
Average	50.0%	52.7%	62.3%	59.4%
Advanced	42.9%	37.8%	27.5%	28.1%

TABLE 4.2 Proficiency in ICT by Gender (n = 356)

	Male	Female
Average	56.06%	55.95%
Advanced	40.15%	25.00%
Limited	3.78%	19.05%

Finally, only 14% of the respondents reported participating in professional development in remote instruction, 45% reported not receiving any training, and 41% did not answer the question.

In summary, the analysis of demographic data shows that, overall, the sample of teachers who chose to respond to the survey is comparable to the general teacher population in terms of gender representation and to a large extent in age distribution. According to Morocco's Ministry of Education Statistical Yearbook for 2019–2020 (The Ministry of Education, Early Education, and Sport, 2020), out of the total lower and upper secondary teacher population of 114,078, female teachers represent 39.3% of that population. This figure is almost identical to the 39.1% of female representation in the current study. Likewise, the age distribution of participants in the survey is similar to that reported in the Statistical Yearbook, especially for teachers under 30 and between 30 and 39, who also represent 20% and 35% of the total teacher population, respectively.

The data also indicated that most of teachers who responded to our questionnaire were not trained in remote instruction. In the remainder of this section, we present the study findings, looking at common trends and probing group-specific patterns by age, gender, number of years teaching, and type of training.

The overarching question that guided this research asked about the respondents' experience of online instruction during COVID and, more specifically, how it compared to face-to-face instruction. Overall, the data suggest that the respondents' experience of online instruction during COVID was more negative than positive. Some of the differences in respondents' experiences can be accounted for by gender, self-reported proficiency in ICT, and training. To garner a sense of the respondents' experience of online vs. in-person instruction, we inquired about their preferred teaching modality (face-to-face, fully online, or hybrid) and their perceptions of student-student interaction in online environments. We also asked the respondents about their opinions of their teaching experience and the perceived differences in students' engagement, interaction, and learning in an online environment, compared to face-to-face settings.

Gender, training, and ICT proficiency

Across gender, age, proficiency with ICT, and training, the responses were resoundingly consistent about rejecting fully online instruction. Two-thirds (66.7%) of the

Moroccan teachers' perceptions of EFL instruction 55

female respondents preferred fully face-to-face instruction compared to 59.4% of the male respondents. Furthermore, 31.5% of the female teachers preferred hybrid, compared to 40.6% of the male teachers. Figure 4.1 depicts the differences in preference for fully online, face-to-face, and hybrid classes between the groups of teachers who reported receiving training in remote instruction and those who did not.

Training in remote instruction seems to be a significant factor shaping the respondents' preferred instructional modes. A chi-square test of independence was performed to assess the relationship between instruction mode preference and online instruction training status (received vs. not received training). There was a statistically significant relationship between the training status and the preferred mode of instruction, $X^2_{(df = 2, N = 151)} = 7.81$, p = .019. In other words, as shown in Figure 4.1, teachers who had not received any training in online instruction were less likely to prefer hybrid instruction (32.46% vs. 51.35%), and more likely to prefer fully face-to-face instruction (67.5% vs. 45.9%).

As shown in Figure 4.2, self-assessment of proficiency in ICT seems to be another factor associated with differences in the teaching mode preference. 87.5% of the respondents who rated their proficiency in ICT as limited preferred full face-to-face instruction. Only 12.5% chose hybrid instruction. Among the teachers who rated their ICT skills as average, 64.63% preferred face-to-face instruction, and 34.15% opted for hybrid instruction. Among teachers who self-reported as having advanced ICT skills, 49.06% chose hybrid, and 50.94% selected face-to-face. None of the groups indicated preferring fully online instruction. While this research design does not permit causal conclusions about the direct attribution of preference of a mode of instruction to self-assessment of ICT proficiency, the teachers' responses suggest that this factor contributes to the determination of the mode of instruction preferred by teachers.

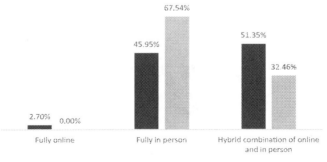

FIGURE 4.1 Teachers' training in remote instruction and preferred instructional modes

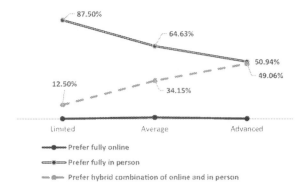

FIGURE 4.2 Teachers' self-reported ICT proficiency and preferred instructional modes

Teachers' perceptions of their experience with online instruction

The respondents' experience of online instruction was contrasted with their face-to-face teaching experience by examining how the two modalities of instruction compare in terms of the perceived amount of learning gained, adjustments made, teachers' perceptions of their success teaching English in an online setting, and the perceptions of the resources available to support fully online classes.

As shown in Figure 4.3, overall, teachers reported that students learned less during online instruction than they did in face-to-face instruction. The teachers who participated in professional development (PD) in remote instruction were also more likely to report gains in learning in online settings, or at least equal gains compared to face-to-face instruction. By contrast, teachers who did not participate in similar PD saw fewer gains in learning in online settings. We ran a

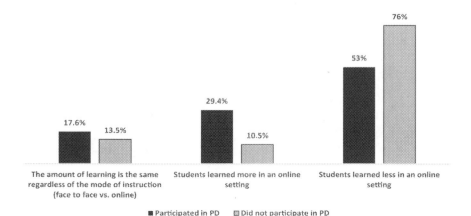

FIGURE 4.3 PD in remote instruction and student learning online

Moroccan teachers' perceptions of EFL instruction   57

chi-square test of the relationship between participation in PD and students' learning experience, and the relationship was statistically significant, $X^2_{(df = 2, N = 138)} = 8.21$, $p = .01$.

With respect to adjusting instruction in online settings, Figure 4.4 shows that teachers who reported advanced proficiency in ICT made more adjustments (40%), or at least about the same number of adjustments (38.5%), compared to teachers who reported limited ICT proficiency. Only 5.2% of the latter group reported making more adjustments to their teaching, and only 7.7% reported they made about the same number of adjustments compared to face-to-face instruction. The difference between the two groups is statistically significant, $X^2_{(df = 2, N = 148)} = 26.4$, $p < .01$.

With respect to the respondents' perceptions of their experience teaching English online, 51.4% of the teachers did not believe their performance teaching English improved when they delivered instruction online. However, teachers who reported participating in the previous PD in online instruction were more positive in their appraisal of their experience.

In terms of the teachers' perceptions of the resources available to them to provide classes fully online, as shown in Figure 4.5, 68.1% rated access to and familiarity with technology as available or at least somewhat available. However, 76.6% rated the support from the school administration as unavailable or somewhat unavailable. Furthermore, 53.3% did not access any training or guidance to deliver engaging EFL lessons in an online setting.

Teachers' perceptions of student learning during online instruction

Apparently, most of the respondents had negative opinions of student learning during online instruction. For instance, 63.7% reported that students were better

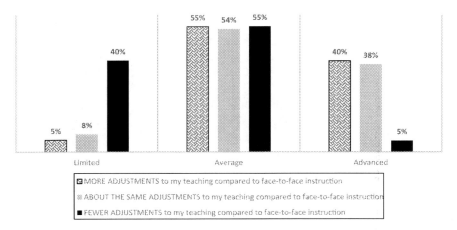

FIGURE 4.4 Teachers' self-reported ICT proficiency and the frequency of their online instructional adjustments compared to face-to-face instruction

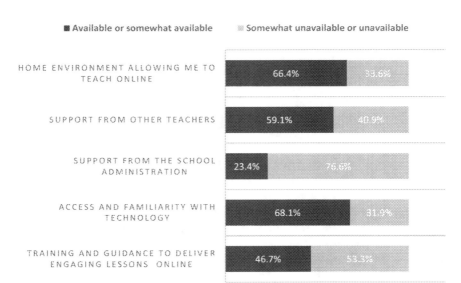

FIGURE 4.5 Teachers' perceptions of resources available for online instruction

able to develop English reading skills in face-to-face settings. In addition, 58.5% reported students were less engaged in online environments, and 70.3% noticed that student-student interaction declined online, compared to face-to-face interaction. While factors such as prior training and proficiency in ICT seem to influence teachers' responses (especially with respect to subgroups that received prior training in online instruction and self-identify as advanced in ICT), their overall effects remain moderate. In other words, that some teachers reported average to advanced ICT proficiency did not change the fact that across all subgroups, there is general agreement that student engagement, interaction, and language skill development did not benefit from online instruction.

While most respondents reported making more adjustments and modifications online compared to face-to-face instruction, they did not rate their strategies as effective. The same negative views characterized their perceptions of student engagement, interaction, and opportunities for the students to improve their reading skills. The analysis, however, unearthed distinctly different behaviors among teachers with advanced ICT skills versus those reporting limited ICT skills.

Our second broad question asked what practices (if any) adopted from the online transition Moroccan EFL teachers implemented in their subsequent face-to-face instruction. To answer this question, we inquired about teachers' use of online tools and likely outcomes with a focus on the lessons from online instruction that were implemented in face-to-face settings. We also asked for specific examples of practices transferred from online to face-to-face instruction. In response to these issues, 47.1% of the teachers reported continuing to use

Moroccan teachers' perceptions of EFL instruction 59

digital tools, while 39.7% reported they rarely do so, and 13.2% said they had ceased to use digital tools. Half (50.4%) reported that their experience teaching online strengthened, to some extent, their connections with other teachers of English. In addition, 28.5% reported a large degree of improvement in teachers' connectedness, although 21.2% reported no improvement. Finally, 63% confirmed implementing lessons learned from online instruction in face-to-face settings.

Respondents were asked to rank the online tools they continued to use after the transition to face-to-face instruction. As shown in Figure 4.6, WhatsApp ranks highest in terms of the number of users, followed by Zoom, Facebook, Microsoft Teams, Google Meet, YouTube, and Google Classroom. To a lesser extent, less than five percent listed Kahoot, TelmidTICE (Morocco's Ministry of Education [MoE] official platform for online instruction), MASSAR (The MoE Management Information System), and Quizlet. When teachers were asked if they used other online tools, they reported using personally recorded videos, Gmail, Edmodo, Messenger, Discord, and Padlet.

Examples of practices adopted by teachers from the online experience after the transition to face-to-face instruction can be gleaned at the levels of knowledge, behaviors, and dispositions, by which we mean the facets of teacher affect – values, beliefs, and attitudes – influencing the use and application of knowledge and skills as defined in accepted standards of teaching (Lang, 2007). At the knowledge level, teachers became aware of the various platforms and online solutions they can use to diversify their teaching. Other tools referenced by teachers include content preparation and presentation tools that are more interactive and visually engaging than chalk/markers and boards. One more knowledge aspect is the realization that online environments accommodate "shy" students who respond better to one-on-one interactions than to interactions in a large group. In this regard, a female teacher with

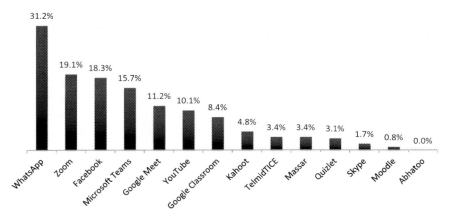

FIGURE 4.6 Ranking of the online tools that teachers continued to use in face-to-face instruction

16 to 20 years of experience noted, "Intensive and extensive reading is more efficient in online settings than in F2F (face-to-face) ones as it enables the learners to work at their own pace and encourages shy students and slow learners to feel heard and fully engaged." Back in the face-to-face setting, awareness that introverted students can thrive differently through alternative digital media is a critical knowledge breakthrough that, arguably, many teachers would not have experienced had it not been for teaching online during the COVID-19 pandemic.

In terms of specific behaviors reported to have continued from the fully online period, some teachers mentioned online tools in the teaching of grammar (e.g., *has/have got*, reported speech, relative pronouns, and modal verbs) and reading (online tools for mind mapping). Other teachers reported using slide decks for presenting, saving, and sharing lessons with students. There was also a reference to flipped learning, a pedagogical approach in which "direct instruction moves from the group learning space to the individual learning space, and the resulting group space is transformed into a dynamic, interactive learning environment" (Flipped Learning Network, 2014, p. 1). Practices of this approach can help weave the advantages of online instruction into face-to-face teaching. At the level of lesson delivery, a female teacher with six to 10 years of experience commented, "I learned to keep my instructions concise and precise." Finally, teachers reported that they continue to use online tools for students to submit homework and ask questions. The percentage of teachers who continue to use WhatsApp and Facebook, as presented in Figure 4.6, supports this continuing trend.

At the level of dispositions, overall, 83.34% of the teachers were not satisfied with the effectiveness of their online teaching strategies, and with the level of student engagement and interaction. Despite the negative perception, the online experience seems to have reinforced the attitude that while online is not the preferable primary mode of instruction, it does represent an idea whose time has come.

In summary, in addition to comments reflecting cognizance of ineluctable change, one major takeaway for some of the respondents was the recognition of the important social dimension fulfilled by face-to-face instruction as well as the need to equip both students and teachers with the necessary technology, connectivity, and administrative support to sustain hybrid learning environments. In other words, COVID was a natural, albeit unfortunate, experiment that seemingly challenged assumptions about face-to-face instruction as the only viable and reliable mode for securing continuity of education, especially during emergencies. Teachers' open-ended responses to our questionnaire reflected a nuanced positive disposition towards hybrid instruction that is contingent upon improving access to technology and strengthening training in hybrid instruction.

Regardless of location, there appear to be recurrent negative opinions from English language teachers about their online experiences (see, e.g., Bentahar & Alalou, 2022, regarding ESL teachers' frustrations in the United States). In Morocco, similar negative perceptions have been reported in the literature, both in secondary schools and university EFL settings. One commonly visible factor is the lack of support from school administrators, which most respondents (76.6%)

deemed "unavailable" or "largely unavailable." Other grounds for the negative perception associated with teaching online amid the pandemic stem from student responsiveness to learning. Perceived low engagement and student-student interaction might have caused teachers to feel discouraged and unenthusiastic about the quality of their overall remote teaching performance. Other scholars (e.g., Bentahar & Alalou, 2022; Jebbour, 2022) have reported similar findings. EFL teachers' lack of support comes at a price.

Teachers' performance online could also be a matter of their expertise, maturity, or seniority. Teachers with less classroom experience tend to be more prone to developing negative attitudes toward ICT (Tou et al., 2020). In looking at our findings, we found the same pattern.

Implications for policy, practice, and future research

There seems to be a disparity between male and female teachers' self-assessed familiarity with ICT. While overall both genders reported having average familiarity with ICT (i.e., 56.06% reported by males and 55.95% by females), only 25% of female respondents described their familiarity as advanced (compared to 40.15% reported by males) and almost 20% of female respondents described their familiarity as limited, as opposed to only 3.78% among males. It is therefore incumbent upon the Moroccan Ministry of Education to ensure that both male and female teachers have access to training that equips and prepares them to integrate technology during trying times in a smooth fashion.

That technology integration during the COVID-19 pandemic was inevitable and practically imposed on experienced and inexperienced language teachers is a reminder it is high time skeptical teachers changed their attitudes to support their students. A teacher with 10 to 15 years of experience noted, "Students are hooked to technology [because its use] in the classroom is mandatory now. Instead of resisting, we [Moroccan teachers] should just find educational and fun ways of integrating technology." Another experienced teacher commented, "We need to change mindsets about teaching online; it must be taken seriously. [Student] parents' associations should be involved. Virtual classes should be set as the regular timetable."

Considering how positively teachers with previous training in ICT felt about their remote teaching experience, it must be noted that with or without emergency or pandemic modes, EFL teachers in Morocco should be prepared to adapt to a change in pace and teaching modalities. After experiencing the COVID-19 pandemic, the need for continuous and up-to-date in-service training is even more urgent for Moroccan teachers to build coping mechanisms in trying times such as the pandemic. Like other teachers worldwide, Moroccan teachers need training that helps them refine their digital skills and adapt to remote teaching techniques (World Bank, 2020). The onus for ICT development falls on the Moroccan Ministry of Education, university-based teacher education programs, *and* the teachers themselves as part of their professional development requirements.

Despite all the challenges reported in our findings, many teachers resumed their face-to-face instruction with new learning and capabilities. In addition to basic teaching by means of WhatsApp and Facebook, areas worth exploring further, as reported in our data, include asynchronous learning, flipped learning, and the use of Google tools to promote student presentational skills, and flashcards to facilitate vocabulary acquisition. In other words, technology is here to stay in the EFL online *and* face-to-face teaching contexts. For future research and given how this and other studies have relied on teachers' opinions to understand practices, attitudes, and successes during the COVID-19 online transition, it would be ideal to also hear from the students.

References

Abidoye, B., Felix, J., Kapto, S., & Patterson, L. (2021). *Leaving no one behind: Impact of COVID-19 on the Sustainable Development Goals (SDGs)*. United Nations Development Programme and Frederick S. Pardee Center for International Futures.

Bentahar, A., & Alalou, A. (2022). An exploration of IEP instructors' perceptions of reading instruction during the COVID-19 Emergency Remote Teaching. *Reading in a Foreign Language, 34*(2), 376–397. https://nflrc.hawaii.edu/rfl/item/552.

Boukhari, O., & Bekkari, H. (2021). Distance learning during COVID-19 pandemic in Morocco: Perceptions of teachers from Kenitra directorate. *International Journal of English Language and Translation Studies, 9*(4), 28–34. http://www.eltsjournal.org/archive/value9%20issue4/4-9-4-21.pdf.

Creswell, J. W., & Plano Clark, V. L. (2007). *Designing and conducting mixed methods research*. Sage.

Flipped Learning Network. (2014, March 14). Definition of flipped learning. https://flippedlearning.org/definition-of-flipped-learning/.

Glossary of Educational Reform. (2016). Student engagement. https://www.edglossary.org/student-engagement/.

Higher Council for Education, Training, and Scientific Research (2021). Enseignement au temps de Covid au Maroc. https://www.csefrs.ma/wp-content/uploads/2021/11/Re%CC%81sume%CC%81-Rapport-Enseignement-au-temps-de-COVID.pdf.

Jamiai, A. (2021). Issues in e-learning during Covid-19 in Morocco: A focus on EFL master students' voices. *International Journal of Social Science and Human Research, 4*(1), 459–467. https://doi.org/10.47191/ijsshr/v4-i1-01.

Jebbour, M. (2022). The unexpected transition to distance learning at Moroccan universities amid COVID-19: A qualitative study on faculty experience. *Social Sciences & Humanities Open, 5*(1), 1–7. https://doi.org/10.1016/j.ssaho.2022.100253.

Lang, W. S. (2007, February). *Disposition: How do you know it when you see it?* Paper presentation. American Association of Colleges of Teacher Education (AACTE), New York.

Perkowski, J. (2013). The role of gender in distance learning: A meta-analytic review of gender differences in academic performance and self-efficacy in distance learning. *Journal of Educational Technology Systems, 41*(3), 267–278.

Sayeh, A. Y., & Razkane, H. (2021). Moroccan high school EFL teachers' attitudes and anxiety on using Microsoft Teams platform. *TESOL and Technology Studies, 2*(2), 29–40. https://doi.org/10.48185/tts.v2i2.267.

The Ministry of National Education, Early Childhood Education, and Sport. (2020). Recueil statistique de l'education 2019–2020. [Education statistical yearbook 2019–2020]. https://www.men.gov.ma/Ar/Documents/RECUEIL%202019-2020.pdf.

Tou, N. X., Kee, Y. H., Koh, K. T., Camiré, M., & Chow, J. Y. (2020). Singapore teachers' attitudes towards the use of information and communication technologies in physical education. *European Physical Education Review*, 26(2), 1–14. https://doi.org/10.1177/1356336X19869734.

UNESCO. (2020). COVID -19 response – hybrid learning: Hybrid learning as a key element in ensuring continued learning. https://en.unesco.org/sites/default/files/unesco-covid-19-r esponse-toolkit-hybrid-learning.pdf.

UNESCO. (2021). *Reimagining our futures together: A new social contract for education.* UNESCO Digital Library.

UNICEF. (2020). Averting a lost COVID generation: A six-point plan to respond, recover and reimagine a post-pandemic world for every child. world-childrens-day-data-and-advocacy-brief-2020.pdf.

World Bank. (2020). Morocco: A case for building a stronger education system in the post Covid-19 era. https://www.worldbank.org/en/news/feature/2020/10/27/a-case-for-building-a-stronger-education-system-in-the-post-covid-19-era.

5

THE COMMUNICATIVE ORIENTATION OF EFL CLASSROOMS

The Tunisian context

Khaled el Houche

Introduction

Ever since its introduction into language discussions in the early 1970s, Communicative Language Teaching (CLT) has gained wide prominence in second and foreign language research literature. As a result, teaching and learning goals were rethought in order to help second language (L2) learners achieve optimal use of the target language, and to meet international standards. Teachers are now trained to incorporate communicative teaching methodologies that depart from decades-long teaching methods which are seen as inefficient and outdated. The learners are expected to take much more active roles in their learning experiences and, as such, participate in the creation of effective L2 classroom learning opportunities which simulate real-world communicative events.

Issues that motivated the research

EFL teachers in Tunisia are expected to implement CLT and involve their learners in communicative lessons which reflect the core features of the approach. Two ways to understand the communicative orientation of these lessons are through the close observation of ELT classrooms and through a survey of EFL teachers' views on their roles, as well as those of their learners.

The present study was motivated by the methodological rethinking and new syllabus designs, as well as their recommendations as outlined in the Tunisian official syllabi (Tunisian Ministry of Education, 2006). Given those changes, I thought it would be useful to investigate the implementation level of CLT principles (such as skills integration, modes of interaction, and learner talking time). Surveying the teachers' opinions and exploring classroom teaching events have allowed me to consider the extent to which teachers' theoretical understandings match their classroom practices. This focus is important since studies on the communicative orientation of EFL classrooms in Tunisia are rare (see, e.g., Ounis & Ounis, 2017).

Research questions

Investigating the communicative orientation of teaching and learning in Tunisia requires a focus on the communicative aspects in Tunisian language lessons. This study investigated teachers' perceptions of their teaching approach and their patterns of interaction during language lessons.

The chapter addresses two research questions:

1. What are teachers' perceptions of their classroom teaching approaches and roles?
2. What are the most frequent patterns of interaction during English lessons?

Research methods

This study is an exploratory, qualitative and quantitative research project based on both questionnaire data and classroom observations. The questionnaire responses provided data about Tunisian English teachers' perspectives on the communicative approach. In addition, three of the respondents were observed during lessons and their talk was recorded and analyzed to reveal the main patterns of their interactions. To conclude, I will contrast the findings from the questionnaire with the results of the observations.

Context

In recent years, there have been several educational developments in English teaching at the elementary level. Three major educational reforms (in 1996, 2002, and 2006) and other initiatives (in 2018 and 2019) reinforced the status of English in the Tunisian official curriculum. The curriculum addresses teaching English to young learners starting from grade 4 Basic Education (age nine) to grade 9 (age 14). These reforms and initiatives were aimed at improving the English proficiency of young learners, following recommendations advocating the introduction of the new language at an early age. These curricular developments were followed by implementing teacher professional development programmes and degrees. The official documents spell out the English teachers' commitment to using communicative principles.

Participants

The participants in the questionnaire part of this study were 44 Tunisian EFL teachers who had varying degrees of experience working in different elementary schools in the region of Tataouine, Tunisia. Twenty-three had passed the CAPES – the French acronym for the Certificat d'Aptitude au Professorat de l'Enseignement du Second Degré (a French certification course vs. a Tunisian selection procedure), while 18 had not. (The remaining respondents did not provide an answer to this question.) Teachers who have passed the CAPES are believed to be professionally able to teach at public schools since they have undergone thorough theoretical and pedagogical training.

A smaller focal group of three seventh-grade teachers was observed during classroom lessons. These teachers had had varying teaching experience. They were selected from among the questionnaire respondents by convenience sampling, which is characterized by the "geographical proximity, availability at a certain time or ease of accessibility" of the participants (Dörnyei & Taguchi, 2009, p. 61).

Data collection procedures

I designed the questionnaire to elicit teachers' attitudes regarding their teaching approaches. The questionnaire included 19 six-point Likert scale items (1 = Strongly Disagree, 2 = Disagree, 3 = Slightly Disagree, 4 = Agree, 5 = Slightly Agree, and 6 = Strongly Agree). Hard copies of the questionnaire were sent, with the help of close teacher colleagues, to almost all the elementary teachers working in different parts of the region, but only 44 copies were collected during and after observation phase of the study.

In observing the three teachers' lessons, I used some of the categories from the Communicative Orientation of Language Teaching (COLT), which was originally developed by Fröhlich et al. to gather data during classroom observations. Categories from Part A of the COLT system "describe instruction at the level of activity" (Fröhlich et al., 1985, p. 32). Part B focuses on "the communicative features of teacher and student interaction" (Fröhlich et al., 1985, p. 32). The coding method developed by Fröhlich et al. (1985) was employed to code language classroom behaviors. That is, the data for Parts A and B were coded during two separate phases: Part A in real time (during the lessons) and part B subsequently, using the audio-recorded data.

The COLT scheme categories include participant organization, topic control, use of the information gap, incorporation of S/T utterances, and discourse initiation. These categories were tallied whenever a participant used a particular behavior.

Data analysis procedures

In analyzing the questionnaire data, I calculated Cronbach's Alpha to determine the internal consistency of the questionnaire. This procedure yielded an alpha value of 0.71, which was considered an acceptable value. Responses to the open-ended items were analyzed for major themes and categorized to reveal salient patterns. The categorization was based on the 44 teachers' questionnaire responses about the types of approaches which frame their teaching practices – teacher-fronted or learner-centered as well as combined or eclectic.

In analyzing the observational data, I tallied the frequency distributions of the various types of interaction during the three lessons. The amount of time for the features of the activities coded in Part A of the COLT system was totaled and then divided by the overall recorded time of that particular lesson to provide the percentage of time allotted to each feature. That percentage reveals the length of exposure to a particular feature in that lesson and gives a general picture about the dynamics of the lesson. For example, a lesson involving group- and pair-work activities for frequent negotiation of meaning is considered more communicative than a highly controlled, teacher-centered lesson in which students mainly respond to teacher-initiated questions and seldom produce original speech.

Likewise, frequency counts provide a view of the three teachers' speech distribution and its communicative features, as identified in Part B of the COLT system. The continuum of classroom speech ranges from form-focused to communicative, with a mid-position where verbal behavior is neither mostly communicative nor completely form-focused.

At the form-focused end of the continuum are language lessons where information gap activities are typically limited. In such classrooms, the giving of information is to some extent predictable, and requesting information yields an answer which is known in advance by the teacher. In addition, students' speech is quite minimal (i.e., answers are always brief).

However, on the communicative side of the speech continuum, the message is largely unpredictable, and speech is sustained, often consisting of long sentences or clauses. More importantly, in sustained speech, the participants negotiate the meaning in their turns. Also, in communicative classrooms, students are expected to suggest and choose topics without total adherence to the textbooks' contents.

Findings and discussion

Teachers' attitudes toward the implementation of CLT

The first research question addressed teachers' attitudes towards the implementation of CLT in their classrooms. To answer that question, teachers responded to Likert scale items and two open-ended questions. The responses to the 19 Likert scale items about teaching approaches were averaged and displayed in the Tables 5.1 and 5.2. In the questionnaire, those items were identified with the letters A through S. The items were mixed as to whether they dealt with teaching approaches or participants' roles. The data are grouped in these tables according to the themes addressed in the questionnaire items. Table 5.1 displays the frequency of responses to items probing teaching approaches, as well as the mean and standard deviation. The lettering from the original questionnaire has been maintained in these tables.

68 Khaled el Houche

TABLE 5.1 Frequency of teachers' responses to items about teaching approaches

Items	SD	D	SLD	SLA	A	SA	N	Mean	SD
A. Language classes should be student-centered not teacher-centered.	2	0	4	1	22	12	41	4.88	0.85
D. The learner-centered approach fosters responsibility and allows the learner to personalize his learning.	0	1	3	12	12	15	43	4.86	0.83
G. The teacher-fronted approach is the efficient method.	4	9	5	12	8	4	42	3.55	0.65
I. The teacher should dominate the classroom situations.	6	10	4	8	5	7	40	3.43	0.67
K. A teacher-fronted class motivates learners to work effectively.	4	12	8	6	8	3	41	3.27	0.67
N. A teacher-centered class is necessary for students to get efficient input.	3	13	8	12	4	4	44	3.30	0.64

The choices displayed in Table 5.1 reveal that the participants favor a learner-centered approach explicitly stated in items A and D, as opposed to a teacher-fronted approach indicated in the remaining items in Table 5.1 (G, I, K, and N). A close look at the mean scores (M = 4.88 and 4.86 in items A and D, respectively) shows that the majority of the respondents agreed that language classes should be student-centered. Conversely, there was substantial disagreement on the items about the benefits of the teacher-fronted approach.

The remaining Likert scale items describe what each approach entails in terms of roles. The respondents expressed their opinions regarding how roles should be according to each area.

In Table 5.2, the responses related to roles are grouped in the three categories that emerged during the analysis: lesson content, classroom responsibility, and interaction patterns.

Three items (C, E, and M) probed the teachers' attitudes vis-à-vis their roles towards the lesson contents. As can be seen in Table 5.2, there is a low mean score (M = 2.95) of agreement on Item E, stating that "teachers should stick to the official syllabus content," whereas there is a high mean score (M = 5.51), indicating agreement with Item C, which states that "the teacher [should] support the lesson with extra material."

Overall, Table 5.2 displays two agreement mean patterns regarding classroom responsibility. Respondents were generally consistent throughout the set of items.

The communicative orientation of EFL classrooms

TABLE 5.2 Frequency of teachers' responses to items about roles

	SD	D	SLD	SLA	A	SA	N	Mean	SD
Lesson Content									
E. The teacher should stick to the official syllabus content.	10	6	8	5	5	3	37	2.95	0.73
C. The teacher supports the lesson with extra material from his own.	0	0	0	1	17	21	39	5.51	1.05
M. Learners shouldn't suggest the content of the lesson.	3	7	12	3	8	2	35	3.34	0.72
Classroom Responsibility									
B. Training learners to take responsibility for their own learning is not important.	9	17	6	4	0	4	40	2.53	0.77
F. The role of the teacher is to impart knowledge.	1	2	0	3	25	11	42	4.95	0.86
H. The success of the lesson depends on the learner's cooperation.	0	0	1	3	10	30	44	5.57	1.0
L. Learners shouldn't correct their peers' mistakes.	9	20	8	1	1	4	43	2.47	0.75
O. The teacher is the facilitator in the communication process.	0	0	0	2	19	21	42	5.45	0.99
Q. The teacher is an organizer of resources and a resource himself.	0	3	2	10	12	16	43	4.84	0.82
S. The teacher plays a central and active role where he monitors the L2, controls the direction and pace of learning.	0	1	2	4	19	17	43	5.14	0.89
Patterns of interaction									
J. The class interactions should be from students to students.	1	5	7	9	13	9	44	4.25	0.7
P. The learner negotiates meaning in the lesson.	0	1	1	9	17	10	38	4.89	0.89
R. The learner shouldn't initiate interactions.	9	12	12	3	0	4	40	2.63	0.75

For instance, when learners are given fewer responsibilities and roles, as in Items B and L, the mean scores are low (M = 2.53 and 2.47, respectively). However, when the learners are involved in the lesson and the teacher is primarily an organizer in the process, the respondents' mean scores are higher. For example, Item O had a very high mean (M = 5.45), indicating that the majority of the respondents believed that the teacher should play the role of "the facilitator of the learning process." Similarly, a large majority of the respondents acknowledge the importance of the teacher's monitoring role in Item S, about the role teachers should play in the lesson. As to source of knowledge, all the respondents agreed that the teacher should not depend solely on the syllabus content but should enrich it with extra material as reflected in Items C and F. This view is further supported by the responses to Item Q, which indicate strong beliefs in the dual role the teacher should play, as both a source of knowledge and an organizer, two major principles within CLT. In the responses to Item H (M = 5.57), almost all the teachers (n = 43) agreed that the "success of the lesson depends on the learners' cooperation," a finding reiterated in responses to Items J and P, as explained below.

As shown in the part of Table 5.2 regarding interaction patterns, the mean scores are relatively high on Items J (M = 4.25) and P (M = 4.89), but low on Item R (M = 2.63). These scores demonstrate first, the agreement of the respondents on the usefulness of meaning negotiations in interactional activities in the lesson, and second, their disagreement about relegating the learners to a subordinate position in the learning process.

In summary, the respondents' answers revealed a positive orientation towards a learner-centered approach for teaching EFL. The teachers showed their understanding of the learner-centered classroom requirements when they expressed their agreement on roles consisting of sharing classroom responsibilities for lesson contents as well as having the learners initiate interactions.

In addition to providing data with the Likert scale items, the teachers were asked to state their favorite teaching styles in response to an open-ended question. Eleven teachers preferred a teacher-fronted style while 23 chose a learner-fronted style. Seven teachers chose both, two people indicated they were eclectic, and one person said none. As such, the respondents showed an understanding of possible appropriate teaching strategies by providing two more styles (eclectic, or saying the classroom situation dictates) than were requested in the question, which asked only about teacher-fronted and learner-fronted styles.

The second (and final) open-ended question asked the respondents to describe roles which might not have been tapped by the questionnaire. Only 37 teachers gave complete answers about the roles teachers play. Their responses incorporated recurring words such as *facilitator* (n = 26), *monitor* (n = 11), *organizer* (n = 10), *guide* (n = 8), *motivator* (n = 5), *initiator* (n = 3), and *supporter* (n = 2).

Likewise, nearly half of the respondents (n = 19) believed in giving the learner an active role. Statements such as "the most important part in the learning process" and "the core of the learning process" are common in the teachers' answers. While seven respondents did not provide an answer, the remaining 18 reported, on the one hand, that the learner should have "an active role" and on the other, the learner should be "a receiver" and "a recipient".

In sum, the questionnaire provided a plethora of responses which revealed the teachers' understanding of the teaching/learning process dynamics in terms of roles. It also showed a variety of opinions as to what the relationship among the classroom parties should be. The questionnaire captured a learner-fronted language orientation from nearly all the teachers.

Patterns of interaction found in the lesson observations

The second research question asked, "What are the most frequent patterns of interaction during English lessons?" To address this question, each of the three teachers in the focal group was observed once. The results are based on a total of 150 minutes of classroom observation, with a mean of 48 minutes per lesson.

Table 5.3 summarizes in percentages the time spent on four types of interactions. The row totals do not equal 100% because other types of individual talk (for instance, students work all on the same task or on different tasks, student-to-teacher talk) are not included in these calculations.

The data indicate that the teacher-to-student interaction pattern dominated in all three observed lessons. This pattern reveals a fairly traditional teaching method where the teacher is responsible for the classroom events most of the time. All three teachers relied heavily on the textbook activities, where they first instructed the pupils to open their books to a given page, then briefly explained what the students had to do, and finally gave them time to complete their individual work. A typical feature among the three classes was that correction was consistently done by two or three pupils sitting in the front seats. The rest seemed reluctant and, in most cases, repeated the correction after the teacher provided it.

The second most frequent pattern of interaction, as the data above reveal, was managerial work. According to the COLT scheme descriptors, this type of talk is checked when the teacher gives instructional directives or comments on students' behavior. The data show that an average of nearly 10% of the lesson time was allocated to giving students varied types of instructions or other related disciplinary comments, which was considered an indication of the teachers' tight control of the classroom events. It may also suggest the inability of a majority of the students to stay on task without their teachers' explanations and close guidance.

TABLE 5.3 Percentages of time for four patterns of interaction

Teacher→Student/Class		Choral Work	Individual Work	Managerial talk
T 1	27.76	1.41	15.5	3.7
T 2	46.12	7	0	16.68
T 3	33.40	4.9	2.38	7.86
Mean	35.76	4.43	5.96	9.41

As for individual work, pupils spent an average of only 6% of lesson time working on their own in their seats on the same textbook tasks without any attempt to modify their contents and their order. As a consequence, the students did not complete their tasks except for two or three high achievers, who would always finish early, and as a result, prompted the teacher to stop work on the task and move to correction, a fact which could possibly explain the low percent of this type of work in lesson time.

Similarly, these three teachers spent relatively very limited time on choral work, which consists of the repetition by the whole class or groups of students of some expressions provided by the teacher or textbook as a model, mainly to improve pronunciation. The scarce occurrence of this pattern might be attributed by the lack of time, which resulted in the teachers focusing first and foremost on the first textbook activities (mainly grammar) without moving to the spelling and pronunciation activities at the end of the unit. The absence of choral repetition may also reflect the teachers' own beliefs on the limited pedagogic worth of this interactional strategy (choral repetition) in fostering L2 speaking skills. In sum, the heavy reliance on the textbook activities in sequence consequently left most of the lessons' linguistic features uncovered and the objectives unachieved. During the observations, none of the lessons ended with a productive activity, whether written or oral. Within the "Three Ps" approach to language teaching (prepare, participate, and practice), bringing the lesson to a close with a production stage is pivotal in the L2 learning process. At that point, the teacher is expected to retreat, and leave the stage to the students to reinvest the recently learned language in a freer way and produce new contextualized forms of that language.

When we consider teachers' verbal behavior, we must define the turns people take during lessons. The *turn* is a basic coding unit for analyzing classroom discourse. This term poses a great deal of fuzziness as a concept, because of the difficulty in identifying its boundaries (i.e., when one turn has ended and another has begun). Nevertheless, discourse analysts agree on the broad workable definition adopted in this study: A turn is "one or more streams of speech bounded by speech of another, usually an interlocutor" (Crookes, 1990, p. 82).

Overall, in the three lessons I observed, there were more teacher turns (449) than student turns (354). This difference could be explained by the small number of students who spoke in these lessons. Most of the time, the teachers' general solicits went unanswered and, as a result, the teachers themselves supplied the answers. There was wide teacher control of the classroom discourse, which was a logical result of the unequal distributions of speech power exchange (Markee, 2000).

The category of sustained speech addresses the length of the interactants' utterances – whether they are minimal or sustained. The former refers to a turn of a word/phrase or clause, whereas the latter refers to a turn which is longer than a clause. The most sustained speech was that of Teacher 1, whose utterances were categorized as 38.46% minimal and 61.53% sustained. For Teacher 2 the figures were 44% minimal and 56% sustained, while for Teacher 3 the figures were

71.29% minimal and 28.57% sustained (the least sustained). While there were large differences among the three teachers, on average, their speech could be characterized as 51.29% minimal and 48.7% sustained.

As an example, Teacher 2 used extended speech (long clauses without a pause) where his whole turn is 124 seconds long as shown in the transcript below. In contrast, Teachers 1 and 3 restricted their utterances to a minimal length (word/clause), 38% and 71% of their turns, respectively. In most cases, the teachers cued the students with word initials to elicit answers, which were usually not provided. Extract 1 provides an example of a teacher's sustained speech, in which T indicates the teachers' turns. A capital L stands for an individual learner and LL represents many learners.

L1: (reading the question from the textbook)
T: Good. So the first question here what do men and women wear? Wear something mean to puts one thing on. I wear clothes. Clothes here we talk about jacket, we can talk about shirts, this is a shirt (pointing to his shirt), and we can talk about (.) trousers, shoes. So we have different clothes clear yes. What men and women we distinguish between these two words. For a man I am a man and a woman is a girl who is a grown up clear yes you are girls and boys. For example eheheh= **[01:28]**
L: (unintelligible)
T: = Faress (boy's name) is a boy because he is (eleven) years old Isslem (girl's name) is a girl okay. When Faress grows up he be became (sic) a man. So man is a singular noun of course we (writing on the board and speaking at the same time) say eh eh man is a singular noun and men is a plural noun of course we don't have (-S) because it's an irregular plural form clear. The plural form of man men okay and **[2:52]**
LL: man men

The notations of 1:28 and 2:52 stand for the time interval (in minutes and seconds) of the speech exchange between the teacher and an individual learner) or many learners. This extract illustrates a common finding in language classroom research, i.e., that teachers talk more than students (see, e.g., Davies, 2011, for a review of the literature on teacher talking time). Exchanges of this kind are not likely to be helpful in guiding learners' L2 development. The teachers' domination of the classroom discourse is a typical feature in the lessons I observed and elsewhere in the Tunisian context (see Abdelslem, 1992). In fact, the high percentages of the features "giving predictable" statements and "asking pseudo questions" might explain the teachers' tendency to extend their utterances, since their questions went unanswered.

When we consider students' verbal behavior, the analysis is limited to the results of the three parameters of CLT: the use of information gaps, sustained speech, and the incorporation of teachers' and/or students' utterances.

The students' contributions consisted overwhelmingly of giving predictable rather than unpredictable information. The teachers' tight control over the textbook activities left no room for the students to digress or diverge in order to vary the topics, which could have given them opportunities to enrich the classroom discourse with unpredictable information. In class 3, there were noticeable attempts to give exchanges with new information, but in classes 1 and 2, the students' contributions were simple answers, which seemingly did not represent any cognitive challenge to them, probably because of the type of activity.

The students' questioning behavior is characterized by the scarce use of referential questions except in some limited instances imposed by the type of activity being used in class 2. Students' contributions consist mainly of giving information. For instance, in class 1 the students asked neither display questions (also called pseudo questions) nor referential questions. In fact, all the questions they asked were pseudo questions from the worksheets and were not generated by the students themselves.

As to whether the students engage in minimal or extended exchanges in their classroom talk, students generally produced more minimal utterances (85%) than sustained ones (15%) during the lessons. An extended turn consists of a paraphrase, an elaboration, or a clarification of a previous language form/structure whether from the teacher, the text, or the student, which occurred only 15% of lesson time. Conversely, the bulk of student verbal behavior (85%) was made up of bits of language in the form of repetitions to a corrected language form or a "yes" or "no" answer to the teacher questions.

To conclude, the analysis of the lesson talk revealed a traditional lock-step method used in teaching English. The discourse reflects tight teacher control over the lessons, thus leaving little space for the students to interact in the process. The results in this section support the reported gap in the EFL classroom research literature between teachers' self-reported beliefs and real classroom practices.

Implications for policy, practice, and future research

In view of these findings, the optimal use of CLT in Tunisian EFL classes should be reassessed. The most important implication gleaned from this study is that what the majority of the 44 EFL questionnaire respondents perceive happens in their classrooms was, in fact, not observed in the lessons taught by the focal group of three teachers. To the extent that the practices of those three teachers are typical of other Tunisian EFL teachers, future work should be directed at reducing this gap.

The second implication consists in the learners' limited talking time. Students' speaking skills need to be further developed, and this goal could be promoted by using various speaking-enhancing instructional materials, rather than sticking to the official textbook contents. Other factors that influence students' talking time (e.g., the typical class size ranges from 25 to 30 pupils) should also be considered.

For future research, the assessment of the implementation of CLT in Tunisian EFL classrooms needs to be further investigated in a comprehensive study. One way to achieve that goal is to select randomly a representative sample of the target population. This technique aims at collecting data from a large number of EFL teachers, so that future decisions would be informed by data from a larger sample. In addition, it would be valuable to observe lessons taught by many teachers whose beliefs had been gathered through questionnaire responses, to see if the ways in which they conduct language lessons match their belief statements.

References

Abdelslem, H. (1992). *Foreign language lesson discourse analysis: The teaching and learning of English in Tunisian schools.* The Edwin Mellen Press.

Crookes, G. (1990). The utterance, and other basic units for second language discourse analysis. *Applied Linguistics, 11*(2), 183–199.

Davies, M. J. (2011). Increasing students' L2 usage: An analysis of teacher talk time and student talk time. Unpublished Manuscript. MA TEFL/TESL Centre for English Language Studies, University of Birmingham. https://www.birmingham.ac.uk/Documents/college-artslaw/cels/essays/languageteaching/Daviesessay1TTTessaybank.pdf.

Dörnyei, Z., & Taguchi, T. (2009). *Questionnaires in second language research construction, administration, and processing* (2nd ed.). Routledge.

Fröhlich, M., Spada, N., & Allen, P. (1985). Differences in the communicative orientations of L2 classrooms. *TESOL Quarterly 19*(1), 27–57.

Markee, M. (2000). *Conversation analysis.* Lawrence Erlbaum.

Ounis, A., & Ounis, T. (2017). Tunisian secondary EFL school teachers' perceptions regarding communicative language teaching: An exploratory survey. *International Journal of Humanities and Cultural Studies, 4*(1), 188–208.

Tunisian Ministry of Education. (2006). *Tunisian official programmes in the Second Cycle of Basic Education.* http://www.edunet.tn/ressources/pedagogie/programmes/nouveaux_programme2011/preparatoire/langues/anglais_college.pdf.

6

MATCHES AND MISMATCHES BETWEEN EGYPTIAN HIGH SCHOOL EFL TEACHERS' GRAMMAR INSTRUCTION PRACTICES AND BELIEFS

Noha Abdelhamied Ibrahim and Muhammad M. M. Abdel Latif

Introduction

Grammar teaching has a prominent place in English-as-a-foreign-language (EFL) and English-as-a-second-language (ESL) learning environments. Regardless of the debate about whether grammar should be a main focus of language teaching or eliminated entirely (e.g., Nassaji & Fotos, 2004), what matters for many teachers working in these educational environments is to help students learn grammar more effectively. That is why EFL/ESL teachers are likely to allocate a considerable part of classroom time to grammar instruction. In Egypt, for instance, Abdel Latif (2012) noted that high school English teachers spent about 45% of their classroom time on grammar teaching.

Compared to research on some other language areas such as reading and writing, not many studies have been published on grammar teaching. Some of these studies have been concerned only with the characteristics of grammar teaching materials (e.g., Cullen & Kuo, 2007; Millard, 2000). Other studies have dealt with learners' and teachers' preferences for grammar instruction. For example, Liviero (2017) found that teachers in an ESL setting in England had varied interpretations of grammar and its teaching. In the Chinese context, Deng and Lin's (2016) research showed discrepancies between high school English teachers' and students' views about grammar instruction. While the teachers preferred communicative grammar teaching, students preferred an integrated mode of communicative and traditional grammar instruction.

A number of studies have indicated some tensions between teachers' grammar instruction beliefs and practices. For example, Farrell and Lim (2005), in their case study of two experienced primary school teachers in Singapore, found that their

DOI: 10.4324/9781003312444-7

grammar instruction beliefs were not reflected in their classroom practices. Similarly, Abduh and Algouzi's (2020) research in Saudi Arabia revealed a negative association between teachers' grammar instruction beliefs and their observed classroom practices. In what may seem to contradict these research findings, the two teachers in Phipps and Borg's (2009) longitudinal study had pedagogical beliefs which generally aligned with their practices. Likewise, Ezzi's (2012) research indicated that Yemeni EFL teachers' grammar teaching beliefs were associated with their instructional practices.

Other authors have also emphasized context-related differences in grammar teaching. For example, the two Argentinean high school English language teachers in Sanchez and Borg's (2014) study implemented a number of grammar instruction strategies which interacted with pedagogical concerns and contextual circumstances. In contrast, Sato and Oyanedel (2019) identified two conflicting beliefs in Chilean teachers' grammar instruction perspectives: their unsuccessful experiences in using pair and group activities in grammar classes, and the contextual barriers making communicative grammar teaching incompatible.

Overall, the above studies suggest that EFL/ESL teachers develop a set of complex grammar instruction beliefs and practices which interact with their previous teaching experiences, on the one hand, and are influenced by some contextual factors, on the other one. Given the context-specific nature of grammar teaching practices and beliefs, it is important to explore them in different international contexts. The study reported in this chapter investigated Egyptian high school EFL teachers' grammar instruction practices and how far they match their pedagogical beliefs.

Issues that motivated the research

Research on English grammar teaching in Egypt is very scarce. The only previous relevant study is perhaps the one reported by Abdel Latif (2017a), who used classroom observation and semi-structured interviews to investigate 12 Egyptian EFL teachers' use of grammar instruction materials, and their beliefs about these materials. He found that the teachers used no textbook materials in 68.3% (i.e., more than two thirds) of grammar-related classroom time instruction, and that they all made very little use of the inductive materials in presenting grammatical structures. Instead, they depended on their own deductive grammar explanations. Given that Abdel Latif's study focused solely on teachers' use of grammar instruction materials, we still need further research to investigate these practices from a different and more comprehensive angle. Trying to address this gap, the present study investigated the way a group of high school English language teachers in Egypt teach grammar, and the matches and mismatches between their grammar instruction practices and beliefs.

Research questions

The present study is guided by two research questions:

1. What are the matches and mismatches in Egyptian high school teachers' grammar instruction beliefs and practices?
2. What are the factors influencing these matches and mismatches?

To answer these research questions, the study drew on classroom observation and post-observation interviews, the approach used in most of the studies reviewed above. Observation was used to identify the way the participating teachers teach grammar to their students, while the interviews were employed to explore their grammar teaching conceptions and beliefs. This approach has in turn helped in identifying potential matches and mismatches between the teachers' grammar instruction practices and beliefs.

Research methods

Context

This study is concerned with English grammar teaching at Egyptian governmental high schools. This type of school is mainly supervised by the Egyptian Ministry of Education and represents about 90% of the schools in Egypt. The English language instruction provided in these schools is not as intensive as the instruction delivered at the other types of schools in the country (e.g., experimental schools, private language schools, or private international schools; see Abdel Latif, 2017b). The students attending such governmental schools receive five hours of English language instruction a week and study a main textbook along with a simplified version of a Western novel. During the data collection stage, high school students in these schools were studying the *Hello! English for Secondary Schools* textbook series, which is based on the communicative language teaching approach. In the textbook in each academic year of this stage, there are 18 units arranged into groups of three units, with a review unit at the end of each; thus the textbook includes a total of 24 units. Each main unit has five lessons (listening, language focus, reading, critical thinking, and communication), and is complemented by another unit in the workbook with additional language and grammar structure exercises.

The data for this study were collected from two schools, a rural school and an urban one, in Fayoum City which is located 100 kilometres southwest of Greater Cairo, the largest metropolitan area in Egypt. The rural school is a mixed one located in southwest of Fayoum City, and it had 850 students at the time of data collection, whereas the urban one is a girls' school located in Fayoum City, which had about 2000 students. Since Abdel Latif's (2017a) study was conducted with a group of teachers in Cairo schools, the potential influence of Fayoum teacher and student population characteristics on English grammar instruction practices and beliefs is another dimension that could add to the originality of the present study. Another originality dimension is related to the grammar teaching issues the present study covers.

Participants

Fifteen teachers took part in this study. Seven teachers were working at the rural school, and eight teachers were working in the urban context. Eight participants were females, and seven were males. They all had a BA degree, in either English language teaching or English literature and linguistics, with the exception of one who was holding an MA degree in TESOL at the time of the study. The participants had teaching experience ranging from 10 to 27 years, and the majority of them were in their thirties and forties during the data collection. Informed consent was obtained from all the teachers who agreed to participate on a voluntary basis, after confirming the confidentiality of the identities and workplaces.

Data collection procedures

The data were collected over a period of one month from the two schools. The first author visited the schools and met the teachers. She invited them to take part in the study, and then she started observing and interviewing the teachers who agreed to participate in the study. Each teacher was observed in two classes; each class lasted for 50 minutes. Prior to attending the classes, the first author did not tell the teachers she was going to observe their grammar instruction but rather their English teaching in general. This choice was intended in order not to influence the teachers' grammar instruction focus or behaviors during the observed classes. In the observations, the first author sat at the back of the class as a non-participant observer, watching classroom interactions and taking notes but not contributing to the interaction itself. She focused primarily on recording and understanding their grammar instruction practices. Each observed class was audio-recorded. While the first author was attending each class, she took two types of fieldnotes. The first consisted of descriptive notes: a description of the classroom events and activities, the role of the teacher inside the classroom, the language (i.e., Arabic, English, or both), techniques and materials the teacher used inside the classroom, and the ways the teacher reacts to students' grammar errors. The second consisted of reflective fieldnotes: her thoughts and reflections on what she has seen and heard in the classroom. In total, the author observed 30 classes, 18 classes in the urban high school grade (grade 10), and 12 in the rural grade (grade 11). Following the observation of each teacher, the first author interviewed them about the observed pedagogical practices and their grammar teaching beliefs. She discussed with each teacher the issues noted in the two observed classes, and the other general issues related to their beliefs about and approaches to grammar teaching, and attitudes towards textbook grammar materials. All the interviews were conducted in Arabic, the native language of the teachers. However, switches to English occurred frequently during all interviews, particularly when discussing teaching materials and classroom activities. The interviews were audio-recorded and each interview lasted for about 30 minutes.

Data analysis procedures

The two authors worked independently on analyzing the observation and interview data, and then collaboratively discussed the themes each one had identified. First, the audio-recorded interviews were translated into English and transcribed by the first author. Second, the two authors independently listened to the grammar teaching-related parts in the audio-recorded classes and read the fieldnotes to identify the pedagogical techniques the teachers followed in grammar instruction. They also read the transcribed interviews to identify the emerging themes. Following this independent data analysis, the two authors exchanged their data analysis files, and then met to discuss the differences in their analysis categories. Finally, the emerging themes identified in the two data types were compared to examine the matches and mismatches between the teachers' grammar pedagogical practices and beliefs. These emerging themes were subjected to further analysis and the early tentative categories were substantiated and refined (Merriam, 1998).

Findings and discussion

The analysis of the observation data revealed five main realities of English grammar instruction in the target context. The interviews with the teachers showed matches and also some mismatches (or tensions) between their instructional practices and beliefs. Below is a description of these five English grammar teaching realities, and how they matched or mismatched the teachers' pedagogical beliefs.

Allocating the largest proportion of classroom time to teaching grammar

In 29 out of the 30 observed classes, the teachers allocated more time to teaching grammar than any other language area. The teachers spent this time on explaining grammar rules on the board or using the textbooks, engaging the students in answering questions about the target rule being explained, getting the students to do textbook grammar activities, and correcting the students' errors. All the teachers switched to Arabic regularly during the observed classes. Some teachers turned the listening lessons into grammar lessons. In other words, the teachers allocated the time of the listening part to covering the grammar rule in that unit, instead of getting students to listen to audios and answer related listening comprehension questions. This phenomenon was also noted in the earlier study reported by Abdel Latif (2012).

In the interviews, all the teachers confirmed the importance of grammar in language learning. According to them, without learning grammar, students will not be able to use English accurately. More importantly, the teachers emphasize the necessity of focusing on grammar instruction because it is the only way to help students get high exam marks. In other words, this context involved *washback* – the influence of tests on teaching and learning (see, e.g., Bailey, 1996). The following interview excerpts summarize the teachers' perceptions of the importance of grammar to their students' English language learning and academic achievement:

> **Teacher 4**: It's all about grammar; the learner can't understand English without getting to know the structure which combines all the components of the language into a meaningful unit….There is no way to skip grammar because it plays a pivotal role in the syllabus and exam.
> **Teacher 7**: No grammar, no English. …This is the goal of the English syllabus in Egypt. In many cases, I don't have time to teach listening or speaking activities.
> **Teacher 15:** Of course, our students can't learn English without grammar. … Grammar is a necessary component in language learning, and without it students get low exam marks.

As noted, the teachers' beliefs about the importance of grammar to their students match their observed pedagogical practices, and the greater amount of classroom time allocated to teaching grammar.

Teaching grammar deductively

Classroom observations revealed that 14 out of 15 teachers taught grammar deductively and explicitly. These teachers almost approached grammar teaching in the same way; the technique they followed encompasses introducing the target grammar rule to the students, explaining the usage and the form of the structure, writing a summary and examples of the target rule on the board, asking the students to write down the explanations given on the board, and getting the students to do textbook activities related to the grammar rule. Most teachers focused mainly on explaining the target grammar rule without getting the students to use it in a communicative mode through speaking or writing activities. Three teachers only used some form of communicative activities at the beginning or the end of grammar instruction. Though one female teacher taught grammar inductively, she implemented a weak version of inductive grammar instruction as she spent a few minutes on writing examples from students' real life on the board and, then asking them to discover the rule by themselves.

In spite of these observed deductive grammar teaching practices, many interviewed teachers reported they like to teach grammar inductively because this helps students to be more actively and communicatively engaged in lesson activities. Many teachers emphasize the importance of inductive grammar instruction; they view it as a way to develop students' communication, and other language skills. This view can be noted, for instance, in the following two interview excerpts:

> **Teacher 5:** I think inductive grammar teaching is a better method for teaching grammar....Students do not only discover grammar rules but they also use them in communication.
> **Teacher 11:** Inductive grammar teaching is a good method to make students discover the grammar rules and meanings by themselves, and to improve their listening, speaking, reading, and writing competence.

Contextual factors seem to have played a key role in this mismatch between the teachers' practices and beliefs. Specifically, some teachers who were interviewed felt that deductive grammar instruction is the simpler method as it saves time and effort, particularly when teaching students of low English proficiency levels. These two interview comments summarize the teachers' rationale for their large dependence on deductive grammar teaching:

> **Teacher 8**: I generally follow the deductive method in teaching grammar. I start with explaining the rules in Arabic, and then give examples; this method takes little time. As you see, the students' level is low and I have to start from scratch... so I think the deductive method is good for overcoming this difficulty.
> **Teacher 12**: First, I write the form of the rule on the white board, and then I explain it to the students. After that, I ask them to generate as many examples as they can; the students do the activities, which all take a short time and help them get prepared for the final exam. I usually follow this method when I teach a difficult lesson or when students' level is low.

Depending largely on non-communicative grammar activities

In the class observations, it was found that the teachers used non-communicative textbook activities in grammar instruction much more frequently than communicative activities. Specifically, the teachers commonly used four types of textbook grammar activities: re-write the sentences, find the errors, fill-in the blanks, and choose the correct answer. Compared to communicative grammar activities or the rules written on the board, the teachers spent far more time teaching these controlled written grammar activities. These results do not concur with Abdel Latif's (2017a) study, in which the teachers spent more than two thirds of their grammar instruction time to teaching grammar without using textbook materials.

The interviews revealed another mismatch between the teachers' observed practices and their beliefs. Fourteen teachers reported they like to teach grammar rules communicatively and in a more contextualized way as this helps their students have a more interesting and real-life learning experience. Below are examples from the teachers' answers to a question about a different approach they like to use in teaching grammar to students:

> **Teacher 2:** If I have the chance to teach grammar differently, I would teach small groups of students so that I would be able to introduce grammar in a more attractive way through real life examples and communication.
> **Teacher 9:** I like to teach grammar through communicative tasks involving role playing and conversations. I do not like to teach just mere examples of grammar rules. This is not useful.
> **Teacher 10:** I would teach grammar rules which have something to do with our real-life situations. ... I don't like to give my students mechanical explanations and exercises on a certain structure which we rarely use in real life, but I like to teach in meaningful texts.

Like the teachers' reported beliefs about inductive grammar teaching, the beliefs they hold about the usefulness of communicative grammar instruction contradict their observed over-dependence on non-communicative grammar activities.

While 12 of the teachers interviewed agree on the importance of the textbook to their students, they were not satisfied with the nature of many grammar activities in it. According to them, these activities are inadequate and do not meet their students' needs. As one teacher summarizes it:

> **Teacher 11**: Many textbook activities neither match the students' levels nor the nature of questions in the exam. The exercises are either too easy in a way to get the students bored or too difficult and this could make them feel frustrated.

Contrary to this more popular view, only three teachers said that textbook activities are good and adequate. These teachers particularly regard the workbook grammar activities as appropriate due to their similarity to exam questions. For example:

> **Teacher 8:** The grammar textbook activities are good enough, specially the exercises in the Workbook. ... I personally depend on them in my teaching. What I like the most are the challenging activities which get the students to practice exam-like exercises, such as "choose the correct answer," "find the error," and "re-write the sentence."

In light of this, washback seems to be a decisive factor influencing the teachers' use of grammar activities in their classes. It is worth noting that there are two completely different types of grammar activities high school students study in Egypt. The first is the communicative activities and this type is included primarily in the students' book. The second is the non-communicative grammar activities found mainly in the workbook; thus, the non-communicative workbook activities are basically designed to help students prepare for their exams.

Delivering teacher-centered grammar lessons

Classroom observations showed that grammar instruction in most classes was a teacher-centered process. In all classes, teacher talk was much more dominant than student talk; the time spent on the teacher's grammar explanations exceeded the time allocated to students' completion of grammar activities. Many teachers provided grammar explanations using a fixed lesson plan without adjusting these explanations to the students' varied proficiency levels.

The teachers' reported beliefs were almost congruent with these observed practices. Their main reasons for the implementation of teacher-centered grammar instruction are avoiding classroom chaos, managing classes with a large number of students, and considering students' language levels. These reasons can be noted in the following interview excerpts:

> **Teacher 1**: It is a good idea to give the students more time to discuss and practice grammar rules in the classroom. ... But as a teacher, I like to have control over what is happening in the classroom; this helps in avoiding classroom chaos and saves time.
>
> **Teacher 14:** With 40 or 50 students in the classroom and very narrow space to move in and check their performance, it becomes so exhausting to implement student-centered tasks. ... The students' low level and the large class size prevent me from trying out any different grammar teaching methods.

Only two of the teachers interviewed view the role of the teacher as facilitating and guiding students' grammar learning. These two teachers think that student-centered classes help in obtaining better learning outputs than do teacher-centered lessons. But as noted, even these two teachers' practices mismatched their beliefs.

Correcting students' grammar errors

It was also noted that the majority of the teachers observed paid attention to correcting the students' grammar errors. In the observed classes, the students were mainly provided with teacher correction rather than peer correction. In most cases, the teachers corrected the students' errors themselves, and did not engage them in many self-correction or peer correction activities. Dealing with the students' errors in this way pertains also to the issue discussed in the previous section, i.e., delivering teacher-centered grammar lessons. The teachers particularly focused on errors the students made during answering textbook activities, i.e., written grammar errors. The individual approaches to error correction, however, varied from one teacher to another. Some teachers paid regular attention to correcting students' grammar errors, whereas others were selective in their errors correction.

In the interviews, the teachers reported that it is essential to correct their students' errors, and to alert them to these errors so the learners can avoid them later on. The following two interview excerpts summarize the teachers' beliefs about correcting students' grammar errors:

> **Teacher 6:** I have to correct errors to help my students who feel it is necessary to know the correct answer, especially in the written work and exercises. I like to repeat the sentence students have made errors in but with their correct forms so that they could figure out the difference by themselves and not to get them ashamed when making errors.
> **Teacher 11:** I think correcting students' errors is an unavoidable thing, but I don't like to correct all errors made by them. It depends on the type of the error; if the error is written, it is crucial to correct it. … Ignoring error correction may cause confusion to my students. … I don't like to correct the students' oral errors to encourage them to speak fluently.

The teachers' emphasis on correcting the students' written errors in the excerpts above is very likely associated with washback; they do so to raise students' awareness of the errors they must avoid in exam-like situations.

Implications for policy, practice, and future research

As indicated in these results, grammar instruction plays a central role in English language education in Egyptian high schools. This study revealed that the teachers in these schools allocate more classroom time to teaching grammar than to teaching any other language area. As for the teachers' approach to grammar instruction, they were generally found to teach grammar deductively, depend largely on non-communicative grammar activities, deliver teacher-centered grammar lessons, and pay regular attention to correcting their students' grammar errors. These results align with those in Abdel Latif's (2012) study; the only exception is teachers' over-dependence on textbook grammar activities in the current study.

This study also showed there are matches and mismatches between the teachers' grammar instruction practices and their beliefs. Table 6.1 gives a summary of these matches and mismatches.

The two tensions noted in the table are between the teachers' practices and their beliefs about inductive and communicative grammar instruction. The teachers' two main reasons for depending on deductive and non-communicative grammar instruction are saving time and the students' low proficiency levels. It is likely that their students have been accustomed to deductive grammar teaching; that is why the teachers may find teaching grammar inductively will not match their students' learning styles and thus will be a waste of time. On the other hand, the other three

TABLE 6.1 Matches and mismatches between the teachers' grammar instruction practices and beliefs

Observed grammar instruction practices	Matched pedagogical beliefs	Mismatched pedagogical beliefs
Allocating the largest proportion of classroom time to teaching grammar.	Grammar is the key to students' English learning and academic achievement.	–
Depending largely on deductive grammar teaching.	This teaching technique is more effective and it is appropriate to students' low proficiency levels.	English grammar should be taught inductively to foster students' engagement and communication.
Drawing heavily upon non-communicative grammar activities.	These non-communicative grammar activities resemble the final exam questions students must answer.	English grammar should be taught communicatively to help students have interesting and real-life learning experiences.
Delivering teacher-centered grammar lessons.	Delivering learner-centered grammar lessons could lead to classroom chaos.	–
Regularly correcting students' grammar errors.	Students' written grammar errors should be corrected to help them avoid these errors in their exams.	–

dimensions of the teachers' practices (i.e., allocating substantial classroom time to teaching grammar, delivering teacher-centered grammar lessons, and regularly correcting students' grammar errors) all align with their pedagogical beliefs. As indicated in Table 6.1, the teachers' main reasons for teaching grammar in this way are washback, effective classroom management, and students' low English levels. Overall, these results concur with previous research findings indicating tensions between teachers' grammar instruction practices and beliefs in many international contexts (e.g., Abduh & Algouzi, 2020; Farrell & Lim, 2005; Sato & Oyanedel, 2019) and the major role of the contextual factors in grammar teaching (e.g., Abdel Latif, 2017a; Phipps & Borg, 2009; Sanchez & Borg, 2014).

The results of the present study indicate that changing teachers' grammar instruction practices in Egypt requires two main reforms. First, there is a need for reforming the high school examination system by including an oral communication component and modifying the assessment of students' English grammar knowledge. This improvement in the examination system would lead to changes in teachers' grammar instruction practices and beliefs. Second, such a change would also require training teachers in inductive and communicative grammar instruction. It is clear from the data that the teachers are willing to teach grammar inductively and communicatively, but they have apparently not received adequate training in these areas. Therefore, training could help them be able to implement these desired grammar instruction practices.

This study is limited in focusing on a small number of high school EFL teachers in Egypt. There is a need for large-scale research investigating Egyptian teachers' English grammar pedagogy and perceptions. It is important to investigate English grammar pedagogy in many Arab countries, given that it is still under-explored in many Arab world regions. These research attempts could have important implications for improving the English grammar instruction Arab students receive.

References

Abdel Latif, M. M. M. (2017a). Teaching grammar using inductive and communicative materials: Exploring Egyptian EFL teachers' practices and beliefs. In B. Tomlinson, M. Hitomi, & F. Mishan (Eds.), *Practice and theory for materials development in language learning* (pp. 275–289). Cambridge Scholars Publishing.

Abdel Latif, M. M. M. (2017b). English education policy at the pre-university stages in Egypt: Past, present and future directions. In R. Kirkpatrick (Ed.), *English language policy in the Middle East and North Africa* (pp. 33–45). Springer. doi:10.1007/978-973-319-46778-8_3.

Abdel Latif, M. M. M. (2012). Teaching a standard-based communicative English textbook series to secondary school students in Egypt: Investigating teachers' practices and beliefs. *English Teaching: Practice and Critique, 11*(3), 78–97.

Abduh, M., & Algouzi, S. (2020). Revisiting grammar teaching in a Saudi EFL context: Teachers' perceptions and practices. *Arab World English Journal, 11*(4), 291–306. https://dx.doi.org/10.24093/awej/vol11no4.19.

Bailey, K. M. (1996). Working for washback: A review of the washback concept in language testing. *Language Testing, 13*(3), 257–279.

Cullen, R., & Kuo, I. C. V. (2007). Spoken grammar and ELT course materials: A missing link? *TESOL Quarterly, 41*, 361–386. https://doi.org/10.1002/j.1545-7249.2007.tb00063.x.

Deng, F., & Lin, Y. (2016). A comparative study on beliefs of grammar teaching between high school English teachers and students in China. *English Language Teaching, 9*(8), 1–10. https://doi.org/10.5539/elt.v9n8p1.

Ezzi, N. A. A. (2012). Yemeni teachers' beliefs of grammar teaching and classroom practices. *English Language Teaching, 5*(8), 170–184. https://doi.org/10.5539/elt.v5n8p170.

Farrell, T. S., & Lim, P. C. P. (2005). Conceptions of grammar teaching: A case study of teachers' beliefs and classroom practices. *TESL-EJ, 9*(2), 1–12.

Liviero, S. (2017). Grammar teaching in secondary school foreign language learning in England: Teachers' reported beliefs and observed practices. *The Language Learning Journal, 45* (1), 26–50. Doi: https://doi.org/10.1080/09571736.2016.1263677.

Merriam, S. B. (1998). *Qualitative research and case study applications in education*. Jossey-Bass.

Millard, D. J. (2000). Form-focused instruction in communicative language teaching: Implications for grammar textbooks. *TESL Canada Journal, 18*, 47–57.

Nassaji, H., & Fotos, S. (2004). Current developments in research on the teaching of grammar. *Annual Review of Applied Linguistics, 24*, 126–145. https://doi.org/10.1017/S0267190504000066.

Phipps, S., & Borg, S. (2009). Exploring tensions between teachers' grammar teaching beliefs and practices. *System, 37*, 380–390. https://doi.org/10.1016/j.system.2009.03.002.

Sanchez, H., & Borg, S. (2014). Insights into L2 teachers' pedagogical content knowledge: A cognitive perspective on their grammar explanations. *System, 44*, 45–53. https://doi.org/10.1016/j.system.2014.02.005.

Sato, M., & Oyanedel, J. C. (2019). 'I think that is a better way to teach but…': EFL teachers' conflicting beliefs about grammar teaching. *System, 84*, 110–122. https://doi.org/10.1016/j.system.2019.06.005.

PART II
Identity and affect

7
EFL LEARNER IDENTITY AND L2 PRAGMATIC CHOICES

Evidence from the Omani EFL context

Fatema Al-Rubai'ey

Introduction

Issues that motivated the research

Speech acts such as requesting, apologizing, and inviting are universal pragmatic behaviors (Blum-Kulka et al., 1989). However, speech acts understood as pragmatic behaviors are problematic for language acquisition because they can have different functions, can be realized in different ways, and can vary across contexts and cultures. Cohen (1996) maintains that speech acts are "an area of continual concern for language learners" (p. 383), because learners must choose from a host of pragmatic strategies, the use of which is context and culture specific. Thus, deviation from the pragmatics norms of native speakers (NSs) is expected as L2 learners might generalize their understanding and use of such strategies in their L1 onto their L2 use.

Among the problems documented in the production of speech acts by NNSs is *pragmatic transfer*, which is defined as "the influence exerted by learners' pragmatic knowledge of languages and cultures other than L2 on their comprehension, production and learning of L2 pragmatic information" (Kasper, 1992, p. 207). Pragmatic transfer is divided into positive and negative pragmatic transfer (Kasper, 1992). Positive pragmatic transfer results from using shared pragmatic norms between the L1 and the target language (TL) that do not result in miscommunication or pragmatic failure (Thomas, 1983). However, when L1-specific pragmatic norms are transferred to the TL, they are considered negative because they could result in deviant use and could cause miscommunication or pragmatic failure. Since positive pragmatic transfer does not lead to pragmatic failure, researchers have focused on negative pragmatic transfer, which is generally called *pragmatic transfer*. Many researchers have attested to

DOI: 10.4324/9781003312444-9
This chapter has been made available under a CC BY-NC-ND 4.0 license.

the negative influence of (negative) pragmatic transfer in L2 communication (e.g., Beebe et al., 1990; Kasper, 1992; Thomas, 1983).

In the few studies that directly examined pragmatic transfer, it was investigated in relation to factors such as L2 proficiency levels and learning context (i.e., ESL and EFL) (e.g., Al-Issa, 2003; Félix-Brasdefer, 2008; Savić, 2014). However, the findings have been inconclusive and indicate a need to consider other factors that might be crucial for understanding pragmatic transfer but have gone unnoticed in previous research, factors such as learner identity.

The identity of the learner has long been a suspected yet under-examined factor affecting L2 learners' pragmatic choices, and thus, pragmatic transfer (Kim, 2014). Some researchers contend that despite L2 learners' awareness of the L2's sociopragmatic rules, they may elect to deviate from those rules by using their L1 pragmatic norms (Ishihara, 2019; Mirzaei & Parhizkar, 2021). Such observations highlight the role of *learner identity*, or "how a person understands his or her relationship to the world, how that relationship is structured across time and space, and how the person understands possibilities for the future" (Norton, 2013, p. 45). Therefore, by examining learners' perceptions (i.e., understanding and assessment) of their performance and asking not only how but also why they make certain pragmatic choices, this study focused on the role of learner identity in pragmatic transfer when refusing in English.

Research questions

This study examined the role of Omani EFL learners' identities in their pragmatic choices and pragmatic transfer when using English, their L2. Specifically, it examined how Omani EFL learners understand their relationship with English and how such a relationship is constructed as conformity with and/or deviation from English pragmatic norms (i.e., pragmatic transfer) when refusing requests or invitations in English. The following research questions were addressed:

1. How do Omani EFL learners define their relationship with (attitude towards) English?
2. How do Omani EFL learners construct their relationship with English through their pragmatic choices (specifically pragmatic transfer) when refusing requests or invitations in English?

Research methods

Context

This study was conducted at Sultan Qaboos University (SQU), at the Department of English Language and Literature. The majority of students at SQU are Omanis, with a small number of students from other Arab countries. Instructors at SQU come from many different nationalities, including both native and non-native speakers of English. Students in the English Department are required to communicate with their professors in English, both inside and outside the classroom.

The Foundation Programme English Language Curriculum Document (2012–2013) at SQU does not explicitly describe English as EFL, ESL, or EIL/ELF, but it seems that British English and American English are the most preferred varieties. That document recommends the use of British and American dictionaries, grammar, and pronunciation in teaching and assessment, but does not explain why these varieties of English are recommended.

Even though English is not recognized as an official language in Oman, it enjoys strong support from the government in institutionalized domains such as business, education, media, and medicine (Al-Busaidi, 1995). English is seen as "a powerful tool for modernization, national development and Omanization" (Al-Busaidi, 1995, p. 220) to replace the foreign workforce in white-collar jobs in Oman, and for Omanis to have better access to education, technology, and the global market.

Data collection procedures

Ten students participated in the study (five females and five males). All the participants were fourth-year Omani students in the English Department at SQU. Their ages ranged from 22 to 23 years old. They spoke Omani Arabic as their first language and had learned English as a foreign language. For the purposes of this report, the participants chose their own pseudonyms.

The participants were required to refuse in English to eight scenarios (four invitations and four requests) using an oral discourse completion task (Blum-Kulka et al., 1989) (henceforth, ODCT). The requests were for help with a workshop, help with an exhibition, directions to the Language Center, and directions to the Deanship of the College of Arts. The invitations were to attend a seminar, a lecture, an open day event, and a media event.

The scenarios in the ODCT included three sociopragmatic variables: absolute ranking of imposition (i.e., requests are more imposing speech acts than invitations), social distance (i.e., familiarity or lack thereof between the participants and their interlocutors; Brown & Levinson, 1987), and cultural distance (i.e., the linguistic and cultural differences between the participants and their interlocutors). Omani interlocutors and American/British interlocutors represented this variable.

Two semi-structured interviews (23 questions) followed the completion of the ODCT. The participants were given the choice of using either English or Arabic in the interviews. The first interview immediately followed the ODCT. It focused on examining the learners' assessment of their refusals in English. During this interview, the refusal responses of each participant were played back to help the speakers recall their responses and comment on them. The second interview was conducted one week later and focused on examining the participants' perceptions of the role of their identities in their pragmatic choices and pragmatic transfer. This chapter reports on the findings of the second interview.

This interview was used to gain in-depth insights about the impact of Omani EFL learners' identity on their pragmatic choices and pragmatic transfer. The interview questions were designed using the three conditions proposed by Norton (2000) for the definition of L2 learners' identities: (1) L2 learners' definitions of their relationship with the L2 language and culture (attitude towards English language, its culture and NSs, and motivation for learning English); (2) how they construct and reconstruct this relationship through L2 use (cases of conformity and non-conformity to L2 pragmatics from the participants' production as well as their perceptions of their refusals in English); and (3) L2 learners' perceptions of future relationship with the L2 (future decisions regarding their pragmatic choices when communicating in English with native and non-native speakers of English).

Unlike the cross-cultural framework used by Blum-Kulka et al. (1989) to examine pragmatic transfer, this study adopts an emic perspective toward the identification and explanation of pragmatic transfer. "An emic perspective attempts to capture participants' indigenous meanings of real-world events" (Yin, 2016, p. 16). The participants were asked if they perceived instances of pragmatic transfer (i.e., Arabic pragmatic strategies of refusals) in their refusals in English. If so, they were asked to explain their pragmatic decisions. Therefore, no data from NSs of English were collected and hence no comparison between the participants' realization of refusals in English and refusals of NSs of English was conducted in this study. The emic perspective was chosen to allow the participants to explain their use of refusals without any external influence.

Data analysis procedures

The refusals strategies produced by the participants were categorized using refusal speech acts classifications from Beebe et al. (1990) and Al-Issa (2003). These refusal speech acts include 11 strategies: Negation, Apology, Excuse, Wish, Solution Suggestion, Assurance, Postponement, Indefinite Acceptance, Gratitude, Compliment, and Consequence Downtoner.

The analysis of the interview focused on the role of the learners' identities in their pragmatic choices and transfer. A thematic analysis was applied to the qualitative data using the three conditions for defining L2 learners' identities proposed by Norton (2000), as noted above.

Findings and discussion

When the participants were asked to identify any instances of pragmatic transfer from Arabic in their refusals in English, they all stated that it was not easy to identify such instances with absolute certainty. They explained that through years of studying English, they had developed their own "personal style" of using English which reflects their choices based on English culture and Arabic culture. For example, Yusuf described his personal style as "neutral," or a style that he could use in both cultures (Arabic and English). Al-Yazan added, "English in our society does not reflect their [NSs of English] culture nor our culture, because it is a mixture of both." Several examples (using Gratitude, Compliment, Wish, and Assurance) were perceived by some participants as refusal styles accepted in both languages.

Cases of pragmatic transfer

Sometimes, however, the students were able to identify instances of pragmatic transfer from Arabic in their refusals in English, using the strategies listed above. It is important to note that these strategies identified as pragmatic transfer represent the participants' emic perspective or personal evaluation of pragmatic transfer in their English refusals. There is no cross-cultural evidence to suggest they are not used by NSs of English.

In relation to the Excuse strategy, for example, all participants agreed that the culture they shared with Omani professors somehow obliged them to comply with the Omani interlocutors' requests and invitations. This expectation of cooperation resulted in the need to justify their refusals in English to the requests of familiar and unfamiliar Omani professors. If they refused without providing justification, their Omani interlocutors might perceive them as uncooperative. Therefore, this pragmatic transfer can be seen as necessary for successful communication in English with Omani professors. Mimi commented, "because it is in the nature of Omanis to help" so an Omani person would think it was unnatural for another Omani not to help. For example, Mimi used the Excuse strategy in her refusal to familiar Omani professors ("I'm sorry but I've already told my family that I'm coming home.") and to unfamiliar Omani professors ("I'm sorry but I'm very late. I'm really sorry.").

It seems that using the Excuse strategy enabled the participants to maintain their self-image as cooperative individuals and members of the Omani culture when refusing Omani interlocutors in English. This interpretation is further confirmed by their perception that the total disregard of Arabic cultural norms when communicating in English, especially with Omanis, would be a form of shedding one's identity. For example, Areej explained, "One has to preserve his principles [cultural values]. It is true that I use their [NSs of English] language but the principles won't change. It is normal to use your own culture when you use your language or English, as if these principles are translated into English when you speak English." Therefore, using Arabic cultural norms such as the Excuse strategy when communicating in English was a way of presenting and preserving one's identity.

Despite the participants' belief that NSs of English are succinct, direct, and straightforward in their refusals, the participants used the Excuse strategy very often in their refusals to the requests and invitations of American/British (A/B) professors. However, the participants were divided about whether the use of the Excuse strategy or frequency of its use is the source of transfer from Arabic. Taif said that her lengthy explanation in refusing the request of an A/B professor ("Sorry doctor. I wish I could do that for you, but I'm busy preparing my midterm paper, which I'm planning to finish this week.") was Arabic pragmatic behavior. Khaled agreed; he stated that it was not only the length of the explanation, but also the idea of justifying a refusal that was influenced by Arabic. Khaled explained that when a NS of English refuses, he/she would "give a direct answer." Cross-cultural studies on refusals by NSs of English and Arab EFL learners found that both groups of speakers use the Excuse strategy in their refusals (e.g., Al-Issa, 2003). However, these studies noted that Arab EFL learners tend to elaborate or use the Excuse strategy more frequently than NSs of English.

The participants gave two reasons motivating their use of the Excuse strategy when refusing A/B professors: concerns for their image as EFL learners and their image as Omanis. In relation to the former, all the participants stated that linguistically it is more difficult to refuse familiar native-speaking English professors than Arab/Omani professors. Most of the participants agreed that giving explanations when refusing their familiar A/B professors is a way to counter any possible misunderstanding that could result from improper pragmatic choices. For instance, Al-Yazan said, "With Arab professors … we have the same language [and] same religion…. An Arab professor will understand even if you make mistakes when you talk to him in English." Taif attributed this understanding to the language acquisition experience shared with their Omani professors. She explained, "Omanis have been through these situations [of learning English], so you feel more comfortable because they will understand your mistakes." When communicating with native-speaking English professors, on the other hand, Taif stated, "I am afraid to commit mistakes with natives [NSs of English] even inside the class. Maybe they will not understand my mistake. I think they would say she is a language specialist and she makes mistakes."

Lack of familiarity between the participants and an A/B professor motivated the use of the Excuse strategy mainly to protect their image and reputation as Omanis. Yusuf, for example, stated, "He is a stranger. He is not from our culture. I think I'm reflecting the culture, Omani culture. I should be more polite by giving so many reasons. He will think that Omanis are kind and so on. He won't have [negative] ideas." In his refusal to unfamiliar A/B professor, he said, "Sorry doctor. I can't really help you. Because I have to go to the library to get resources. Because I don't have a car, I depend on my friend [to give me a ride]. He is also busy. He has half an hour to get me there."

Even though the Wish, Assurance, and Solution Suggestion strategies are not frequently used in refusing requests, two of the participants affirmed that concerns for their image as Omanis when refusing the request of an unfamiliar A/B professor motivated their use of these strategies. For example, Abdulla refused by saying, "I'm sorry. I cannot help you because somebody is waiting for me, but I hope somebody will guide you." He commented, "It is Omani style because I was concerned about our image as Omanis.... I feel that if I said to him this [wish], it will give him [a good] idea about Omanis in general." Taif explained, "If you don't help a foreigner, he might think that all Omanis are like that." As a result, she felt she had to assure her unfamiliar A/B interlocutor by saying, "I wish I could, but my friend is waiting. Could you please ask someone around? They will help you."

Two participants stated that suggesting using a Solution to unfamiliar A/B professor was an Arabic pragmatic behavior. For example, despite Al-Yazan's argument that "It does not matter for foreigners if you suggest for them or not," he used a Solution in his refusal to unfamiliar A/B professor's request, "I'm so sorry doctor. I have some work to do now. I'm busy. So, you can ask someone to direct you." Taif agreed with Al-Yazan's perception of using this strategy to maintain a positive image of Omanis. However, Reem and Areej, who also used this strategy, affirmed that suggesting a Solution was an acceptable behavior in both Arabic and English.

The fact the participants choose to use these strategies in spite of their perception of them being non-English pragmatic norms of refusals highlights the role of their identity in their pragmatic choices. Those choices were motivated by a desire to play particular roles or identities (Norton, 2013). These include the desire to appear as polite and cooperative individuals, to be seen as individuals who are representing the Omani community and culture, and to be good EFL learners. These different identity roles were invoked by the participants' evaluation of the relevance of all or some of the context-related details, such as degree of familiarity and cultural distance. The influence of the context of interaction on identity enactment supports Hall's (2012) observation that the relevance of our identities is "dynamic and responsive to contextual conditions" (p. 33).

When refusing invitations, eight participants stated that the use of the Gratitude and Compliment strategies in combination with Negation and Apology is an acceptable pragmatic behavior when refusing invitations in both languages. However, Fajir and Ali perceived the use of Gratitude and Compliment as influenced by Arabic, while adding Negation and Apology is an English style. For example, Fajir used the Compliment strategy in saying, "That would be very useful, but I cannot attend," and the Gratitude strategy in saying, "Thank you, doctor, for the invitation. But I cannot come because I have something important on that day." Fajir explained that Compliment and Gratitude were used to express appreciation for the invitations; however, they would also imply a refusal in Arabic similar to that conveyed by Regret ("Sorry" and "I am sorry"). Ali agreed and stated, "If I start with it [Gratitude], it will indicate directly that I don't want to attend. Starting with 'Thank you' is a direct refusal. It is like saying 'No.'" He refused one of the invitations by saying, "Thank you doctor for suggesting, but you know I have to submit my ... my...the final paper next week. So I cannot attend."

All the participants agreed that when the Gratitude, Compliment, Indefinite Acceptance, and Postponement strategies are used in isolation or in combination, they could result in the production of indirect refusal to invitations in Omani Arabic. Therefore, when these strategies are used to refuse invitations in English to Omanis and NSs of English, it is a transfer from Arabic. For example, Reem stated that she could refuse by combining Gratitude with Indefinite Acceptance, "<u>Thank you. I'll try</u>," while Fajir combined Gratitude with Postponement: "<u>Thank you doctor for the invitation. I'll see</u>." Seven of the participants also used the pragmatic marker Consequence Downtoner of "Insha'Allah," which means "God Willing." The participants stated that they could use "Insha'Allah" in isolation or in combination with these strategies when refusing public invitations. For example, Mimi used it alone, while Ali used it in combination with Indefinite Acceptance in saying, "<u>I'll try to attend, Insha' Allah</u>."

All of the participants perceived these strategies as equally suitable refusal responses in English with Arab/Omani people and NSs of English for two reasons. First, their responses posed no negative effect on the interlocutors' face (Brown & Levinson, 1987), because invitations were less imposing than requests. The transfer of these strategies, therefore, was triggered by the participants' evaluation of perceived degree of imposition of type of speech act only. Accordingly, they preferred using responses that were more positive (those that do not indicate immediate rejection). Reem explained, "Arabs don't say 'No' to your face [when invited] …. It is kind of polite to reply positively." Yusuf confirmed this understanding: "It is a public invitation and confirming attendance is not necessary. In our culture we believe it is polite not to reject immediately." The absence of degree of imposition and hence lack of threat to the face of their interlocutors empowered the participants to transfer presumably Arabic pragmatic norms when refusing invitations more easily compared to refusing requests. This perceived transfer could be a form of the students' attempt to utilize and display their linguistic and cultural capital (Darvin & Norton, 2015). Jenkins (2006) also affirmed that NNSs of English might utilize their bilingual and multilingual resources to meet their communication needs and goals.

Second, the local context influenced their pragmatic choices when refusing the invitations of A/B professors. The participants explained that their interlocutors were either Omanis or Arabs, with whom they shared the same culture, or foreigners (including NSs of English) who they assumed were familiar with the local Omani culture and hence they would understand and accept their refusals. All the participants stated that differences in the context of interaction (i.e., in English-speaking countries) might result in transferring less from Arabic, and hence conforming more to the pragmatics norms of NSs of English. However, the participants affirmed that they would do so only if they realized that their transferred pragmatic norms were causing misunderstanding or offence. Reem stated that she would "transfer Arabic politeness to English unless my Arabic politeness might be offensive to NSs; then I would use their politeness." Whether the context is EFL or ESL, it seems that these students' desire to be perceived as polite is the deciding factor in their pragmatic choices.

While the influence of the Omani EFL learners' identities on their pragmatic decisions is present, some of the disagreement on what constitutes pragmatic transfer from Arabic could indicate a lack of pragmatic awareness (Bardovi-Harlig & Dörnyei, 1998) of what is pragmatically acceptable when refusing in English. This disagreement includes type of strategy (such as Excuse or Wish), aspect of strategy (such as the frequency of using the Excuse), and the style of combining these strategies (such as Gratitude and Compliment in combination with Negation and Apology or with other strategies). Lack of pragmatic awareness is also implied by the participants' inability to sometimes distinguish between Arabic and English pragmatic norms, which they described as a neutral style. This possible lack of pragmatic awareness could be caused by language proficiency as well as the influence of the local context on pragmatic decisions. Previous research attested to the influence of proficiency level and the learning context on English language learners' pragmatic performance (Roever & Al-Gahtani, 2015).

The first research question asked about Omani ELF learners' relationship with English. All the participants had a positive attitude to English language, culture, and NSs. They saw the value of English in its utility as an international tool for communication, thus granting them chances to communicate with people from other cultures, access to educational resources, and opportunities for access to jobs that require English. English was not just a second language for the participants; rather, it was a second language with international value and status. They stated that this international status empowered them to speak with people locally and internationally. Areej said, "English is the most common language. The most widespread [language]." Ali commented, "It opens horizons for you. You can communicate with anyone from different nationalities." This instrumental motivation made the participants passionate about acquiring the English language.

All the participants stated that they would maintain the use of Arabic pragmatic norms when communicating in English for two reasons: their desire to maintain their culture and identity and their perception that using Arabic cultural norms when communicating in English was appropriate. For example, Abdulla said, "Your identity is Omani. You have to use these things [Arabic pragmatic norms] whether you want or not." Taif added, "There is no insult to English when I use my culture with it. English culture is important as well. If I change the English use to the Arabic use completely it won't sound like English. Nonetheless, I have to bring my culture when I speak in English."

Overall, it seems participants' views of language and culture as inherently related fit with the sociocultural perspective on language and culture (Hall, 2012). Perhaps participants see their discursive interaction as a realization of culture because "culture is located not in the individual mind but in the activity" and specifically in the discursive activity (Hall, 2012, p. 17). The embodiment of culture through language use is an enactment of identity and vice versa. Identity is not only the students' sense of self, but a way to illustrate their perception of their sense of self (Norton, 2013). Therefore, pragmatic choices could be seen as their enactment of their identity.

Implications for policy, practice, and future research

This study contributes to the growing literature on pragmatic transfer in SLA by uncovering the role of learners' identities in their realization of refusals in English and their perceptions of their refusals, particularly in triggering pragmatic transfer. The findings have implications on how we conceptualize pragmatic transfer. For example, what has been commonly described as pragmatic transfer in L2 pragmatics studies might be an attempt by learners to express their identity and not a reflection of their pragmatic competence (or lack thereof) in the L2.

Also, this study contributes to our understanding of how learners as social beings select and decide on the pragmatic norms that are most relevant to their communication. As a result, the findings suggest revisiting predetermined notions of successful communication and competence in mainstream SLA (Taguchi, 2019). Jenkins (2006), for example, asserted that we cannot afford to neglect the sociolinguistic reality of L2 learners of English, because common assumptions in SLA about L2 learners' desires to conform to the norms of English NSs and only communicate with English NSs are not necessarily true. The majority of users of English in the world are NNSs of English. Jenkins (2006) argued that L2 learners might not only desire to use English to communicate with NNSs of English, but they might also use their bilingual and multilingual resources to meet their communication needs and goals. Therefore, what defines competence when communicating in English is not the monolingual norms of English NSs, but rather the bilingual and multilingual resources of NNSs. Accordingly, pragmatic transfer can be understood as necessary and beneficial for successful communication rather than as an "error" to be corrected.

In addition, by focusing on learners as social beings, this study brings their sociolinguistic reality and social communication needs to the forefront of L2 pragmatics research. These findings can inform our understanding of L2 pragmatics learning and use as a social process. For example, Lantolf (2000) asserted that the cognitive development of language learning and use does not reside in the brain, but rather in social interaction. Thus, understanding learners as social beings is vital to understanding their language development, and hence, L2 pragmatics development as a social process. Also, such an understanding can support social approaches to teaching and assessing L2 pragmatics, which are based on purposeful (i.e., geared towards meeting learners' needs) social interaction.

It is beyond the scope of this study to offer definite approaches for L2 pragmatics pedagogy; however, some general implications arise from the findings. First, the results affirm that the conformity to NSs norms "may be neither a goal nor a requirement for today's globalized communication" (Ishihara, 2019, p.

168). Therefore, the conceptualization of pragmatic transfer as an "error" or "failure" (Kasper, 1992) to be corrected or viewed as impolite behavior is problematic because pragmatic transfer could be an enactment of identity. Accordingly, English teachers should be aware that EFL learners' pragmatic choices and hence pragmatic transfer could be a realization of the different desires of their multiple identities.

Second, L2 teachers should be aware that feedback on pragmatics is a "delicate matter" (Thomas, 1983, p. 14). Correcting and criticizing the pragmatic transfer of L2 learners, which resulted from their evaluation of contextual or sociopragmatic variables, could be seen by L2 learners as a criticism or a challenge to their cultural beliefs and values. Thomas (1983) remarks that "while foreign learners are fairly amenable to correction which they regard as linguistic, they are justifiably sensitive about having their social (or even political, religious, or moral) judgment called into question" (p. 104).

Third, L2 teachers should be aware that what they might view as a pragmatic transfer and hence an error or impolite behavior could, in fact, be an excellent utilization and display of pragmatics knowledge or "symbolic capital" (Darvin & Norton, 2015, p. 45) by L2 learners interacting in their local context. Therefore, Darvin and Norton advise teachers "to reflect on the importance of treating the linguistic and cultural capital of learners as affordances rather than constraints and to question and re-evaluate the taken-for-granted value system, they use to assess this capital" (p. 45).

This study set out to examine the influence of Omani EFL learners' identities on their pragmatic transfer when refusing in English. The identity of these learners is linked to their language uses when refusing in English. L2 learners are active agents whose identities, cultures, and contexts of interaction are indispensable to their pragmatic decisions and pragmatic transfer. In light of this observation, Omani EFL learners' perception of pragmatic transfer when refusing in English can be understood as an enactment of their identity.

References

Al-Busaidi, K. A. K. (1995). *English in the labour market in multilingual Oman with special reference to Omani employees.* Unpublished doctoral dissertation, University of Exeter.
Al-Issa, A. (2003). Sociocultural transfer in L2 speech behaviors: Evidence and motivating factors. *International Journal of Intercultural Relations, 27,* 581–601.
Bardovi-Harlig, K., & Dörnyei, Z. (1998). Do language learners recognize pragmatic violations? Pragmatic versus grammatical awareness in instructed L2 learning. *TESOL Quarterly, 32*(2), 233–259.
Beebe, L. M., Takahashi, T., & Uliss-Weltz, R. (1990). Pragmatic transfer in ESL refusals. In R. Scarcella, E. Anderson, & S. D. Krashen (Eds.), *On the development of communicative competence in a second language* (pp. 55–73). Newbury House.
Blum-Kulka, S., House, J., & Kasper, G. (1989). Investigating cross-cultural pragmatics: An introductory overview. In S. Blum-Kulka, J. House, & G. Kasper (Eds.), *Cross-cultural pragmatics: Requests and apologies* (pp. 1–34). Ablex Publishing Corporation.

Brown, P., & Levinson, S. C. (1987). *Politeness: Some universals in language usage* (Vol. 4). Cambridge University Press.

Cohen, A. (1996) Speech acts. In S. L. McKay & N. H. Hornberger (Eds.), *Sociolinguistics and language teaching* (pp. 383–420). Cambridge University Press.

Darvin, R., & Norton, B. (2015). Identity and a model of investment in applied linguistics. *Annual Review of Applied Linguistics, 35,* 36–56.

Félix-Brasdefer, J. C. (2008). *Politeness in Mexico and the United States.* John Benjamins.

Hall, J. K. (2012). *Teaching and researching language and culture* (2nd ed.). Pearson.

Ishihara, N. (2019). Identity and agency in L2 pragmatics. In N. Taguchi (Ed.), *The Routledge handbook of second language acquisition and pragmatics* (pp. 161–175). Routledge.

Jenkins, J. (2006). Points of view and blind spots: ELF and SLA. *International Journal of Applied Linguistics, 16,* 137–162.

Kasper, G. (1992). Pragmatic transfer. *Second Language Research, 8*(3), 203–231.

Kim, H. Y. (2014). Learner investment, identity, and resistance to second language pragmatic norms. *System, 45,* 92–102.

Lantolf, J. P. (2000). Introducing sociocultural theory. In J. P. Lantolf (Ed.), *Sociocultural theory and second language learning* (pp. 1–26). Oxford University Press.

Mirzaei, A., & Parhizkar, R. (2021). The interplay of L2 pragmatics and learner identity as a social, complex process: A poststructuralist perspective. *TESL-EJ, 25*(1), 1–27.

Norton, B. (2000). *Identity and language learning: Gender, ethnicity and educational change.* Longman/Pearson.

Norton, B. (2013). *Identity and language learning: Extending the conversation* (2nd ed.). Multilingual Matters

Roever, C., & Al-Gahtani, S. (2015). The development of ESL proficiency and pragmatic performance. *ELT Journal, 69*(4), 395–404, https://doi.org/10.1093/elt/ccv032.

Savić, M. (2014). *Politeness through the prism of requests, apologies and refusals: A case of advanced Serbian EFL learners.* Cambridge Scholars Publishing.

Taguchi, N. (2019). Second language acquisition and pragmatics: An overview. In N. Taguchi (Ed.), *The Routledge handbook of second language acquisition and pragmatics* (pp. 1–14). Routledge.

Thomas, J. (1983). Cross-cultural pragmatic failure. *Applied Linguistics, 4*(2), 91–112.

Yin, R. K. (2016). *Qualitative research from start to finish* (2nd ed.). The Guilford Press.

8

CULTURE, MOTIVATION, AND SELF-EFFICACY IN THE SUDANESE EFL CONTEXT

Elham Yahia and Aymen Elsheikh

Introduction

Globalization and the emergence of English as a major international language have contributed to the development of different motives to learn English. This is because learning English is viewed as bestowing a lucrative source of income in addition to its importance in travel and social media for reasons of interpersonal communication. These orientations are of value because, as Gardner (1985) noted, students' attitudes towards a specific language and its users are bound to influence how successful they will be in incorporating aspects of that language. Since the early 1980s, the motivation for language learning has been a burgeoning area of study in many contexts. However there seems to be dearth of studies that investigate motivation alongside culture and self-efficacy.

Issues that motivated the research

This research was motivated by a paucity of studies into the issues that contribute to successful language learning in Sudan. Of particular interest to us are the constructs of motivation, culture, and self-efficacy, and how they can contribute to successful language learning. As both of us are Sudanese nationals living and working in the diaspora (in the US and Qatar), the impetus for this research is also a reflection on our past English language learning experiences as we grappled with concerns similar to those that the participants in our study experienced.

According to Hofstede, culture is

> the collective programming of the mind which distinguishes the members of one group from another, which is passed from generation to generation; it is

DOI: 10.4324/9781003312444-10

changing all the time because each generation adds something of its own before passing it on.

(Hofstede, 1980, pp. 21–23)

The mind is typically programmed according to the values, beliefs, behaviors, attitudes, customs, traditions, and other cultural norms. In this chapter, and for the purposes of our data analysis, culture is seen as the way of thinking, behaving, and valuing. For example, if teachers are viewed positively in a given community, this valuing of teachers could be considered a cultural norm. In Sudan, a predominantly Muslim country, respect for teachers is ingrained in the social imagination, because the Prophet Muhammad is considered the great teacher and those who follow in his footsteps are duly respected.

Motivation, one's desire to achieve a certain task, is widely held to be crucial to learning success. However, the behaviors, feelings, and cognition by which motivated individuals exhibit their interest in completing tasks vary widely (Masgoret & Gardner, 2003). Ryan and Deci (2000) defined *motivation* simply as the intensity and direction of one's effort. *Motivation* is also defined as the sum of the forces that account for the arousal, selection, direction, and continuation of behavior (Eccles & Wigfield, 2002). Although motivation in second language education has been widely researched (see, for example, Dörnyei, 2020; Dörnyei & Ushioda, 2011), the relationship between motivation, self-efficacy, and culture has been under-researched in English as a foreign language (EFL) contexts. In addition, the notion of investment should be incorporated into the study because it complements the construct of motivation (Norton, 2013). By *investment* we refer to how learners choose to express who they are (their identity) by engaging in language learning tasks so they achieve their desired outcomes, such as successful learning, which may lead to an increase in their social and economic capital. In other words, investment is viewed as part and parcel of motivation, but it takes a more socio-political and cultural dimension, as learning a language (and the drive to learn) is not a purely psychological act.

The layman's definition of *self-efficacy* is the belief in one's ability to achieve certain tasks. Bandura and Locke (2003) defined *self-efficacy* as individuals' confidence in their ability to solve problems or accomplish tasks. Bandura (1997) argued that self-efficacy involves "beliefs in one's capability to organize and execute the courses of action required in managing prospective situations" (p. 2). According to Bandura's theory, students are more likely to become engaged in learning a foreign language if they believe that it will provide them with the skills to achieve material and other goals in life.

Research question

The purpose of this study was to examine how the constructs of culture, motivation, and self-efficacy may contribute to language learning. Therefore, two research questions were posed:

1. How do five Sudanese college students describe their educational and language learning experiences?
2. What are the interrelationships among self-efficacy, motivation, and culture in the context of their English language learning in Sudan?

Research methods

Context

Sudan is a developing country located in Northeast Africa. It gained independence from Great Britain in 1956. Because of this colonial history, English is considered the country's second language. Arabic is the official language, although Sudan is linguistically diverse and has many other local languages.

Ever since independence, successive governments have paid little attention to education. The past and current rulers of Sudan have not considered education their primary concern, even though the country has had one of the highest growth rates amongst Sub-Saharan African countries and a rapidly rising per capita income: GDP of US $750 (United Nations Development Program, 2022). This GDP, however, changes every year depending on the economic situation of the country. As education is crucial for development, the expectation is that the government will spend more on it, but this has not been the case in Sudan. Also, since we are both Sudanese nationals and are aware of the socioeconomic and political situation in our country, we believe the GDP figure provided by the United Nations Development Program (UNDP) is an overestimate. The rich resources of the country are in the hands of the powerful few and the country's infrastructure is extremely underdeveloped, with a poverty rate of 65% or even more (United Nations Development Program, 2022).

The history of higher education in Sudan dates to the 1900s with the establishment of a colonial college. According to the website of the Ministry of Higher Education and Scientific Research (MHESR, 2022a), there are currently 39 public and 116 private higher education institutions (MHESR, 2022b). This study was conducted at one of the public universities.

Over the years, the education system has undergone many changes. These changes reflect change in the political regime. In the last 40 years, Sudan has experienced three different political regimes. The educational ladder went from six years of elementary school, three years of middle school, and three years of high school to eight years elementary, three years middle school, and three years high school. In 2021, the system was switched back to 6+3+3. In this current model and the one that preceded it, the English language is introduced in Grade 5 (where the average age of children is 11). It is taught as a subject and Arabic is the medium of instruction at all levels, including higher education (especially in public institutions).

In 2019, when popular protests brought down the longest military rule in the history of the country, a joint civil and military government was formed. As a result, and in an effort to make the teaching profession more attractive, the government doubled teachers' salaries. However, inflation rates have skyrocketed in the last few years because of political instability. As a result, and due to lack of government spending, the education sector nationwide lacks basic resources, such as textbooks, adequate classrooms, and trained teachers. In addition, there are not enough elementary schools to meet the needs of the growing population, and the available schools are severely under equipped by all measures. What is more, many of the teachers are neither qualified nor suitably trained to meet their students' learning demands, and this problem reflects the status of the country's higher education system. Since the adoption of the open education policy in 1991, which contributed to relaxing admission requirements and the opening of dozens of public and private higher education institutions, these institutions have been run as businesses. As long as the admissions fees and other fees are paid by the students, the educational standards can be lowered so that paying students can graduate. This lowering of standards produces ill-equipped future teachers.

Participants

The participants in this study are five college students, three females (A, B, and C) and two males (D and E). All were majoring in English language and translation at National Liberty University (NLU), a pseudonym for a large public university in Sudan. Upon graduation, they should be qualified to teach English as a foreign language and/or become translators. The participants varied in terms of geographical origins, age, gender, and level of English language proficiency. At the time of the study, the participants ages ranged from 19 to 23. Participants A, B, and D were in their sophomore year and participants C and E were in their senior year.

The participants were all living in the outskirts of Khartoum, the capital of Sudan, and had to commute for at least one or two hours daily to get to school. All were considered as having low socio-economic status (see the participants' profiles below). Besides struggling with lengthy commutes to school, they are also the oldest children in their households. By Sudanese cultural standards, the oldest child is the one who carries all the responsibilities. Below is a brief profile for each participant.

Participant A is 20 years old and is originally from Western Sudan. Her father died when she was five years old, and she was raised by her mother, who is an artisan, with some help from time to time from her uncle on her father's side. Her relatives also chipped in when there was a dire need, which is a standard cultural norm in Sudan. Participant A is not married, as she was determined to complete her higher education first and secure a high paying job as an EFL teacher.

Participant B is 22 years old and comes from the Blue Nile area, which has recently witnessed serious conflict and political instability. She is divorced with two children. Her father is a mechanic and her mother is housewife. Her personality exhibits a remarkable resilience, which may have contributed to her sense of self-efficacy and hence the success in learning English. Beside going to school, she also had worked at two jobs as to provide for her two children. From time to time, she also received help from her father to provide for her children.

Participant C is 19 years old, the youngest of the participants. She was born and raised in Northern Sudan, on a small island. Her father used to work as a clerk at the municipality of Khartoum, so the family moved from the island to Khartoum, the capital of Sudan. When her father passed away, they moved to a small house located 50 miles away from Khartoum. She has a strong and determined personality and these traits may have contributed to the development of her sense of self-efficacy. Her determination was what drove her to continue her education despite the challenges she faced as a divorced woman with two children in a conservative, male-dominated society.

Participant D is 21 years of age and comes from central Sudan. He is unmarried and is the oldest of his siblings. When he was 12 years old, his father died, so he had to work to support his mother and siblings. He faced many obstacles while continuing his education. The political instability of the country contributed to his struggle, as he was always targeted as an activist and opposer of the government. Despite the challenges, he continued his education. He decided to study English and to become an English teacher due to his strong desire to make a difference in the way the language is being taught in Sudan. As an EFL student, he maintained high levels of enthusiasm.

Participant E is the oldest participant (23 years old). He is not married. His father was a government official and his mother was a teacher. Both parents placed a high value on education, seeing it as a means to acquire personal prosperity as well as a way to advance the country. His passion for learning English was motivated by his desire to become a United Nations interpreter. He grew up in a household that encouraged and loved education. His family viewed education as the sole way to prosperity and advancement of individuals and the country as well, so this may have contributed to his determination and self-efficacy to learn English and pursue a university degree. He was very determined to achieve his goal, believing that one day he would be a famous interpreter. His love for English literature was reflected in his extensive vocabulary.

Data collection procedures

Formal interviews were conducted to document the educational and language learning experiences of these five Sudanese college students and to determine what a qualitative examination of their stories might contribute to our understanding of the interrelationships among students' culture, self-efficacy, and motivation. As noted above, all the participants were studying English in one of Sudan's public universities. Although access to the participants was facilitated by the Department Head, the first round of interviews was somewhat awkward. The administration of the university was worried that the presence of a researcher might expose weaknesses in the system. However, the participants began to be more open in the subsequent interviews when trust had been established, and they appeared to feel more comfortable about the researcher's presence in their school.

The participants were interviewed one-on-one by the first author in rooms used by the Faculty of English Language and Translation at NLU. All the interviews started with a review of the participants' information, such as name, marital status, parents' education, etc. The first interview lasted for about 55 minutes and the second and third interviews lasted for about 75 minutes. In addition to the audio-recording, we made hand-written notes during the interviews. All the participants spoke in Arabic, except for Participant E who, at times, switched to English, expressing the belief that this practice would help him to improve his oral skills. We translated all the excerpts from these interviews. Letters are used (A, B, C, D, and E) to protect the participants' identities. The translated excerpts were chosen based on the participants' reference to the constructs of the research (motivation, culture, and self-efficacy) as well as their socio-economic backgrounds.

The first interview focused on obtaining information regarding the participants' personal backgrounds and experiences of learning English in public schools. The second one focused on broader life experiences (e.g., the participants' social life, family status, tribal affiliations, and socio-economic status). The third interview inquired into the participants' general opinions about learning English, their views and beliefs regarding self-efficacy, and their motivation to learn EFL. In this chapter, we focus primarily on this interview. While telling their personal stories, some of the participants provided comments that described and evaluated English language learning and teaching practices in Sudan, as well as their cultural norms.

Data analysis procedures

The data in this study were analyzed using a grounded approach to qualitative data analysis techniques. A manual open coding system was used (Strauss, 1987). We broke the data into smaller samples. Based on the samples, we identified themes and gave each one a specific color coding. Examples of the themes include "motivational indicators" (yellow color coding). These indicators consisted of instances in which the participants referred to their motivation of learning the language. Similarly, self-efficacy (green color coding) and cultural influence (blue color coding) themes were identified based on the participants' data that reflected such themes. We created additional codes whenever the data did not fit under the above-mentioned themes. Examples of such additional codes include family influence (orange color coding) and the participants' socio-economic background (purple color coding).

Findings and discussion

Four of the five participants (A, B, C and D) indicated that they planned to pursue careers as EFL teachers and they commented on their imagined future teaching practices. Participant E stated that he intended to become a translator. His intention is consistent with previous research conducted in the Sudanese context (Elsheikh, 2012) in which some students favored translation over teaching.

Participant B had this to say about becoming an EFL teacher: "I want to be an English teacher; it's a good job; and I can buy for my mother and my sisters everything they need. They don't have to struggle like me." Participant B's motivations seem to be an economic desire to fulfill family members' needs. This view reflects the collectivist aspect (Hofstede, 1980) of the Sudanese culture, with its emphasis on family relationships. Although teaching is not a lucrative career in Sudan (or in many other countries), Participant B, was interested in becoming an EFL teacher for the financial stability it would bring. This positive relationship is what motivated her as an English language learner. She clearly saw the economic benefits of teaching. This motivation ought to be taken seriously, given the dire socioeconomic predicament in the Sudanese context.

These financial aspirations were also shared by Participant C. She said,

> If you know how to speak English, this will open many doors and job opportunities for someone like me. It's very hard to get a job these days; while there is a high demand for teachers of English, it will definitely guarantee that I will have a job with decent money.

Although Participant C expressed interest in EFL teaching, she might consider other more lucrative jobs since she believes that knowledge of English could "open many doors and job opportunities," especially given her low socio-economic status. She recounted during the interview, "My father is a mechanic; he works very hard to provide us with what we need in the house, but his salary is low. This is one of the reasons that I want to work to help him."

It appears that Participant D is aware of the sociopolitical context of the Sudanese educational system, where there is a dearth of EFL teachers for a host of reasons, such as the lack of proper qualifications and of professional training. He felt assured that, upon graduation, he would obtain an EFL teaching post.

The lucrative job opportunities that can be secured based on knowledge of English are what drove Participant E to imagine a career as an interpreter. He said,

> I want to be a translator; maybe I'll score a job at the UN or travel the world freely since I know the language. English is a very rich language and will make me feel rich. I know someone who is currently working at the UN as a translator; everyone in our village sees him as the rich and famous person in the village.

In addition to the financial aspect of working as an interpreter with an international organization like the UN, traveling around the world is another source of motivation to learn the language. This desire clearly stems from the status of English as an international language, as it is currently viewed as the language of travel and tourism. Even though teachers' salaries have recently increased, this increase is being eroded by inflation. Therefore, teaching, to some, still remains an unattractive career financially, and this unattractiveness is likely another reason that contributed to Participant E's imagined career as an interpreter.

Another example of the relationship between culture and the motivation to learn and/or teach English comes from Participant A:

> To learn English is very good, and to teach English is even better. People in our community look at the person who speaks English with a lot of respect. They also respect the teachers in general, let alone if you speak and teach English; that's way better.

In addition to the recognition that learning English carries certain benefits, perhaps because of its status as an international language, Participant A is aware of not only how those who speak English are viewed by the community, but also the revered status of teachers in general. As noted above, respect for teachers is an integral part of Sudanese culture, because the Prophet Muhammad is considered the great teacher, so teachers today are seen as following in his footsteps.

The male participants (D and E) were forthcoming, not only in commenting on their family background but also in sharing their experience of learning English. Their level of proficiency is well advanced despite the fact that English was not introduced to them until Grade 5. Participant D was excited to learn English, so he would memorize the alphabet through rehearsing the alphabet song. This practice is an example of how self-efficacy and motivation were both developed early in the learning process, probably because of the positive attitude toward the language, which goes back to Gardner's (1985) assertion about attitudes and their role in incorporating aspects of the language.

Although all five participants had great respect for their teachers (an attitude derived from the Sudanese culture, as explained earlier), they didn't think their teachers were good enough at introducing the language subject matter. They also thought their teachers lacked general instructional skills, such as controlling the class and giving effective instructions to students. As a result, only a few students were able to succeed and pass the different English courses in which they were enrolled. A quote from Participant C, who was in her senior year, reflects this view:

> I felt that I didn't learn much English at this university, and the teachers were extremely unorganized. Besides, their ways of teaching were very traditional. And after I reached this far in my higher education, I can say that they were not trained either.

Despite these shortcomings, the participants seemed to value their experience of learning English in high school as well as in college. They explained that their home environment and their valuable experience with education in general were what motivated them to overcome daily obstacles stemming from their low socioeconomic status as well as their struggles related to political instability. For example, Participant D's love for learning, his confidence, and his self-esteem were inspired by his educated parents. This type of inspiration and self-efficacy are what structured the participants' future goals as they imagined a different and more engaging teaching style: "Our teaching is going to be fun. We will do everything in class; we'll sing and maybe dance too. I like music, and I like to sing. I will teach English as it should be taught," said Participant D.

That comment from Participant D could also be related to his critical stance on his teachers' teaching styles, which he explained as follows:

> My teachers are not updated in the teaching techniques they are using. I mean they are still following the old-fashioned teaching techniques. This is the twenty-first century, and many things are different now, including teaching modalities and techniques. The generation of learners is also different. They are very well-versed in using technology. Therefore, it would be more appealing to them if certain things are incorporated in teaching, such as digital photo stories, drama, or music.

Participant D is not only aware of the needs of his generation and their learning preferences but also the use of active learning techniques in the English language teaching (ELT) profession such as, but not limited to, the student-centered approach and incorporating technology in classroom. Similar observations were made in Elsheikh's (2012) study, in which the participants expressed the need for their teacher educators to use best practices and incorporate the use of technology in their teaching. This awareness from the participants is due to the heavy emphasis placed on courses in linguistics, literature, and translation with very little emphasis on courses in ELT pedagogy and best practices.

As can be seen from the findings, the participants' cultural, socio-economic, and educational backgrounds played an important role in shaping their academic and future professional lives. These backgrounds shed light on why they wanted to be teachers (or in one case, an English interpreter) and be free to travel the world and move up the socioeconomic ladder. Their attitudes and motivation to learn English played a major role in helping them adopt a positive view of their future classroom practices, which is clearly evident from Participant D's assertion, "Our teaching is going to be fun. We will do everything in class; will sing and maybe dance too. I like music, and I like to sing. I will teach English as it should be taught".

Implications for policy, practice, and future research

Policy and decision makers should be aware of findings from this and other educational research, so they can incorporate the results into teacher education and schools' curricula. For example, teacher education programs should utilize more engaging and entertaining techniques in their instruction, such as the use of technology, especially the use of music, and listening to songs in English as a viable and effective way of learning English and motivating learners (Dzanic & Pejic, 2016). ELT curriculum planners should, in turn, ensure that the curriculum includes interesting teaching materials, such as the assumption of learning English to secure more lucrative jobs by featuring stories from different individuals who moved up the socio-economic ladder by virtue of learning and excelling at English. Utilizing the learners' cultural, social, educational, and personal backgrounds should also figure in the curriculum so the students are more interested in investing time and effort into the learning process.

The participants' real-life experiences, their self-efficacy, and culture influenced their motivation to learn English as a foreign language. It was interesting to note that all participants viewed the pursuit of higher education and learning English as a crucial way to change their lives and solve many of their problems (i.e., finding a better job with more income, such as a translation job with the UN, as imagined by Participant E). All five participants tended to speak about their educational journey vis-à-vis the learning of English. These reflections could be a valuable lesson for practitioners and teacher educators to gauge the interest of their own students and provide them a space in the classroom to recount their personal experiences so that such stories can be utilized for teaching and learning purposes.

All participants agreed that English is an international language, the use of which would enable them to have access to better career opportunities, and, accordingly, financial stability. This realization has pushed them to invest, to use Norton's (2013) term, in learning English. Therefore, with the international status of the English language, and the advent of globalization, most of the time learning English in Sudan is strongly connected to economic concerns (Elsheikh, 2012). Teachers could develop strategies that may capitalize on this relationship, so they can motivate their learners to acquire the language.

Another implication of this research is the role and relevance of identity in language learning and teaching (Elsheikh, 2016; Elsheikh & Yahia, 2020). Participant E, for example, imagined himself to be a particular kind of teacher in the future. As he rejected the identity of the teacher who lacked subject matter and pedagogical content knowledge (Shulman, 1987), he aspired to be an entertaining teacher who would use best practices, such as singing and music, in his teaching. Identity in ELT and its pedagogical implications could be incorporated in Sudanese teacher education programs so future teachers are aware of their identities' relevance and how they could enhance their future classroom practices.

Finally, this study is an extension of the ongoing discussion over the relationship between students' motivation, culture, and self-efficacy when learning English as a foreign language. Therefore, it further adds to the knowledge about whether students' motivation to learn English as a foreign language might be influenced by their cultural and socio-economic backgrounds. As this study was conducted in the higher education context, future studies in public school settings might shed more light on the level of motivation and whether it is connected to culture.

References

Bandura, A. (1997). *Self-efficacy: The exercise of control*. Freeman.
Bandura, A., & Locke, E. (2003). Negative self-efficacy and goal effects revisited. *Journal of Applied Psychology*, *88*(1), 87–99.
Dörnyei, Z. (2020). *Innovations and challenges in language learning motivation*. Routledge.
Dörnyei, Z., & Ushioda, E. (2011). *Teaching and researching motivation* (2nd ed.). Longman.
Dzanic, N. D., & Pejic, A. (2016). The effects of using songs on young learners and their motivation for learning English. *NETSOL New Trends in Social and Liberal Sciences*, *1*(2), 40–54. doi:10.24819/netsol2016.8.
Eccles, J., & Wigfield, A. (2002). Motivational beliefs, values, and goals. *Annual Review of Psychology*, *53*, 109–141.
Elsheikh, A. (2012). *Case studies of Sudanese EFL student teachers' knowledge and identity construction* (Doctoral Dissertation). Indiana University.
Elsheikh, A. (2016). Teacher education and the development of teacher identity. In J. Crandall & M. Christison (Eds.), *Teacher education and professional development in TESOL: Global perspectives* (pp. 37–52). TIRF & Routledge.
Elsheikh, A., & Yahia, E. (2020). Language teacher professional identity. In C. Coombe, N. Anderson, & L. Stephenson (Eds.), *Professionalizing your English language teaching* (pp. 27–38). Springer.
Gardner, R. C. (1985). *Social psychology and second language learning*. Edward Arnold.
Hofstede, G. (1980). *Culture's consequences: International differences in work-related values*. Sage.
Masgoret, A., & Gardner, R. C. (2003). Attitudes, motivation, and second language learning: A meta-analysis of studies conducted by Gardner and associates. *Language Learning*, *53*(1), 123–163.
MHESR (Ministry of Higher Education and Scientific Research). (2022a). Private higher education institutions in Sudan. http://www.mohe.gov.sd/index.php/sport/2022-10-20-11-17-04.
MHESR (Ministry of Higher Education and Scientific Research). (2022b). Public higher education institutions in Sudan. http://www.mohe.gov.sd/index.php/sport/2022-10-20-11-09-21.
Norton, B. (2013). *Identity and language learning: Extending the conversation*. Multilingual Matters.
Ryan, R. M., & Deci, E. L. (2000). Intrinsic and extrinsic motivations: Classic definitions and new directions. *Contemporary Educational Psychology*, *25*(1), 54–67. https:// https://doi.org/10.1006/ceps.1999.1020.
Shulman, L. S. (1987). Knowledge and teaching: Foundations of the new reform. *Harvard Educational Review*, *57*, 1–22.
Strauss, A. L. (1987). *Qualitative analysis for social scientists*. Cambridge University Press. https://doi.org/10.1017/CBO9780511557842.
United Nations Development Program. (2022). *Sudan National Human Development Report*. https://www.undp.org/sudan/publications/human-development-report-2021-22.

9

AN ENGLISH LANGUAGE TEACHER CANDIDATE'S TENSIONS IN THE CONTEXT OF TURKEY

What does an identity-oriented practicum course offer?

Özgehan Uştuk and Bedrettin Yazan

Introduction

Learning to teach is a trajectory of becoming, an identity work in action for language teacher candidates. As teacher candidates learn to teach, they constantly negotiate and enact identities, which inform their pedagogical choices and practices. Teacher learning is a situated activity and process in which "[a] three-dimensional learner […] combines life, learning, and practice" and creates an individual understanding of the world and herself or himself, and maintains an ongoing construction of their relationships to those combined aspects (Olsen, 2016, p. 18). It is not only a process of constructing professional knowledge and skills but also a holistic process of becoming a teaching professional (Barkhuizen, 2017; Danielewicz, 2001). Teacher learning is developing a professional identity, or "learning an identity" (Beijaard, 2019, p. 1).

Issues that motivated the research

In teacher education programs, practicum or clinical experiences are critical components of teachers' professional learning because such experiences tend to be the initial introduction to the classroom setting where teacher candidates can road-test their emerging teacher identities (Çomoğlu & Dikilitaş, 2020; Elsheikh, 2016; Yazan, 2015). That is, immersed in classroom practice, they can relate their existing beliefs, values, priorities, and positionings about language teaching to their theoretical knowledge (Martel, 2015; Olsen, 2016; Uştuk, 2022a). Facilitating this process, language teacher educators, as faculty, mentors, or supervisors, can explicitly bring in an identity-oriented approach to teacher-learning throughout the practicum and help teacher candidates understand the complex

DOI: 10.4324/9781003312444-11

relationship between identity, learning, and practice (see Martel & Yazan, 2021). Therefore, practicum courses offer important spaces for language teacher education programs to center teacher identity as a "central organizing principle" (Varghese et al., 2016, p. 557).

Teacher identity is a disputed concept that lacks a clear, widely agreed upon definition (Barkhuizen, 2017). That said, we draw on Yazan's (2018) review of existing definitions and understand teacher identity in the context of this study as a dynamic construct that is (re)enacted in social settings and through social interaction. Identity relies on teachers' agency, conceptualizations about themselves, social positionings, and interactions. The term *identity work* refers to the agentic aspect of identity (re)construction processes that centers teachers as the subject of the process. Identity is inevitably fraught with tensions that teacher candidates need to navigate as they learn to teach, and such tensions might become more intensified during practicum experiences (Alsup, 2006, 2019; Menard-Warwick, 2014; Smagorinsky et al., 2004; Uştuk & Yazan, 2023). In this context, we use the word *tensions* to refer to teachers' feeling of in-betweenness and the internal struggles of being pulled in different directions related to mismatching professional experiences, emotions, ideologies, and aspirations (Alsup, 2006; Berry, 2007).

Identity-oriented learning activities may help teacher candidates better understand those tensions and engage in agentive identity work during the practicum. To support his students' identity work, Özgehan redesigned an existing practicum course in a university-based English as a foreign language (EFL) teacher education program in Turkey, to ensure that all class activities have the identity work as their explicit focus (e.g., Flip recordings, collages).

Research question

In this chapter, we draw our data from a larger qualitative case study focused on the said identity-oriented practicum course, to examine the experiences of one of the teacher candidates as our focal case. We rely on Activity Theory (Engeström, 2001, 2015; Roth & Lee, 2007) as our theoretical base, to explore how Nihat (pseudonym), an EFL teacher candidate from Turkey, mediated his dialogic engagement to enact his professional identity and navigate identity tensions. More specifically, we use the concept of identity-in-activity (Cross & Gearon, 2007; Dang, 2013) and address this research question: How does an EFL teacher candidate engage in identity work as he navigates tensions through teacher-learning activities in an identity-oriented TESOL practicum course?

Activity Theory is a conceptual approach to understanding human activity as being mediated. According to the scholarship of Sociocultural Learning and Activity Theory, human activity is mediated by instruments, which can be technical or psychological *tools*. One example of psychological tools is language; individuals use languages to mediate actions, and activities mediated by psychological tools are reflective and require consciousness of individuals (Engeström,

2015). On the other hand, *activity* is "an evolving, complex structure of mediated and collective human agency" instead of "[a] brief event with a definite beginning and end points" (Roth & Lee, 2007, p. 198). In this sense, the concept of activity as in Activity Theory is in alignment with our understanding of teacher identity, which is a dynamic construct that is in constant flux rather than an endstate. That said, activity is analyzed by juxtaposing activity system elements. The elements include Vygotky's mediated activity triangle – namely the subject, the object, and the mediation tools. Additionally, other elements of the activity system (rules, community, and division of labor) extend Vygotky's original triangle and provide a more elaborate system to depict human activity (Engeström, 2015, p. 63) and reveal the social resources in the system.

The following are the fundamental elements of Vygotsky's mediated activity (Johnson, 2009): (1) *subject* is the focal agent of the activity, (2) *object* is the goal of the subject, (3) *mediation/tools* are technical/physical or psychological/conceptual tools that the subject uses to reach the object, (4) *rules* are implicit or explicit norms that regulate how the activity is operated, (5) *community* is the slate of people that are directed by the same goal and influence and/or are influenced by the outcome of the activity, and (6) *division of labor* is the definition of roles and responsibilities that the subject and other community members take within the activity.

By situating identity work within the activity (in relation to the six components), we acknowledge challenges the teacher candidates encounter when they find themselves in the middle of conflicting activity systems, especially in practicum experiences (Cross & Gearon, 2007; Dang, 2013). As teacher candidates work towards the object of the system and learn to serve language learners, they negotiate different meanings to understand their role and responsibility within the system. Their interactions with other members of the communities lead them to attend to questions such as these: What does it mean to be a language teacher? What does it mean to teach languages to a specific group of learners in their socio-educational context? Their answers to those questions are central to the teacher candidates' identity negotiation and help them construct their "dynamic self-conception and imagination of themselves as teachers, which shifts as they participate in varying communities, interact with other individuals, and position themselves (and are positioned by others) in social contexts" (Yazan, 2018, p. 21).

Teacher candidates' identity work within the activity system involves how they understand their situatedness as the subject vis-a-vis other dynamic components and how they act based on that understanding (Cross & Gearon, 2007). This discursive construction and the enactment of professional identity are both parts of their growth in the program, which is rife with tensions emergent in the system. Against this theoretical backdrop and responding to the calls in teacher identity research, we believe that teacher trainees should become cognizant of the situated and dynamic nature of professional identities in the activity system.

Research methods

We used a qualitative case study design with a constructivist approach (Merriam & Tisdell, 2016) and conceptualized the case as a "bounded system" (p. 38) whose borders we can delineate to focus entirely on our phenomenon of interest within that system. In our study, the case is Nihat, an EFL teacher candidate in the identity-responsive EFL practicum course Özgehan taught in a university-based teacher education program. We situated Nihat's identity work within the context of this program. We also considered the macro-level context (i.e., the policy-level, such as the national practicum system) that subsumes the meso-level context (i.e., the institutional level, such as the practicum school and district) and the micro-level context (i.e., classroom level, such as practicum classes) that Nihat interacted with directly.

Context

Our case study is situated in an undergraduate level TESOL practicum course in two semesters of the 2020–2021 academic year in Turkey. The required activities were (1) weekly online meetings of the practicum cohort and the university supervisor, (2) weekly observations of classes at a public school, and (3) teaching practice at that school, monitored by the school mentor. The class community included eight EFL teacher candidates in the practicum cohort (including Nihat), one university lecturer as the supervisor (Özgehan), and one experienced teacher as the mentor teacher (the terms *mentor* and *cooperating teacher* are used interchangeably here) in whose classes Nihat taught.

In collaboration with Bedrettin, Özgehan designed identity-oriented activities to guide the teacher candidates' learning experience. We intended these activities to foster dialogic engagement as a group, as well as collaborative and individual reflection on language learning and teacher identities. To this end,

1. The practicum cohort members engaged with each other in an online Flip community throughout the year (in which each trainee produced six video tasks in total). This engagement involved posting videos responding to a prompt posted by the lecturer about the participants' prior experiences of language learning and teaching (e.g., *Talk about the teachers who you think influenced your current practices*). The practicum participants also commented by text or video on each other's responses.
2. Participants also completed arts-based activities, such as creating collages and memes, through which they were asked to express their beliefs, values, and priorities about language learning and teaching. Additionally, they selected pieces of art (e.g., a painting, a literary work, a sculpture) as an expressionist think-about activity (emphasizing the teacher-candidate as the subject of the *activity*) and reflected on how that artwork resonates with language teacher education.

3. Participants worked on individual teaching philosophy statements (TPSs); however, as a collaborative process writing activity, they exchanged feedback with each other and reflected on their statements collaboratively.

With these activities, the object of the identity-oriented practicum course, as an activity system, was to pedagogize identity through the teacher-learning activities the teacher candidates completed during the practicum.

Participant

Our focal case in this study is Nihat. We invited him as a participant as he was a local, had had his K-12 education in Turkey, and was learning/speaking English as a foreign language. His qualities and background made him a good representative of the teacher candidate profile that Özgehan most commonly works with. Also, he voluntarily accepted to be the case-participant. We examine his experiences in navigating the tensions in the activity system of the year-long TESOL practicum course and in constructing and enacting his professional identity as an EFL teacher. As a senior in the program, Nihat wanted to become a teacher of English because he was interested in the U.S.-American culture and language. He has family members who live in the U.S. Having visited them as a high schooler motivated him to study English language teaching. He observed that his formal language education in Turkey relied mostly on grammar-based instruction, and he wanted to adopt a more communication-oriented approach to instruction in his language teaching practice.

Nihat's own language learning was a very dehumanizing experience, which he believes was because of his teachers' pedagogical approaches. His language teachers were quite distanced from their students and did not make any effort to establish a friendly rapport with English language learners. Therefore, Nihat kept asking what kind of teacher-student relationship would support language learning the best and his answer was part of his imagined teacher identity. His goal was to develop a practice that would "help [him] find a way" (Flip video #1) to address such questions about instructional methods and humanizing pedagogy.

Data collection procedures

We collected data from Nihat's six Flip videos along with his interaction within his small group, his lesson plans, and his arts-based activity products (memes, collages, and art piece think-aloud memos). After he completed the course requirements, Özgehan conducted a semi-structured interview with Nihat to have a conversation to evaluate his teacher-learning experience in the activity system of the TESOL practicum course in 2020–2021.

Data analysis procedures

We mainly used an analytical coding framework that relied on Activity Theory. Merriam and Tisdell (2016) suggest that this kind of coding is closely related to an analytical interpretation and reflection on meaning and is conducted by creating preliminary lists of emerging codes based on these interpretations and reflections. However, they also caution that such lists might be very long, misleading, and unfocused. To overcome this problem, we started coding the data by going through data sets independently to find the emerging code clusters. After deciding on the focal code clusters, we grouped them to create themes by cross-checking the data sets.

We also used non-textual, graphics-based data that were collected through the arts activities, such as creating memes and collages. They were also coded in this process, focusing on the semiotic cues (e.g., signs and symbols) represented in those visual outcomes of these activities.

Findings and discussion

Our pedagogical goal in this practicum course was to pedagogize identity in English language teacher education practices. As noted above, our research question in this study was, "How does an EFL teacher candidate engage in identity work as he navigates tensions through teacher-learning activities in an identity-oriented TESOL practicum course?" Our analysis showed that Nihat completed those activities in two ways. First, he enacted his aspired language teacher identities by developing a professional discourse of his own (i.e., using terms and concepts related to language teaching in his linguistic practice). Second, his ongoing identity work informed his participation in practicum activities, such as classroom observations and practice teaching.

Enacting an aspired identity by developing a professional discourse

By completing identity-responsive activities such as creating memes and collages, Nihat found space to develop a professional discourse of his own about language education. More specifically, he critically evaluated the professional discourses to which he had been introduced in his experience as a language learner (e.g., learning a foreign language to pass a test) or his teacher education background. This latter context included teaching language structures mostly explicitly with materials designed for EFL learners or following coursebooks designed for preparing language learners for tests. Nihat realized that these discourses did not fit in his instructional beliefs, values, and priorities as part of his emerging teacher identity.

Aware of potential tensions between what he was exposed to in the activity systems of the practicum and what he brought to the activity system as its subject, Nihat problematized and re-conceptualized authoritative professional discourses and worked towards creating his voice. For example, Özgehan expected teacher candidates to create a collage demonstrating an ideal study/workplace for an EFL teacher. Nihat chose to create a digital collage that pictures him standing in that ideal study room (see Figure 9.1).

Such a portrayal is important for the demonstration of Nihat's imagined language teacher identity. As part of this task, he elaborated on his collage in a class meeting, as shown in Excerpt 1 from a think-aloud session:

> I have a world map with the countries that I one day would like to go marked on it. Then I have a widescreen computer where I will be watching TV shows on Netflix, and on Twitter, I'll get into popular culture, which is continuously evolving among English native speakers so that I will have a better understanding of the language. Through Discord, I will get to communicate with native speakers who I meet online. On Spotify, I will listen to my favorite playlist and simultaneously follow the lyrics line by line for listening comprehension and I can also sing along by imitating the singer's accent so that I can have better pronunciation. I have headphones that will accompany me through all these so it better be a comfortable one. I'll have a dog, which I am expecting to positively affect me. Finally, I'll have a hard copy Oxford monolingual dictionary. We don't need it anymore as it's already online and we get to find a word much faster when compared to a hard copy but as a sign of respect, it deserves the top shelf.

As the subject of the activity, Nihat focused on his study room as an area where he learns more about native speaker variations and culture from different real-life

FIGURE 9.1 Nihat's digital collage

resources. For him, it was important to use English as a part of his everyday life (object). He mediates this activity with applications such as Netflix, Twitter, Spotify, and Discord in a cozy and safe learning environment, another object for his aspired teacher self. Nihat points to a hard copy dictionary and remarks on the old-school way of language learning, which only has a symbolic place in the room on the top shelf; it has a place in the room but is not used for practical reasons (i.e., mediatory use), but rather as decor. In many ways, Nihat built his study room as a safe haven where he can learn English having a fun time connected to the broader virtual world of English-speaking communities.

Nihat maintained his focus on language learning in a safe environment that resonated in his TPS as well. This view is shown in this excerpt from his teaching philosophy statement:

> I will dedicate time to my students to explore new resources from real life and go through the ones I already know to help students in this process. All these given, structure-based instruction is what I am going to avoid in class. Of course, I am aware of the fact that communicative language teaching demands experience and predisposition. I think I could overcome the predisposition part using humor, which my practicum students like, as I did in my past experiences.

In his TPS, Nihat repeated his aspired teacher role as a provider of a comfortable learning atmosphere where it is possible to learn languages by using real-life resources. He said he would create a learning environment where the instructional focus would be on meaning rather than forms. Such a goal was probably because of the heavy emphasis on grammar teaching that is dominant in the ELT classroom in Turkey, as it was the case of Nihat's own learning experience. He also mentioned his experiences in the practicum and stated that this approach of creating a relaxed learning environment (e.g., by using humor) works, as it worked when he was at school. Building connections across his past experiences as a learner, his current ones, and his aspired teacher identities, Nihat's identity work became more vibrant and active through identity-oriented activities in the practicum.

Juxtaposing the aspired and the performed identities

Secondly, identity-oriented practicum activities enabled Nihat to juxtapose his aspired identities and his teaching practice. In addition to the relevant data above, he discussed his advocacy for communication-oriented instruction in the Flip videos. He said, "[one of his former teachers] made him very anxious while speaking in the target language" and said that teacher only implemented long drilling activities that were focused on select grammar topics. In the identity-oriented teaching practicum, however, he taught four classes, none of which was particularly communicative, and all of which predominantly included structure-based activities. This choice was curious for us as teacher educators since we expected him to show the agency to transfer his active identity work into his teaching, which was hardly the case in Nihat's practicum. Özgehan brought this issue up during the interview at the end of the semester. First, Nihat reflected on the TPS writing process, as shown in this excerpt:

> When I was writing [the TPS] up, these had been the stuff that I used to think about. This was an opportunity to write them down and it made them more concrete. However, I am not fully content with myself as a teacher. I think this TPS is a work in progress. I am also a work in progress as a teacher, right? I need to develop but I also need to develop myself, right? But it was a good start. This is what the feedback said too. So I am developing.

In this comment, Nihat likened his development as a teacher to the process of authoring his teaching philosophy. He also relied on feedback from the practicum community to validate his insights. Participation in such a response group helped him grow a reflexive understanding of his teaching identity and practices.

In the next quote, Nihat further explained why he had refrained from using practicum lessons to put his philosophy into practice:

> Maybe I did not feel ready to get out of my comfort zone in the practicum. I didn't feel the ownership of the lessons, to be honest. Also, I don't see myself as a teacher with a magic wand in his hand. I want to be present to my students as a friend, as a resource when they fail. I was thinking about it. I am not pretentious, claiming that my students and I will only succeed. No, I do not want that. I used to feel guilty about feeling that way so I wasn't even able to turn this thought into an utterance before. But I want [the students] to have a fun time and see how foreign language competence brings quality to life in my classrooms in the future. Unfortunately, [practicum lessons] were not my classes.

This excerpt ends with a clear expression of one of Nihat's tensions which resulted in his lack of ownership of his practicum lessons. This tension was related to his frustration regarding the controlling nature of the mentor and practicum school, and the mismatch of his teaching philosophy and contextual expectations. According to him, this situation constrained him from building up a close and peer-to-peer relationship with his students, as he would normally strive to do. More specifically, Nihat did not feel so motivated when he was assigned to teach a part of the coursebook by his mentor teacher.

However, what was interesting for us was to see that his teacher learning (as identity work) was not dependent solely on the change in his pedagogical choices and instruction. As the identity-oriented activities unfolded, his beliefs, predispositions, and philosophy became more concrete on the conceptual level. Even though he did not feel much ownership for his practicum lessons (inferring the lack of agency to put his teaching philosophy in his practice), his identity-agency nexus still included a teacher learning activity whose outcome was a clearer understanding of Nihat's aspired teacher identity. Based on Engeström's extended system of mediated activity (see 2015, p. 63 for the original figure), it is possible to depict and summarize Nihat's activity system with Nihat as its subject and application of other activity system elements as follows:

Mediation/Tools: Identity-responsive tasks (such as Flip Community, arts-based assignments, process writing of TPS);
Outcome (of the object): Enacting a professional identity and a teacher self;
Rules: Participation in the tasks and fulfilling the practicum assignments (i.e., teacher and observing);
Community: Practicum cohort that consists of eight teacher-candidates, mentor, and supervisor;
Division of labor: Teacher-candidates reflect on their own work as well as their peers' and give/receive feedback.

Nihat, as the subject of the activity, intended to succeed in the practicum assignments, such as teaching and observing, as well as the identity-oriented activities that mediated the process. This mediation was regulated by the course rules, such as participation and timely submissions within the practicum community. The community members (i.e., the practicum cohort) informed each other's identity work through providing/receiving feedback related to the identity-responsive activity performances. Nihat's mediated activity resulted in an outcome of a teacher-learning trajectory that was interwoven with his ongoing identity work such as getting clear about what kind of impact he wants to create as a teacher. As he stated, he clarified for himself that he wants his future students "to have a fun time and see how foreign language competence brings quality to life in my classrooms in the future."

Examining Nihat's identity work and enactment trajectory in his practicum experience through Activity Theory enabled us to see teacher learning in the identity-oriented TESOL practicum. Teacher learning as identity work (Olsen, 2016) emerges when the teacher candidates are regarded as the subject of the activities that they engage in during the TESOL practicum. For example, rather than regarding teacher candidates and their teaching practices (e.g., practicum teachings) as events to be observed and evaluated by university supervisors or school-based mentors, practicum activities in which teacher candidates are viewed as the subjects of the activity afforded them opportunities to develop their discourses and pedagogical (and linguistic) philosophies/ideologies. Supporting previous studies, such as Dikilitaş and Çomoğlu (2020) and Smagorinsky et al. (2004), we found that TESOL teacher practica may provide an agentic space for teacher candidates where they can develop professional discourses, knowledge, and identity when teacher identity is systematically taken as a central component of the practica.

In sum, the findings related to Nihat's identity work in the practicum revealed that the identity-oriented activities supported Nihat in negotiating a professional voice that activated a reflexive process of enacting aspired identities. His identity tensions originated from the mismatch of authoritative discourses and his teaching philosophy. The former included what Nihat was taught in his studies in a transmissive way (e.g., *teachers are expected to follow curricula and deliver course content*). The latter, his teacher philosophy, was what he shaped in the practicum school contexts by interacting with students and other stakeholders (the mentor and the supervisor) and in building peer-to-peer relationships and learning English through extracurricular real-life engagements. This tension was not unique to him. Nihat's experience supported previous research that tensions are closely related to language teachers' identity work as they are embedded in their past and present experiences as well as future aspirations (Ilieva & Ravindran, 2018; Martel & Yazan, 2021; Uştuk, 2022b).

On the other hand, our findings also revealed that the active negotiation of professional identities is not automatically projected upon teaching practices. As in Nihat's case, teacher candidates need opportunities to take ownership not only of the professional voice that they develop but also of the teaching context and practice.

Implications for policy, practice, and future research

When examined as an activity system, teacher learning opportunities can be redesigned in a way that puts the teacher candidate in the central position of the activity of becoming a language teacher. The space where the activity system unfolds (e.g., in practicum settings) needs to provide opportunities for teacher candidates to become agentic subjects of their identity work. Nihat's experience showed us that the strict curricular and school policies or mentor teachers' coursebook or standardized test-driven practices and expectations of their mentees may hinder the teacher candidates from experimenting or taking ownership of their teaching practices. Becoming the subject of the activity, the mediatory tools and the other activity elements (i.e., rules, community, and division of labor) facilitate the subject's trajectory toward the object and beyond that, the outcomes. This perspective acknowledges teacher candidates' experiences, meanings, and understandings as being (at least) equally important as authoritative discourses of language teaching.

The subject in the activity system is not necessarily the source of the activity. The subject is in a reflexive relationship with the other elements of the activity (e.g., Nihat's engagement with the practicum community). This understanding may help teacher educators to put teacher reflexivity (De Costa, 2015) into practice in initial TESOL teacher education. Our experience also showed that systematic reflection on teacher identity and reflexivity may not suffice to impact teacher candidates' practices, as in Nihat's case: Identity-oriented teacher education should strive to create a *praxis* (Freire, 2005), action and reflection combined in the context of one activity.

To this end, we propose teacher educators in TESOL programs devise ways to incorporate the teacher candidates' ongoing identity work with teaching practices in the practicum. One great challenge would be the limitations of time and resources, which is just another 800-pound gorilla for teacher educators to deal with among many other challenges. However, returning to the title of this chapter, an identity-oriented practicum course can offer opportunities for novice teachers to develop professional discourses and growth in understanding of their pedagogical philosophies and ideologies, as well as teacher reflexivity, which are all very valuable outcomes.

Scaffolding reflection through identity-responsive activities informs the teacher candidates' identity work and operationalizes teacher learning (Olsen, 2016; Beijaard, 2019), but does not necessarily create immediate results in the on-site practices of the TESOL practicum (e.g., EFL lessons). As reported in Uştuk and Yazan's study (2023), some of Nihat's colleagues from the same cohort engaged in some agentic actions by projecting the ongoing identity work on their practicum activities and by sorting out a reconciliation between the teacher candidates' emerging philosophies and the institutional context. Thus, we propose further studies to create a praxicum (i.e., a practicum that is based on *praxis*: action and reflection; see López-Gopar et al., 2022; Pennycook, 2004) for identity-oriented teacher education. Echoing Varghese et al. (2016), we also recommend that higher education policymakers and program coordinators in Turkey (and beyond) regard identity as a central organizing principle while designing TESOL teacher education programs (undergraduate or graduate) especially in the practicum modules and professional development certificate programs.

Acknowledgments

We are grateful to the teacher candidates who participated in our efforts to pedagogize teacher learning activities in the practicum offered in the 2020–2021 academic year, and particularly to Nihat.

References

Alsup, J. (2006). *Teacher identity discourses*. Lawrence Erlbaum Associates.
Alsup, J. (2019). *Millennial teacher identity discourses*. Routledge.
Barkhuizen, G. (Ed.). (2017). *Reflection on language teacher identity research*. Routledge.
Beijaard, D. (2019). Teacher learning as identity learning: Models, practices, and topics. *Teachers and Teaching*, 25(1), 1–6. https://doi.org/10.1080/13540602.2019.1542871.
Berry, A. (2007). *Tensions in teaching about teaching: Understanding practice as a teacher educator*. Springer.
Çomoğlu, İ., & Dikilitaş, K. (2020). Learning to become an English language teacher: Navigating the self through peer practicum. *Australian Journal of Teacher Education*, 45(8), 23–40. https://doi.org/10.14221/ajte.2020v45n8.2.

Cross, R., & Gearon, M. (2007). The confluence of doing, thinking and knowing. In A. Berry, A. Clemans, & A. Kostogriz (Eds.), *Dimensions of professional learning* (pp. 53–67). Sense Publishers. https://doi.org/10.1163/9789087901257_006.

Dang, T. K. A. (2013). Identity in activity: Examining teacher professional identity formation in the paired-placement of student teachers. *Teaching and Teacher Education, 30,* 47–59. https://doi.org/10.1016/j.tate.2012.10.006.

Danielewicz, J. (2001). *Teaching selves: Identity, pedagogy, and teacher education.* State University of New York Press.

De Costa, P. (2015). Tracing reflexivity through a narrative and identity lens. In S. B. Said & E. Park (Eds.), *Advances and current trends in language teacher identity research* (pp. 135–147). Routledge.

Dikilitaş, K., & Çomoğlu, İ. (2020). Pre-service English teachers' reflective engagement with stories of exploratory action research. *European Journal of Teacher Education,* 1–17. https://doi.org/10.1080/02619768.2020.1795123.

Elsheikh, E. (2016). Teacher development and the development of teacher identity. In J. Crandall & M. Christison (Eds.), *Teacher education and professional development in TESOL: Global perspectives* (pp. 37–52). TIRF & Routledge.

Engeström, Y. (2001). Expansive learning at work: Toward an activity theoretical reconceptualization. *Journal of Education and Work, 14*(1), 133–156. https://doi.org/10.1080/13639080123238.

Engeström, Y. (2015). *Learning by expanding: An activity-theoretical approach to developmental research, second edition* (2nd ed.). Cambridge University Press.

Freire, P. (2005). *Pedagogy of the oppressed.* Continuum International Publishing.

Ilieva, R., & Ravindran, A. (2018). Agency in the making: Experiences of international graduates of a TESOL program. *System, 79,* 7–18. https://doi.org/10.1016/j.system.2018.04.014.

Johnson, K. E. (2009). *Second language teacher education: A sociocultural perspective.* Routledge.

López-Gopar, M. E., Sughrua, W. M., Cordova, V. H., González, A. J. R., & Vera, G. R. (2022). Mexican student-teachers' "English" language praxicum: Decolonizing attempts. *International Journal of Educational Research, 115,* 102022. https://doi.org/10.1016/j.ijer.2022.102022.

Martel, J. (2015). Learning to teach a foreign language: Identity negotiation and conceptualizations of Pedagogical Progress. *Foreign Language Annals, 48*(3), 394–412. https://doi.org/10.1111/flan.12144.

Martel, J., & Yazan, B. (2021). Enacting an identity approach in language teacher education. In M. Bigelow & K. Paesani (Eds.), *Diversity and transformation in language teacher education* (pp. 35–62). CARLA, University of Minnesota.

Menard-Warwick, J. (2014). *English language teachers on the discursive faultlines: Identities, ideologies and pedagogies.* Multilingual Matters.

Merriam, S. B., & Tisdell, E. J. (2016). *Qualitative research: A guide to design and implementation* (4th ed.). Jossey-Bass.

Olsen, B. (2016). *Teaching what they learn, learning what they live: How teachers' personal histories shape their professional development.* Routledge. https://doi.org/10.4324/9781315631684.

Pennycook, A. (2004). Critical moments in a TESOL praxicum. In B. Norton & K. Toohey (Eds.), *Critical pedagogies and language learning* (pp. 327–346). Cambridge University Press. https://doi.ord/10.1017/CBO9781139524834.017.

Roth, W. M., & Lee, Y. J. (2007). "Vygotsky's neglected legacy": Cultural-Historical Activity Theory. *Review of Educational Research, 77*(2), 186–232. https://doi.org/10.3102/0034654306298273.

Smagorinsky, P., Cook, L. S., Moore, C., Jackson, A. Y., & Fry, P. G. (2004). Tensions in learning to teach: Accommodation and the development of a teaching identity. *Journal of Teacher Education*, *55*(1), 8–24. https://doi.org/10.1177/0022487103260067.

Uştuk, Ö. (2022a). How massive open online courses constitute digital learning spaces for EFL teachers: A netnographic case study. *Teaching English with Technology*, *22*(3–4), 43–62.

Uştuk, Ö. (2022b). Drama-in-teacher-education: A "metaxical" approach for juxtaposing EFL teacher identity and tensions. *Language Teaching Research*. https://doi.org/10.1177/13621688221118644.

Uştuk, Ö., & Yazan, B. (2023). Tensions in an identity-oriented language teaching practicum: A dialogic approach. *TESOL Quarterly*. https://doi.org/10.1002/tesq.3234.

Varghese, M., Motha, S., Park, G., Reeves, J., & Trent, J. (2016). Language teacher identity in (multi)lingual educational contexts [Special issue]. *TESOL Quarterly*, *50*(3), 545–571. https://doi.org/10.1002/tesq.333.

Yazan, B. (2015). "You learn best when you're in there": ESOL teacher learning in the practicum. *The CATESOL Journal*, *27*(2), 171–200.

Yazan, B. (2018). A conceptual framework to understand language teacher identities. *Journal of Second Language Teacher Education*, *1*(1), 21–48.

PART III
Academic writing

10
METADISCOURSE IN ACADEMIC ABSTRACTS WRITTEN BY ALGERIAN, SAUDI, AND NATIVE ENGLISH RESEARCHERS

Tarek Assassi

Introduction

Like tertiary education institutions worldwide, Algerian and Saudi universities hire instructors and professors based on their qualifications both to teach and to conduct research. As Algerian scholars writing research reports in English, we have wondered about the challenges faced by other non-native writers. Flowerdew (2019) has noted that "academics are coming under increasing pressure to publish internationally" (p. 260). He adds that "given the global dominance of English, this very likely means publishing in English-medium journals and with publishers which publish in English" (p. 260). This concern raises the issue of "the possible disadvantage of those scholars whose first language is not English and who therefore have the additional burden of having to develop adequate proficiency in an additional language, English" (p. 249).

Santos (1995) asserts that "researching and research reporting are usually thought of as distinct activities. They cannot be split apart, i.e., the research cycle is not complete until the results have been communicated" (p. 481). Therefore, communicating research is as important as conducting it. In this sense, communicating research outcomes in a written form requires the use of an academic writing style, respecting its characteristics, from form and organization to the function of every statement. The effective writing process should result in a piece of appropriate, academically written text. To produce effective academic writing, it is important to use a number of metadiscourse devices. *Metadiscourse* is defined as "the range of devices writers use to explicitly organize their texts, engage readers, and signal their attitudes to both their material and their audience" (Hyland & Tse, 2004, p. 156). Metadiscourse is important because it "embodies the idea that communication is more than just the exchange of information, goods or services, but also involves the

DOI: 10.4324/9781003312444-13

personalities, attitudes, and assumptions of those who are communicating" (Hyland, 2005, p. 3). Different types of metadiscourse markers help authors to create organized texts and develop relationships with their readers.

From a broad perspective, *metadiscourse* refers to the system by which language producers interact via language use with the audience. According to Hyland (2010), *metadiscourse* refers to the manner language is used out of consideration for our readers or hearers, based on our estimation as speakers or writers of how best we can help our audiences comprehend what we are saying or writing. In written texts, metadiscourse markers are words or phrases that help build a relationship between the writer and the reader through connecting and organizing texts, delivering evidence, and expressing attitude, thus ensuring coherence via a smooth flow of ideas.

Frame markers are one important kind of metadiscourse marker used in generating effective academic writing. *Frame markers* provide a basic element of written discourse and offer information about "text boundaries or elements of schematic text structure" (Hyland & Tse, 2004, p. 168). They are used to serve four major functions: labeling text stages (e.g., *to summarize*); showing topic shifts (e.g., *in connection with*); sequencing (e.g., *to begin with, lastly*); and declaring the writer's goal (e.g., *the main aim, the primary focus*) (Hyland, 2005).

Three other examples of metadicourse markers are transitions, endophorics, and evidential devices. Transitions, such as *and, but,* and *thus,* are used to create logical semantic relations between clauses in full sentences. Endophorics (e.g., *as stated below*) are used as references to other parts of the text. Academic writers use endophorics to cross-reference different pieces of information within their writings. Evidential devices contrast with endophorics because they are used to refer to sources or pieces of information from other texts. For example, authors use evidential devices (e.g., *according to X*) to support their claims with statements of other authors.

Issues that motivated the research

It is important to note that metadiscourse markers play a major role in organizing academic texts. Research shows that non-native researchers writing in English tend to use a limited number of these markers, most notably longer and formulaic sequences (Khalili & Aslanabadi, 2014). This pattern may occur because those authors do not focus on these markers' organizational usefulness in academic writing (Khalili & Aslanabadi, 2014). Unfortunately, very few studies have been conducted on the functional nature of metadiscourse devices, most notably in Saudi and Algerian researchers' articles in applied linguistics.

The database used in this study consisted of abstracts of published journal articles. This choice was based on the immense importance given to abstracts by editors, reviewers, publishers, and authors, because the abstract acts as the face of the research paper and the summary of the whole article. Research papers' abstracts are thus important tools for promoting the visibility of scientific endeavors. However, little research has been carried out on how abstracts can be characterized in terms of their textual organization.

We wished to gain detailed and well-grounded insights on the use of metadiscourse markers in research abstracts written by Algerian researchers and to learn how their use of these devices compares to abstracts written by native and other non-native writers. We believed that investigating the frequency of use and the functional use of these markers in Algerian and Saudi researchers' abstracts in comparison to those of native English writers would help us understand the writing processes of these different discourse communities.

Consequently, we have noticed a burgeoning interest in studying discourse analysis and analyzing corpora in general, and in analyzing metadiscourse in particular. In addition, Abdulaal (2020) states that metadiscourse addresses "how speakers and writers use language to explicate communicative situations, and how they count on their perception of communicative situations to make their intended meanings crystal clear to their interlocutors" (p. 195).

The complexity of defining and delimiting metadiscourse as a concept (Duruk, 2017) has led researchers to design models to classify and elaborate its linguistic dimensions. Table 10.1 is adapted from a model suggested by

TABLE 10.1 Hyland's taxonomy of metadiscoursal devices

Category	Function	Examples
Interactive resources	Help to guide the reader through the text	
Transitions	Express semantic relation between main clauses	In addition / hence / but / thus / and
Frame markers	Refer to discourse acts, sequences, or text stages	finally / to conclude / my purpose is
Endophorics	Refer to the information in other parts of the text	noted above / see Figure / in section 2
Evidential devices	Refer to source of information from other texts	according to X / (Y, 1990) / Z states
Code glosses	Help readers grasp the meanings of ideational material	namely / e.g., / in other words
Interactional resources	Involve the reader in the argument (formulaic language)	
Hedges	Withhold the writer's full commitment to proposition	might / perhaps / possible
Boosters	Emphasize force or writer's certainty in proposition	in fact / definitely / it is clear that
Attitude markers	Express writer's attitude to proposition	unfortunately / I agree / surprisingly
Engagement markers	Explicitly refer to or build a relationship with the reader	consider / note that / you can see that
Self-mentions	Explicit reference to the author(s)	I / we / my / our

Source: Hyland, 2005.

Hyland (2005), in which he divides metadiscourse devices into two main categories: interactive and interactional markers. The former category includes devices such as *transition markers*, which help guide the reader through the text. The latter includes devices such as *hedges*, which help writers demonstrate their perspective, allow the readers into the argument, and enhance the audience's engagement.

It is important to be aware of the use of metadiscourse markers and the research focus on this specific indicator of writing quality in academic research. Researchers around the world have investigated the use of metadiscourse markers in different academic texts. For instance, the occurrence of metadiscourse markers has been studied in academic essays (Hyland, 2007), theses/dissertations (Aimah et al., 2019; Hyland, 2010), argumentative essays (Anwardeen et al., 2013), and textbooks (Hyland, 1999; 2005) generated by native and non-native writers of English. Burneikaité (2008) and Bal-Gezegin and Baş (2020) elaborated that in comparison to British students, text connectives were among the most often used markers in postgraduate essays created by Lithuanian non-native English writers. These discourse markers were mostly utilized to signal text stages rather than to express writers' goals. Zakaria and Malik (2018) analyzed metadiscourse devices employed by 50 Arab international students in Malaysia. The findings showed these students' academic written materials involved greater use of interactive devices.

One of the few contrastive studies on metadiscoursal devices in research articles is Marandi's (2003) work. It resulted in no statistically significant differences in the use of frame markers or connectors in the English articles produced by native Persian and native English writers. Likewise, Mirshamsi and Allami (2013) examined research papers of both Persian and English authors. They reported no statistically significant differences in these groups' use of various metadiscourse devices.

Many researchers have focused on specific sections of research papers written in English. Lee and Casal (2014) investigated the results and discussion sections of English and Spanish writers' texts. They discovered that the Spanish authors used a significantly greater number of metadiscourse markers than the English writers. Duruk (2017) examined the frequency of interpersonal metadiscourse markers in the academic written discourse of Turkish MA students specializing in English language teaching. The outcomes revealed the use of hedges, boosters, and attitude markers, while attitude markers were used more frequently than other markers by the Turkish writers. Aimah et al. (2019) focused on the introduction section in Indonesian university EFL students' final projects. They discovered those students tended to use more interactive markers (such as transitions and evidential devices) than interactional ones (e.g., hedges and boosters). The outcomes indicated the attention students gave to guiding readers through the text by establishing their interpretations rather than by involving the readers in the arguments.

One aspect that motivated the present investigation is the scarce research on metadiscourse devices in the abstract sections of published research. In our literature review, we found that Martin-Martin (2003), Ren and Li (2011), Saeeaw and Tangkiengsirisin (2014), and Santos (2019) focused on the rhetorical variation in abstract and discussion sections. Akbaş (2012) investigated metadiscourse devices in doctoral dissertation abstracts and compiled a corpus of abstracts composed by native English and Turkish non-native English speakers. The results indicated that native English writers' abstracts contained the highest frequency of metadiscourse devices when compared with their native Turkish counterparts' abstracts. Farjami (2013) confirmed that surveying journal abstracts seems to provide a practical and valid reservoir of condensed information. As a database, abstracts are practical for reasons of ready availability and terseness, and valid because this genre, as Swales and Feak (2009) suggest, "shows best the features of specialized communication between experts in the related field" (p. 1).

Another issue that motivated this research is the limited number of studies conducted on Algerian scholars' use of metadiscourse markers in academic research papers. We reviewed reports produced by Algerian researchers in the field of applied linguistics and discourse analysis. Given the relatively small number of papers by Algerian authors published in high-indexed journals, we decided to study the occurrence and effect of metadiscourse markers on Algerian researchers' quality of manuscripts. Examples of Algerian studies include Bouchemet's (2019) investigation of interactional metadiscourse in the introductory and concluding sections of applied linguistics master's theses written by Algerian students. He found a difference in the distribution and features of the markers used in these two sections. Similarly, Boudersa (2014) examined Algerian undergraduate students' expository essay writing quality concerning the use of connective expressions as metadiscourse markers. She found that the quality of students' writings is not bound to the use of metadiscourse markers. The fewer connective markers students used, the better their writing quality was deemed to be. These two studies are the only ones we found published by Algerian scholars investigating metadiscourse in academic writing.

Research questions

The current study sought to address the following research questions:

1. How similar are metadiscourse markers produced by Algerian and Saudi researchers to those of native English writers, specifically in the abstract section of published articles?
2. In comparison to the native English writers' abstracts, which formulaic metadiscourse devices do Algerian and Saudi researchers with a frequency similar to that of the native English writers?

Research methods

Context

To address our main objective, a mixed-methods approach was chosen. To identify metadiscourse markers and their functions in the abstract section of research papers written by Algerian, Saudi, and native English writers, a qualitative method was employed. We used the framework shown in Table 10.1 to categorize every metadiscourse marker that we found in the database with regards to its function.

Subsequently, a quantitative approach was used to calculate the frequency of the various functions of metadiscourse devices in the abstracts. We then compared and contrasted the metadiscourse devices in the abstracts of the three groups of researchers.

Data collection procedures

We relied on a two-step plan to compile the study corpus, which consisted of the abstracts of sixty research papers, 20 for each group (Saudi, Algerian, and Native English-writing researchers). For comparison and contrast aims, we made sure of the comparability of the Algerian research articles group with the other two groups. That is, in the corpus, all the articles are similar in word count and belong to the field of applied linguistics.

The articles were downloaded from well-recognized and peer-reviewed international journals specializing in linguistics, language, and education. We focus only on specialized articles that were published in recent issues (2000–2020). While the majority of the Native and Saudi articles were downloaded from high-indexed journals, 18 of the 20 Algerian articles were downloaded from two main sources. The first is the *Algerian Scientific Journals Platform*, which is a platform of the indexed journals in Algeria, and the second is the *Arab World English Journal* (see Table 10.2). The two remaining articles by Algerian authors were downloaded from *Language Policy*.

TABLE 10.2 The characteristics of the compiled corpus

Abstract Authors	Native Writers (n = 20)	Saudi Writers (n = 20)	Algerian Writers (n = 20)
Number of Words	3790	3610	3815
Sources for Corpus Compilation	International Journal of English Linguistics, Applied Linguistics, Annual Review of Applied Linguistics, Arab World English Journal, Modern Language Journal, and Applied Linguistics	International Journal of English Linguistics, Applied Linguistics, Annual Review of Applied Linguistics, Arab World English Journal, Modern Language Journal, and Applied Linguistics	Algerian Scientific Journals Platform (Journal of Translation and Languages, Journal of Human Sciences), Arab World English Journal, and Language Policy

Data analysis procedures

After the collection and organization of the data, and compilation of the research corpus, we gathered the abstract sections of the articles into one document for analysis. We read the selected sections carefully and highlighted the metadiscourse markers based on Hyland's (2005) classification system. After 20 days, we reread the compiled corpus with a colleague to cross-check the highlighted devices and their functions in the text. In the last stage, we read the sections one final time to validate the data categorization and prepare the data for tabulation.

Findings and discussion

In this section, we discuss the categorization of interactive and interactional metadiscourse devices in our database. By analyzing the abstracts written by Native, Saudi, and Algerian authors, and by relying on Hyland's (2005) categorization framework (see Table 10.1), we sought to understand the frequency of the metadiscourse markers used in the three groups' research abstracts. Table 10.3 displays the frequency and percentage of both interactive and interactional metadiscourse markers in the abstract section of Algerian researchers' articles.

The distribution of the Algerian authors' metadiscourse markers in Table 10.3 shows the relatively larger number of interactive markers (n = 222) used by Algerian scholars in comparison to their use of interactional markers (n = 111). Transitions are the most frequently used markers for both interactive markers and for metadiscourse markers in general (27.6%). Engagement markers, on the other hand, are the least frequently used markers in the Algerian authors' research abstracts.

TABLE 10.3 The frequencies of interactive and interactional metadiscourse devices in abstracts written by Algerian scholars

Discourse Devices		Algerian Abstracts	
		Total Number	Percentage %
Interactive	Transitions	92	27.6
	Frame markers	58	17.4
	Endophorics	20	6.0
	Evidential devices	25	7.5
	Code glosses	27	8.1
Interactional	Hedges	39	11.7
	Boosters	21	6.3
	Attitude markers	29	8.7
	Engagement markers	6	1.8
	Self-mentions	16	4.8
Total		333	

Next, Table 10.4 shows similar results for the Saudi researchers' abstract sections. We can see that interactive markers are used much more often than interactional markers. With 71 transition markers used in the Saudi abstracts, this specific interactive marker is the device most often employed in the abstracts of this group. In comparison to attitude markers, engagement markers, and self-mentions, and hedges are used infrequently as interactional markers.

Table 10.5 shows the dominant use of interactive markers (n = 244) in comparison to interactional markers (n = 122) in the abstracts produced by native English

TABLE 10.4 The frequencies of interactive and interactional metadiscourse devices in abstracts written by Saudi scholars

Discourse Devices		Saudi Abstracts	
		Total Number	Percentage %
Interactive	Transitions	71	24.3
	Frame markers	41	14.0
	Endophorics	4	1.4
	Evidential devices	43	14.7
	Code glosses	52	17.8
Interactional	Hedges	16	5.5
	Boosters	42	14.4
	Attitude markers	14	4.8
	Engagement markers	3	1.0
	Self-mentions	6	2.1
Total		292	

TABLE 10.5 Frequencies of interactive and interactional metadiscourse devices in abstracts written by native scholars

Discourse Devices		Native Abstracts	
		Total Number	Percentage %
Interactive	Transitions	63	17.2
(n = 244)	Frame markers	72	19.7
	Endophorics	22	6.0
	Evidential devices	63	17.2
	Code glosses	24	6.6
Interactional	Hedges	36	9.8
(n = 122)	Boosters	21	5.7
	Attitude markers	26	7.1
	Engagement markers	6	1.6
	Self-mentions	33	9.0
Total		366	

scholars. More specifically, frame markers are more prevalent than transitions as interactive devices. Hedges, as interactional discourse devices, are used more than any other device in the same category. Engagement markers are the least frequently used discourse marker by far compared to all the markers in both categories.

We used the two-way chi-square statistic to check for statistically significant differences among the three groups of authors' use of metadiscourse markers. The results indicated that there is no statistically significant difference between the number of metadiscourse markers in either of the two main categories (i.e., Interactive and Interactional) among Native, Algerian, and Saudi authors' abstracts. Table 10.6 provides a detailed count of metadiscourse markers in the three groups of abstracts (Native, Saudi, and Algerian).

Transitions are the most frequently used markers in both Saudi and Algerian abstracts, and both groups seem to be using this specific marker more than the native authors. Frame markers are the most frequently employed marker in the Native writers' abstracts. In addition, the count of endophorics in the Algerian abstracts is close to that in the natives' abstracts, while the Saudis authors' use of this device is almost double that of the other two groups. Evidential devices are among the most frequently employed devices in the native authors' abstracts, but Saudi and Algerian abstracts use far fewer of these markers than the number employed by natives. Algerian abstracts are close to native abstracts as far as the use of code glosses is concerned, while Saudi abstracts have fewer code glosses than the abstracts of either the native authors or the Algerian authors.

In the main category of interactional metadiscourse markers, the use of hedges used in Algerian abstracts is close to the natives' writers count, while the Saudi abstracts used fewer hedges than either of the other groups. Unlike hedges, boosters are used in the Saudi abstracts in a number close to that of the native writers. The Algerian researchers' use of attitude markers is more similar to their

TABLE 10.6 Metadiscourse markers in Native (N), Saudi (S), and Algerian (A) abstracts

	Native Abstracts "N"	Saudi Abstracts "S"	Algerian Abstracts "A"
1. Transitions	63	71	92
2. Frame markers	72	41	58
3. Endophorics	24	52	20
4. Evidential devices	63	43	25
5. Code glosses	22	4	27
6. Hedges	33	6	39
7. Boosters	6	3	21
8. Attitude markers	26	14	29
9. Engagement markers	36	16	6
10. Self-mentions	21	42	16

native counterparts' than it is to the Saudi authors' use. Both the Saudi and Algerian abstracts had a lower count of engagement markers compared to that of the native writers. Finally, the number of self-mentions in Saudi abstracts is higher than either the Algerian or native use.

We will summarize our main research results by providing a brief elaboration of the two research questions addressed in this study. The first research question addressed the use of metadiscourse markers, both interactive and interactional, in Algerian, Saudi, and Native authors' research abstracts in the field of applied linguistics. We have noted that the Saudi abstracts were closer to those of the Native authors in the employment of transitions only. The use of the remaining interactive and all interactional discourse markers in Saudi abstracts was far from that of both the native and Algerian abstracts. The Saudi researchers' use of transitions may be interpreted as an indication of the attention they pay to keeping a smooth flow of ideas in a coherent and organized manner.

The second research question inquired about the comparative frequency of use of specific metadiscourse markers among the three groups. In some categories, the Algerian authors' abstracts have a frequency of metadiscourse markers similar to that of the Native authors' abstracts. The relatively high use of endophorics by the Saudi researchers may indicate a sense of academic responsibility to avoid any form of plagiarism through citing and cross-referring sources. The use of frame markers seems to show the Algerian authors' use of efficient sequencing and organization skills to create in-text interactiveness. The Algerian authors also tended to elaborate and explain data through the use of code glosses, perhaps to maintain a strong relationship with the reader. The use of hedges, which is similar in the Algerian and Native abstracts, seems to indicate a careful distinction between facts, allegations, and claims. Finally, the number of attitude markers used in Algerian abstracts was very close to that in the native abstracts, and we believe this finding indicates the tendency towards expressing perspectives and evaluation of shared propositional information. Also, self-mentions in the Algerian abstracts were closer to the native rate and further from the Saudis'.

Ultimately, the use of metadiscourse markers as formulaic expressions by the Algerian researchers in the abstract section is not far from the use of these markers by natives, yet it is quite far from the Saudis. This contrast is important because we need to situate the Algerians' use of metadiscourse markers in the literature and in comparison with counterparts in different parts of the world.

Implications for policy, practice, and future research

One of our concerns in conducting this study was the small number of articles by Algerian authors published in high-indexed applied linguistics journals. We investigated the use of metadiscourse markers in the abstracts of Algerian, Saudi, and Native researchers specializing in applied linguistics. We used a mixed-methods approach to examine these devices in both frequency and function, resulting in different frequencies of use among the three groups of authors. What we concluded from our findings is that, unlike Saudis, Algerian researchers approach persuasion using rhetorical conventions similar to those of the Native authors.

Based on our experience, we believe that the Algerian researchers have less international academic interaction, have had less experience in publishing papers in high-indexed journals in the field of applied linguistics, and are provided with fewer materials and opportunities in academia than the Saudis or the native authors. Yet, they are still close to natives in using metadiscourse markers appropriately in the abstract section. Thus we can infer that the use (or lack of use) of metadiscourse markers in the abstracts of Algerian writers specializing in applied linguistics is probably not a factor in the relatively low frequency of publication in high-indexed journals in their field.

This issue raises implications for future research. For example, the lower number of Algerian authors' publications in high-indexed journals could be due to a small number of manuscripts being submitted by Algerian authors. Or perhaps Algerian authors' work is rejected more frequently than that of other non-native writers. It was beyond the scope of this study to investigate these possibilities.

A broader question is whether native English researchers' studies are accepted for publication in English-medium journals more often than research reports by non-native writers. Again, the relative number of submissions by native and non-native researchers would be a key factor to determine. But given the many challenges of writing in a foreign language, it is possible that specific mentoring in research reporting would be helpful. As Flowerdew (2019) noted, non-native writers face "challenges in writing for publication which are shared by EAL [English as an additional language] and L1 writers, but EAL writers have an additional set of linguistic challenges, which do not apply (to such an extent) to L1 writers" (p. 258). Furthermore, given the importance of publications for university promotion and tenure decisions in many countries, support for non-native writers submitting manuscripts for publication could have a profound impact on their professional lives.

If equity of publishing opportunities is a matter of concern, perhaps journal editorial boards should consider adopting policies of proportional acceptance (e.g., if X percent of manuscript submissions come from non-native writers, then X percent of the items selected for publication should be those written by non-native writers). However, this suggestion will certainly raise concerns that – no matter what authors' native language may be – acceptance for publication should be determined by well-written papers reporting on important and well-designed research projects.

Finally, in this chapter, we have tried to shed light on the importance of metadiscourse markers in academic research in general and in the abstract section in particular. As our literature review shows, metadiscourse markers serve many important functions in academic writing, and some of those functions contribute directly to the readers' understanding of the concepts being reported. For this reason, we encourage educators to emphasize metadiscourse markers in their teaching to help their students produce better and more organized academic writing.

References

Abdulaal, M. A. A. (2020). A cross-linguistic analysis of formulaic language and meta-discourse in linguistics research articles by natives and Arabs: Modeling Saudis and Egyptians. *Arab World English Journal*, *11*(3). 193–211. https://dx.doi.org/10.24093/awej/vol11no3.12.

Aimah, S., Mulyadi, D., & Ifadah, M. (2019). Metadiscourse markers written in introduction section of final project of Unimus learners. *English Review: Journal of English Education*, *7*(2), 109–118. doi:10.25134/erjee.v7i2.1717.

Akbaş, E. (2012). Exploring metadiscourse in master's dissertation abstracts: Cultural and linguistic variations across postgraduate writers. *International Journal of Applied Linguistics & English Literature*, *1*(1), 12–26.

Anwardeen, N. H., Luyee, E. O., Gabriel, J. I., & Kalajahi, S. A. (2013). An analysis: The usage of metadiscourse in argumentative writing by Malaysian tertiary level of students. *English Language Teaching*, *6*(9), 83–96. doi:10.5539/elt.v6n9p83.

Assassi, T., & Benyelles, R. (2016). Formulaic language for improving communicative competence. *Arab World English Journal (AWEJ)*, *7*(2), 163–176.

Bal-Gezegin, B., & Baş, M. (2020). Metadiscourse in academic writing: A comparison of research articles and book reviews. *Eurasian Journal of Applied Linguistics*, *6*(1), 45–62. doi:10.32601/ejal.710204.

Bouchemet, T. (2019). Interactional metadiscourse in applied linguistics master theses: A corpus-based comparative study. *Human Sciences Journal*, *51*, 57–70.

Boudersa, N. (2014). Connective expressions as metadiscourse markers of writing quality in undergraduate students' expository writing. *Human Sciences Journal*, *25*(2), 57–70. http://revue.umc.edu.dz/index.php/h/article/view/1621.

Burneikaité, N. (2008). Metadiscourse in linguistics master's theses in English L1 and L2. *KALBOTYRA*, *59*(3), 38–47. doi:10.15388/Klbt.2008.7591.

Duruk, E. (2017). Analysis of metadiscourse markers in academic written discourse produced by Turkish researchers. *Journal of Language and Linguistic Studies*, *13*(1), 1–9.

Farjami, H. (2013). A corpus-based study of the lexical make-up of applied linguistics article abstracts. *Journal of Teaching Language Skills*, *32*(2), 27–50.

Flowerdew, J. (2019). The linguistic disadvantage of scholars who write in English as an additional language. *Language Teaching*, *52*(2), 249–260. https://doi.org/10.1017/S0261444819000041.

Hyland, K. (1999). Talking to students: Metadiscourse in introductory course books. *English for Specific Purposes*, *18*(1), 3–26. doi:10.1016/S0889-4906(97)00025-2.

Hyland, K. (2004). *Disciplinary discourses: Social interactions in academic writing*. University of Michigan Press.

Hyland, K. (2005). *Metadiscourse: Exploring interaction in writing*. Continuum.

Hyland, K. (2007). Applying a gloss: Exemplifying and reformulating in academic discourse. *Applied Linguistics*, *28*(2), 266–285. doi:10.1093/applin/amm011.

Hyland, K. (2010). Metadiscourse: Mapping interactions in academic writing. *Nordic Journal of English Study*, *9*(2), 125–143.

Hyland, K., & Tse, P. (2004). Metadiscourse in academic writing: A reappraisal. *Applied Linguistics*, *25*(2), 156–177.

Khalili, A., & Aslanabadi, M. (2014). The use of metadiscourse devices by non-native speakers in research articles. *Journal of Applied Linguistics and Applied Literature: Dynamics and Advances*, *2*(2), 21–34.

Lee, J. J., & Casal, J. E. (2014). Metadiscourse in results and discussion chapters: A cross-linguistic analysis of English and Spanish thesis writers in engineering. *System, 46*(1), 39–54. doi:10.1016/j.system.2014.07.009.

Marandi, S. (2003). Metadiscourse in Persian/English master's theses: A contrastive study. *Iranian Journal of Applied Linguistics, 6*(2), 23–42.

Martin-Martin, P. (2003). A genre analysis of English and Spanish research paper abstracts in experimental social sciences. *English for Specific Purposes, 22*(1), 25–43.

Mirshamsi, A., & Allami, H. (2013). Metadiscourse markers in the discussion/conclusion section of Persian and English master's theses. *The Journal of Teaching Language Skills, 5*(3), 23–40.

Ren, H., & Li, Y. (2011). A comparison study on the rhetorical moves of abstracts in published research articles and master's foreign-language theses. *English Language Teaching, 4*(1), 162–166.

Saeeaw, S., & Tangkiengsirisin, S. (2014). Rhetorical variation across research article abstracts in environmental science and applied linguistics. *English Language Teaching, 7,* 81–93.

Santos, M. B. (1995). Academic abstracts: A genre analysis. Unpublished Master's thesis, Federal University of Santa Catarina, Brazil.

Santos, M. B. D. (2019). The textual organization of research paper abstracts in applied linguistics. *Text, 16,* 481–499. http://dx.doi.org/10.1515/text.1.1996.16.4.481.

Swales, J. M., & Feak C. B. (2009). Abstracts and the writing of abstracts. *Michigan ELT.* http://www.press.umich.edu/titleDetailDesc.do?id=309332.

Zakaria, M. K., & Malik, F. A. (2018). *Metadiscourse in academic writing of pre-university Arab students at the International Islamic University Malaysia (IIUM).* MATEC Web of Conferences. doi:10.1051/matecconf/201815005086.

11
INTRODUCING A CURRICULUM-BASED TUTORING MODEL IN THE FOUNDATION ENGLISH PROGRAM AT QATAR UNIVERSITY

Mansoor Al-Surmi, Pakize Uludag, and Mohammad Manasreh

Introduction

Issues that motivated the research

The process of composing a text requires using linguistic abilities, organizing structure, and generating content geared towards various academic purposes (Grabe, 2001). In process-based writing classrooms, students complete a variety of writing tasks through the stages of prewriting, drafting, revising, and editing (Nunan, 1999). During this hierarchical process, novice writers with developing linguistic abilities might experience cognitive and social challenges, such as understanding task instructions and responding to instructor feedback (Hinkel, 2003). To address these challenges, writing centers play an essential role in addressing learners' linguistic and rhetorical challenges, functioning as a supplement to traditional writing instruction in higher education contexts (Faigley, 2015; Williams, 2004; Williams & Severino, 2004).

Students participate in writing center tutorials since doing so gives them access to one-to-one writing instruction and scaffolding (Thompson, 2009; Thompson & Mackiewicz, 2014). Nordlof (2014) defined *scaffolding* in the context of writing center tutorials as "the approaches tutors might take to help students reach the limits of their zones of proximal development" (p. 56). The fact that students do not feel the pressure to obtain a grade from writing center tutors helps minimize anxiety by creating a collaborative and "safe and stress-free environment" during writing center visits (Moussu, 2013, p. 59). This type of help leads to higher motivation for using the services offered at writing centers and increases passing rates of students enrolled in university-level composition courses (Niiler, 2003; Pfrenger et al., 2017).

DOI: 10.4324/9781003312444-14

While providing individualized feedback to students is one of the major purposes of writing centers, the amount and type of feedback can vary in terms of its focus and relevance. Studies exploring student perceptions of writing center pedagogy have found discrepancies between the type of feedback expected and what is provided. For example, Winder, Kathpalia, and Koo (2016) reported that more than 60% of the students who participate in writing center tutorials were concerned about developing their higher order skills, including textual organization and argumentation. However, Bell and Elledge's (2008) study, which analyzed the writing center interactions between tutors and tutees, revealed that around 50% of the tutorial sessions were dedicated to providing feedback on grammar and sentence-level errors rather than targeting students' higher order skills. A study by Eckstein (2016) compared the perspectives of L1 and L2 students about feedback provided in writing center tutorials. The results revealed that L2 students expected to receive more feedback on grammar while L1students thought they received more grammar help than they expected.

Students' perceptions have also been investigated to identify whether they consider writing center tutorials helpful for the development of their writing ability. For example, Bell (2000) used interviews and questionnaires to investigate students' perspectives about the usefulness of writing center tutorials across three time intervals (i.e., immediate, short, or long terms) after their tutoring sessions. The results suggested the majority of the students found the tutorials to have been helpful even two months after their writing center visits. In addition, they were able to use feedback they received in other assignments. A study by Carino and Enders (2001) explored the correlation between the frequency of writing center visits and students' overall satisfaction with the help they received from tutors. The frequency of visits was not related to students' satisfaction with the tutorials or their perceptions of the tutors' ability. However, the frequency of visits correlated significantly with students' perception that their writing ability had improved.

Overall, previous student perception research seems to offer contradictory findings regarding students' expectations and gains from tutorial sessions. Thus, further studies are needed to shed light on students' expectations from writing center visits along with the factors which might affect their participation in writing center tutorials (Salem, 2016). The present chapter contributes to this line of research by investigating students' perceptions of the role of traditional writing centers compared to a more curriculum-based supporting system (i.e., aligning tutoring with student learning outcomes of particular English courses in a specific context).

Current writing center models

Traditionally, writing center tutorials are offered through an on-campus center, which collaborates with the departments that offer composition courses. The departments that offer the writing courses typically run the tutorials in writing centers. To improve students' academic writing skills, and reduce the pressure on L2 writing instructors, various alternatives to traditional writing center tutorials have been developed over the years.

One approach adopted at higher education institutions in the last few years is to offer a one-credit elective course that is taken along with the writing course (Bielinska-Kwapisz, 2015; Salem, 2016). On the one hand, credit-bearing academic tutorials are effective since they can increase students' motivation to participate in tutorials and encourage them to pay more attention to tutors' feedback (Gray & Hoyt, 2020). On the other hand, registering in these elective tutorials has been shown to trigger negative feelings among students (e.g., feeling inferior) (Osman, 2007).

A second alternative to the on-campus writing center visits is to offer virtual tutorials through an online platform (Breuch & Racine, 2000; Palmquist, 2003). Online writing centers can address the needs of learners with different learning styles, and reduce the anxiety associated with in-person tutorials (Van Waes et al., 2014). This method can also increase the number of students who take advantage of writing center resources virtually instead of walking into an on-campus writing center. Online writing centers have become even more popular during the post-COVID era; however, one important constraint could be the disparities in students' equal access to technology. In addition, for accommodating virtual visits, writing centers need to train tutors and increase the number of staff to assist with logistics such as appointments.

The student tutoring scheme: A unique tutorials model

Considering the potential issues with the current writing center models and reflecting on our students' issues with academic writing courses, we developed a new approach to writing tutorials in the English Foundation Program at Qatar University. This model, known as *the Student Tutoring Scheme,* differs from conventional approaches, first, in that it was specifically developed for L2 students as a curriculum-based alternative (drawing on the curriculum of the writing courses offered in the department) to the writing center practices available on campus. Second, it was not limited by a booking system or time limit for each session. Third, it was available to students with a longer time across the day than the university writing center hours. Finally, its tutors were the teachers of the writing courses offered in the department themselves.

The sub-program under which the scheme was established offered two process-based English academic writing courses. Arabic-speaking students enrolled in those courses engage in a multi-stage writing process, while teachers take a background role, review student drafts, and provide oral and written feedback during class time. The challenge for both teachers and students in the classroom environment was not having enough time to give and receive adequate feedback. Before the Student Tutoring Scheme was introduced, students used to resort to the university writing center once they needed more support with their writing assignments. However, the feedback they received from the writing center tutors was not always consistent with the feedback from their course instructors. Powers and Nelson (1995) associated this mismatch with the fact that L2 writing programs and university writing centers operate at different levels and might be isolated from one another. Lack of collaboration between writing center tutors and writing course instructors makes it difficult for tutors to tailor their practices and fulfill the needs of L2 writers.

Additionally, studies have suggested a strong relationship between tutors' expertise in the discipline as well as their knowledge of the curriculum and the effectiveness of the tutoring sessions (e.g., Dinitz & Harrington, 2014). In this particular context, feedback given by writing center tutors with a generalist approach would often fail to address the specific problems in student drafts, as reported by the course instructors. This situation created communication problems and affected the student motivation negatively. Hence, reflecting on what we do and why we do it, the Student Tutoring Scheme arose as a response to rethinking traditional writing center pedagogy. In the English Department, we created an internal system in which writing course instructors offered tutorials to the students enrolled in academic writing courses. Students were provided with a schedule of the tutoring hours, and they were able to participate in tutorials based on their available hours.

Research questions

An important task is to examine the effectiveness of the curriculum-based tutoring model from the students' perspectives. This chapter, therefore, focuses on students' tutoring perceptions and expectations and is guided by the following over-arching question: Is there a difference in students' perceptions of the in-house program tutoring vs. the university writing center tutoring? In particular, we ask

1. At what stage of the writing process do students seek tutoring?
2. What aspects of the writing process do they seek help with?
3. What are students' expectations of these tutoring sessions?

Research methods

Context

As part of the core curriculum program of Qatar University, undergraduate students take two academic writing courses. In the first course, the focus is on essay writing, critical reading analysis, academic vocabulary, and paraphrasing. In the second course, students learn how to summarize short articles, read them critically, and write short response papers. They also write a brief term paper (around 1,000 words), in which paraphrasing, source information integration, and referencing skills are emphasized.

These courses are offered by the English Department at the Foundation Program of the university. Due to the large number of students enrolled in these courses and considering the limited capacity of the university writing center, the department designed this in-house tutoring service, where the teachers of these courses served as tutors. Teachers served three hours of tutoring each week as part of their workload. Using SharePoint Software, teachers kept an in-house online record of students who participated in the tutorials.

Participants

The data for this study were collected from 272 students enrolled in English-medium undergraduate degree programs at Qatar University, including health sciences, medicine, general sciences, pharmacy, engineering, and business. Students are admitted to these majors with a minimum of a 5.5 IELTS score. These students typically take two academic writing courses in their freshmen or sophomore year. Their ages ranged from 18–26 and approximately 93% of these students come mainly from Arabic speaking L1 backgrounds.

Data collection procedures

At the end of a three-semester program, a tutoring survey (in English) was developed and sent to students enrolled in the writing courses. The survey consisted of 15 close-ended questions (with a possibility to add open-ended comments for two items). They were a mix of some items adapted from the literature (i.e., Carter-Tod, 1995; Winder et al., 2016) and some created to examine students' perceptions of the two models employed at Qatar University. The goal for both models was to determine (1) at what stage of the writing process leaners seek tutoring, (2) what aspects of the writing process they seek help with, and (3) what their expectations of these tutoring sessions are. In addition, we wanted to learn what model of tutoring services students preferred and whether they preferred tutoring to be offered by course teachers or writing center tutors.

Data analysis procedures

Students' responses to the survey questions were analyzed quantitatively using descriptive statistics. Frequency counts and percentages were used to compare students' ranking of stages and aspects of writing they seek help with when visiting the in-house tutoring program vs. the university writing center. Moreover, frequency counts and percentages were used to compare students' responses of each item across a Likert-scale regarding their expectations. The students open-ended comments were analyzed qualitatively, focusing on pre-determined themes: positive and negative statements regarding the in-house tutoring program vs. the university writing center. Our findings are discussed below.

Findings and discussion

Stage of the writing process

The first research question asked about the point of the writing process at which students try to seek help. Table 11.1 shows the ranking of the stages for both the writing center (WC) and the in-house tutoring (IT) sessions based on the highest percentages, which have been underlined. Overall, results show that there was no difference in students' stage ranking by tutoring type. The majority of respondents ranked stage 4 (*After you have completed a draft, for assistance in revising*) first for both types of tutoring. Stage 5 (*After you have revised a draft, for assistance with editing/formatting*) came next in order, while stage 3 (*After you have written some and need some assistance to go on*) was ranked third. Clarifying an assignment or visiting before the beginning of writing were ranked last in terms of utilizing both the writing center and the in-house tutorials.

This finding is not surprising as clarifying an assignment or receiving help at the planning stage are typically done in the classroom. Course instructors usually make sure task instructions are clear, and, in many cases, students are asked to work on an outline as part of the writing process. Therefore, very few students would seek tutoring for assignment clarification. In fact, the majority of these students seem to have visited the services when they have a complete draft rather than when they have written a part of the assignment. This pattern could be because writing instructors encourage their students to have someone else check their drafts before submission. Moreover, students tend to be more motivated to revise their subsequent drafts rather than the initial ones.

Aspects of the writing process

As part of the questionnaire, students rank ordered the aspects of the writing process they seek help with during their writing center vs. in-house tutorial visits. As shown in Table 11.2, language structure was ranked first by students for both services, while getting started, understanding instructions or requirements, and in-text citation/referencing were ranked later. However, there were some differences in the other aspects. Those students who visited the writing center ranked seeking help on organization before content development and integration (i.e., integrating information from sources into their writing), while those who participated in the in-house tutoring sessions ranked seeking help with content development before organization.

Overall, these students considered three main aspects of the writing process as important during their tutorial visits: (1) language structure, (2) idea development, and (3) requirements and referencing. Most students prioritized having correct language structure and then having their ideas flow smoothly, including those integrated from sources. This finding is in line with previous studies where the

TABLE 11.1 Students' stage ranking by tutoring service type

Rank		1		2		3		4		5	
Stage*		WC	IT	WC	IT	WC	IT	WC	IT	WC	IT
1	To help clarify an assignment	14%	23%	19%	13%	15%	13%	**26%**	25%	**26%**	**27%**
2	Before you begin to write	23%	20%	12%	16%	10%	5%	17%	27%	**38%**	**32%**
3	After you have written some and need some assistance to go on	19%	15%	16%	20%	**43%**	**51%**	17%	12%	6%	2%
4	After you have completed a draft, for assistance in revising	**39%**	**30%**	24%	24%	8%	16%	17%	18%	12%	12%
5	After you have revised a draft, for assistance with editing/formatting	17%	16%	**34%**	**24%**	18%	22%	13%	15%	18%	23%

(*All items adapted from Carter-Tod, 1995.)

Introducing a curriculum-based tutoring model 151

TABLE 11.2 Students' writing aspect ranking by tutoring service type

Rank		1		2		3		4		5		6		7	
	Aspect*	WC	IT	WC	IT	WC	IT	WC	IT	WC	IT	WC	IT	WC	IT
1	Getting started, brainstorming, exploring	15%	23%	15%	15%	5%	8%	2%	2%	11%	5%	10%	10%	**42%**	**37%**
2	Understanding instructions or requirements	13%	13%	13%	21%	7%	8%	14%	5%	10%	9%	**36%**	**35%**	7%	9%
3	Content and idea development	10%	15%	11%	11%	31%	**27%**	15%	18%	**25%**	20%	3%	7%	5%	2%
4	Organization, structure, and overall coherence	18%	10%	**30%**	18%	14%	18%	17%	**31%**	10%	12%	3%	7%	8%	4%
5	Language structure: grammar, word choice, punctuations, and mechanics	**43%**	**21%**	6%	12%	10%	20%	9%	12%	9%	19%	16%	7%	7%	9%
6	Integrating evidence into my writing	3%	7%	13%	14%	22%	**20%**	**24%**	13%	17%	17%	13%	**20%**	8%	9%
7	In-text citation and referencing	10%	17%	13%	12%	12%	4%	16%	17%	15%	14%	11%	11%	**23%**	**25%**

*Items 1, 2, 4, and 5 adapted from Winder et al. (2016).

students' main concern was to fix their grammatical issues (e.g., Winder et al., 2016). On the other hand, they needed less help with understanding the task instructions and using references. Materials and handouts for such aspects were typically available and accessible to these students, which helped them work independently rather than seeking guidance from a tutor.

Expectations of tutorials

Students' expectations were examined through a series of statements using a Likert scale with five levels. Students were asked whether they strongly agree, agree, disagree, strongly disagree, or neither agree nor disagree with each statement. As shown in Table 11.3, there was no difference in students' expectations of in-house and writing center tutorials. They perceived that utilizing the tutoring services would improve their grades and that it is the job of tutors to fix their grammatical mistakes, proofread and correct their drafts, and help them to understand the assignments, find their mistakes, and become better writers. Similar results were reported in Carter-Tod's (1995) study where students perceived writing centers as a one-stop fix-it-all. This view, Moussu (2013) indicated, is a result of students' preference for authoritative teacher's feedback. The same view might have been adopted by the students in this study since they come from a traditional classroom environment where teachers are thought to have such knowledge authority.

Our results also show that students overall believed that tutors need to understand the content of the assignment to be able to help them (item 7 in Table 11.3). However, it should be noted that students who visited the university writing center strongly agreed with the statement about the need for tutors to understand the content of the assignment (88%) than those who reported having participated the in-house tutoring sessions (51%). Moreover, about 27% of the students who visited the in-house tutoring program responded neither agree nor disagree to the same question and about 21% of them reported that they disagree. This difference might be attributed to the familiarity of the course instructors' with the content of the assignments as opposed to writing center tutors. This fact was evident in the comments students provided when asked about which tutoring model they preferred and why (see the *Model and Tutor Preference* section). Many students reported that they prefer the in-house tutoring program since the tutors are their teachers. For example, one student said, "I believe that having a session with my class teacher is much more convenient as he would be able to provide help more efficiently since he is the one tutoring me".

Model and tutor type preference

Students were asked to indicate which model they would prefer for getting tutoring support. The majority of students preferred in-house tutoring (54%) over the writing center (46%). Students also provided open-ended comments

TABLE 11.3 Students' tutoring expectations by tutoring service type

Statement*	Strongly Agree WC	Strongly Agree IT	Agree WC	Agree IT	Neither Agree Nor Disagree WC	Neither Agree Nor Disagree IT	Disagree WC	Disagree IT	Strongly Disagree WC	Strongly Disagree IT
1 A visit to the writing lab/tutoring sessions should improve my assignment grade.	43%	**48%**	**46%**	40%	8%	10%	2%	1%	1%	1%
2 A visit to the writing lab/tutoring sessions should help me to become a better writer.	36%	35%	**51%**	**51%**	9%	11%	2%	2%	1%	1%
3 The writing lab/tutoring sessions is/are there to fix my grammar.	36%	32%	**45%**	**49%**	15%	14%	2%	4%	2%	1%
4 The writing lab/tutoring sessions is/are there to proofread and correct my paper.	43%	33%	**46%**	**53%**	8%	12%	2%	1%	1%	1%
5 The writing lab/tutoring sessions is/are there to help me better understand how to find errors in my own writing.	43%	40%	**46%**	**47%**	5%	11%	3%	1%	3%	1%
6 The writing lab/tutoring sessions is/are there to help me better understand how to improve my writing.	41%	38%	**49%**	**52%**	6%	8%	3%	1%	1%	1%
7 In order to be of assistance, the writing lab/tutoring sessions tutor should understand the content of my paper.	**52%**	21%	36%	**30%**	9%	27%	2%	21%	0%	1%

*All items adapted from Carter-Tod (1995).

elaborating on their answers (comments are reported verbatim – original grammar, spelling, and word choice) as shown below, with the positive and negative comments about in-house tutoring shown first:

Positive:

> "My first choice is tutoring because taking feedback from several professors helps in viewing my paper from different point of views and discover new mistakes."
>
> "The tutoring sessions is more beneficial than the writing center as the prof. knows exactly what is required of us regarding the assignments and such."
>
> "The tutoring session, are by some other teacher so you can get additional guidance and comments."

Negative:

> "I had a tutoring session with one of the teachers, he just gave me a feedback without even correcting grammar mistakes or at least looking at the format of the paper."
>
> "I think that I would most likely go to the office hours of my instructor, that is because the tutoring sessions are not well organized and planned."
>
> "Increase tutoring session hours during the week, and specify for each student a limited time with the teacher, at least 15 minutes so all students can review their paper."

Next we share the positive and negative comments about the university writing center:

Positive:

> "The writing center, because they understand Arabic and if i have good ideas but I don't know how to write them in English they can help me."
>
> "In the writing center... They are lots of student to share ideas with."
>
> "Comparing tutoring sessions to the writing center.. writing center helped me more in improving my term paper."

Negative:

> "Second choice is writing lab because it's inconvenient; very far away and needs booking in advance."
>
> "I haven't been to the writing center, coz of the appointment taking system, so it comes last."
>
> "The writing centre offers 30 minutes of assistance per session, which in my opinion, is not enough time to go through the entire paper thoroughly and proofread it."

In terms of whether students preferred to have the teachers conduct the tutoring sessions, 87% of the respondents said yes. Some of the comments students wrote are as follows:

> "Because he (teacher) will have the same way of telling the info."
> "Yes, because he would understand his students more and would know exactly what they are looking for. Also the teacher would know exactly what the students need to improve on."
> "Because we already know him/her."
> "He or she knows the actual progress."

Overall, more students seem to prefer the in-house tutoring scheme and would like to have their teachers conduct the tutoring sessions. Because the tutors were the course instructors themselves, many students believed that they were able to give more effective feedback than the writing center tutors. This view is also supported by the fact that in previous research students reported a mismatch between feedback received from tutors in the writing lab and from their teachers in class. This contrast is particularly important when it comes to the assignment requirements, where the tutor's expertise is crucial in ensuring effective tutoring sessions (see Dinitz & Harrington, 2014).

Another important aspect reported was students' frustration with the booking system and session time of the university writing center. Some students reported that they felt discouraged to visit the writing center because they have to book in advance and the time is limited to 30 minutes. The in-house tutoring system, on the other hand, offered a walk-in service since teacher tutors were available throughout the day. However, even though many students appreciated the convenience of the in-house system, some thought that the sessions were not well organized and that a booking system with time limits could improve the service.

Implications for policy, practice, and future research

The present study reported on implementing a unique tutoring scheme in the English Department, Foundation Program, at Qatar University. Introducing a curriculum-based model was the result of the competing concepts of centralization versus decentralization of services seen in many institutions. The English Department management at this university, motivated by the disadvantages of the centralized tutoring service, had decided to implement such an in-house curriculum-based tutoring program and to find out whether decentralizing the service could make a difference in students' perceptions and hence their satisfaction. For policymakers, the results of this experiment can provide information to reflect on the current institutional tutoring practices and to weigh in the advantages and disadvantages of each scheme. It can also inform their decisions on improving or altering current practices to better serve students' challenges in writing courses.

Our results showed that students are more likely to use the in-house tutorial service and prefer to have their teachers as tutors. However, results should be treated with caution since we did not compare the students' performance in the two systems. In other words, while students' preferred the in-house system, it is not clear whether it had an impact on their performance. Future research could examine whether such a curriculum-based teacher-tutor approach, compared to the university traditional tutoring system, can make a difference in students' writing performance. Future research could also investigate the underlying factors contributing to students' preferences. The present study attempted to do so by having an open-ended question for students to comment on their preferences, but follow-up interviews could be conducted to explore such factors in more depth. All in all, despite the limitations, this study sheds light on a different approach to writing tutoring and contributes to our understanding of effective tutoring practices.

References

Bell, D. C., & Elledge, S. R. (2008). Dominance and peer tutoring sessions with English language learners. *Learning Assistance Review, 13*(1), 17–30.

Bell, J. H. (2000). When hard questions are asked: Evaluating writing centers. *The Writing Center Journal, 21*(1), 7–28. https://www.jstor.org/stable/43442109.

Bielinska-Kwapisz, A. (2015). Impact of writing proficiency and writing center participation on academic performance. *International Journal of Educational Management, 29*(4), 382–394. https://doi.org/10.1108/IJEM-05-2014-0067.

Breuch, L. A. M. K., & Racine, S. J. (2000). Developing sound tutor training for online writing centers: Creating productive peer reviewers. *Computers and Composition, 17*(3), 245–263. https://doi.org/10.1016/S8755-4615(00)00034-7.

Carino, P., & Enders, D. (2001). Does frequency of visits to the writing center increase student satisfaction? A statistical correlation study – or story. *The Writing Center Journal, 22*(1), 83–103. https://www.jstor.org/stable/43442137.

Carter-Tod, S. (1995). The role of the writing center in the writing practices of L2 students. Unpublished Dissertation. Virginia Polytechnic Institute and State University.

Dinitz, S., & Harrington, S. (2014). The role of disciplinary expertise in shaping writing tutorials. *The Writing Center Journal, 33*(2), 73–98. https://www.jstor.org/stable/43443372.

Eckstein, G. (2016). Grammar correction in the writing centre: Expectations and experiences of monolingual and multilingual writers. *Canadian Modern Language Review, 77*(3), 360–382. http://doi.org/10.3138/cmlr.3605.

Faigley, L. F. (2015). Why writing centers work: Address delivered at the South-Central Writing Center Association Conference 13 February 2015. *Praxis, 12*, 2–7.

Grabe, W. (2001). Notes toward a theory of second language writing. In T. Silva & P. Matsuda (Eds.), *On second language writing* (pp. 39–58). Routledge.

Gray, R., & Hoyt, J. (2020). Changing attitudes: Impact of mandatory tutoring in writing centers. Curiosity. *Interdisciplinary Journal of Research and Innovation, 1*(1). https://doi.org/10.36898/001c.12711.

Hinkel, E. (2003). *Teaching academic ESL writing: Practical techniques in vocabulary and grammar.* Routledge. https://doi.org/10.4324/9781410609427.

Moussu, L. (2013). Let's talk! ESL students' needs and writing center philosophy. *TESL Canada Journal*, *30*(2), 55–68. https://doi.org/10.18806/tesl.v30i2.1142.

Niiler, L. (2003). The numbers speak: A pre-test of writing center outcomes using statistical analysis. *The Writing Lab Newsletter*, *28*(7), 6–9.

Nordlof, J. (2014). Vygotsky, scaffolding, and the role of theory in writing center work. *The Writing Center Journal*, *34*(1), 45–64. https://www.jstor.org/stable/43444147.

Nunan, D. (1999). *Second language teaching & learning*. Heinle & Heinle.

Osman, G. D. (2007). Student perceptions of the effectiveness of a mandatory remedial tutorial program in a developmental program at a historically black university (Doctoral Dissertation). Available from Proquest Dissertations and Theses Database. (UMI 3286867).

Palmquist, M. (2003). A brief history of computer support for writing centers and writing-across-the-curriculum programs. *Computers and Composition*, *20*(4), 395–413. https://doi.org/10.1016/j.compcom.2003.08.013.

Pfrenger, W., Blasiman, R. N., & Winter, J. (2017). "At first it was annoying": Results from requiring writers in developmental courses to visit the writing center. *Praxis: A Writing Center Journal*, *15*(1), 22–35.

Powers, J., & Nelson, J. (1995). L2 writers and the writing center: A national survey of writing center conferencing at graduate institutions. *Journal of Second Language Writing*, *4*(2), 113–138. https://doi.org/10.1016/1060-3743(95)90003-9.

Salem, L. (2016). Decisions... decisions: Who chooses to use the writing center? *The Writing Center Journal*, *35*(2), 147–171. https://www.jstor.org/stable/43824060.

Thompson, I. (2009). Scaffolding in the writing center: A microanalysis of an experienced tutor's verbal and nonverbal tutoring strategies. *Written Communication*, *26*(4), 417–453. https://doi.org/10.1177/0741088309342364.

Thompson, I., & Mackiewicz, J. (2014). Instruction, cognitive scaffolding, and motivational scaffolding in writing center tutoring. *Composition Studies*, *42*(1), 54–78.

Van Waes, L., Van Weijen, D., & Leijten, M. (2014). Learning to write in an online writing center: The effect of learning styles on the writing process. *Computers & Education*, *73*, 60–71. https://doi.org/10.1016/j.compedu.2013.12.009.

Williams, J. (2004). Tutoring and revision: Second language writers in the writing center. *Journal of Second Language Writing*, *13*(3), 173–201. https://doi.org/10.1016/j.jslw.2004.04.009.

Williams, J., & Severino, C. (2004). The writing center and second language writers. *Journal of Second Language Writing*, *13*(3), 165–172. https://doi.org/10.1016/j.jslw.2004.04.010.

Winder, R., Kathpalia, S. S., & Koo, S. L. (2016). Writing center tutoring sessions: Addressing students' concerns. *Educational Studies*, *42*(4), 323–339. https://doi.org/10.1080/03055698.2016.1193476.

12

TEACHING ACADEMIC WRITING IN THE ONLINE ENVIRONMENT

Challenges and benefits in the context of higher education in the UAE

Doaa Hamam and Christine Coombe

Introduction

The idea of teaching academic writing online in EF/SL contexts is not considered new or especially innovative. In fact, it was in use even before the pandemic. When the pandemic hit in March 2020, it became evident that online classes might be the future of teaching and learning due to pandemics and other factors, such as cost and logistics. Academic writing is important because it is the base of most other subjects and is a necessary skill required to obtain most degrees. Therefore, there is a specific focus on delivering and enhancing writing classes, especially in the online environment.

Issues that motivated the research

When the pandemic hit in 2020, both teachers and students were asked to move their classes online and had less than two weeks to do so. Everyone was overwhelmed and had doubts about whether this shift to online teaching was doable. Today, now that this stressful time has passed, many teachers have reflected on their experiences online and admit that overall the online teaching experience was successful. However, we wanted to dig deeper into this belief and analyze the challenges faced at that time as well as the benefits gained by teachers. It is for this purpose that we conducted this research.

Almost all universities in the UAE have English as the Medium of Instruction (EMI) for their courses, and teachers are generally supportive of this model. However, it is worth mentioning that some students, especially those with limited English abilities, have found this model problematic. In the UAE, the EMI model generally works well due to the nature of the diverse and international population of the country (Mouhanna, 2016).

It should be noted that even before the pandemic, universities in the UAE had adopted various models of online learning for their EMI courses, such as blended or hybrid learning. *Blended learning* refers to a course that combines online learning and face-to-face classes and includes material that supports the face-to-face classes. In contrast, *hybrid learning* includes face-to-face and online classes in a systematic approach, so students attend face-to-face classes for certain period of the course and do the rest of the work through the online material.

Sharma and Barrett (2008) provided three reasons for using a blended learning approach when teaching students how to write in a foreign language. The first is the fact that the learners expect to use technology in their language courses. The second is the flexibility that this mode of learning offers students, because it supports their ability to learn anywhere and at any time. The third reason is the direction that the authorities (e.g., Ministries of Education) are taking. As such, because of the importance of academic writing in EAP programs, offering it online might require a different pedagogy from the face-to-face instruction, as well as numerous resources for the model to be successful.

To deliver successful academic writing classes in the online environment, certain guidelines are recommended. In this chapter, we explore these guidelines and highlight the challenges and benefits of online classes.

Successful online academic writing classes need to be designed carefully so that they can be delivered effectively online. To achieve good course design, various resources to support teaching and learning must be available (such as the Learning Management System or LMS, a stable internet connection and a robust infrastructure, as well as tools and platforms for activity and course design). In addition, since such courses depend on technology, online resources (e.g., software licenses) and technical support must also be readily available.

Furthermore, academic writing classes typically incorporate peer collaboration. In the past, it was easy to ask students to work in pairs or groups in the physical classroom, but in online classes, students need to have a suitable platform for peer collaboration.

Feedback is another issue in online academic writing classes. Traditionally, teachers have given oral or written feedback on their students' writing samples, but we have seen more innovative ways to give feedback in online classes, such as providing audio or video feedback.

Another concern with the internet is the issue of plagiarism. There is no doubt that the advent of the internet and the development of user-friendly devices and programs like ChatGPT have exacerbated students' unethical behavior, from the blatant "cutting and pasting" of a few sentences without proper citation to purchasing a ghost-written essay. It is easy for students to cut and paste content and present it as if it were their own, and with the introduction of artificial intelligence (AI) writing tools, it has become even more difficult to track students' plagiarized work. However, the beauty of technology is that we also have plagiarism/AI content detectors, which help teachers discover copied and pasted content.

Technology will continue to produce such tools; however, besides the ethical considerations, the use of such tools may negate one of the important functions of writing, i.e., that it is regarded as a thinking process (Richardson, 2001). In addition, not every higher education teacher feels ready to use technology to teach academic writing online; therefore, professional development is critical to help teachers improve their knowledge about online teaching and provide the right tools.

Benefits of online academic writing classes

Some research has documented benefits of online academic writing classes. For instance, a study by Iwasaki et al. (2019) explored e-learning efficiency in improving 12 Japanese students' academic literacy skills in the context of higher education. These authors concluded that e-learning helped students improve their academic literacy, which, in turn, helped improve their academic writing skills. That study also compared the writing problems encountered during online and face-to-face classes, and the results revealed that there were no statistically significant differences in the students' scores in these two conditions. However, Iwasaki et al. also emphasized the importance of having a comprehensive learning environment to support students, especially in e-learning. Their study concluded that online tutoring helped in promoting the learners' autonomy.

Jun and Lee (2012) designed a three-week online academic writing course in the context of higher education in the USA. Their research revealed that students found the flexibility of their online classes to be a distinct advantage, especially the convenience of choosing the time and the place to study in an online writing course. Likewise, the teachers in that study mentioned some strengths of using online platforms in their writing courses. They described the students' enjoyment in exchanging comments with their peers and being able to access the online material at any time.

In a study by Dung (2020) during the COVID-19 outbreak, 205 students in Vietnam were surveyed to determine the advantages and disadvantages of online learning at Hong Bang International University. The results showed that several courses could be offered online efficiently, one of which was Academic Writing. In Greece, Jimoyiannis et al. (2018) concluded that an online academic writing intervention was an effective learning activity and helped the students improve their cognitive and learning presence.

Several studies have investigated the role of feedback in the online environment. In research by Tuzi (2004) in the USA, students reported that they benefited from e-feedback, and the researcher stated that although students preferred to have oral feedback, the e-feedback was more effective and helped students produce larger chunks of writing. In a study by Chong (2019), Hong Kong college students also benefited from e-feedback as it allowed them to engage and respond to the teacher's feedback. A more recent study by Saeed and Al Qunayeer (2022) conducted with undergraduates in Saudi Arabia reported that "interactive feedback also contributed to students' discussion of issues in their writing, engagement in accurate text revisions, and negotiation of feedback" (p. 360).

Challenges in online academic writing classes

Previous research has shown that students did not encounter major issues in their online academic writing classes (Ganobcsik-Williams et al., 2022; Hysaj & Hamam, 2020). It was found that no issues were encountered because of the robust infrastructure of the institution where they studied and the availability of various resources like the LMS, internet, and subscriptions to technological tools among others. Some students, such as those in the investigation by Jun and Lee (2012), did note challenges. They felt there was less interaction with the teacher in the online course and there were no immediate answers to their questions or solutions to their problems. The students also mentioned that the instructions given by their teachers were sometimes confusing and that they could not establish a connection between certain tasks and the essay assignment.

Yet another study by Sam'ah (2022) found that although teachers in Indonesia had positive reactions towards teaching academic writing online, there were many challenges, such as the instability of the internet connection and students keeping their cameras off. Another issue was that students lacked encouragement from their teachers in the distance or online environment. Indonesian students also expressed the same sentiment in a study conducted by Rohayati and Rustandi (2021). These students sometimes lacked motivation to do the required work.

In contrast, Rahmat et al. (2022) mentioned that one problem in online academic writing classes in Malaysia was the heavy cognitive load required. These authors reported that one strategy to reduce the cognitive load is to use color codes and graphic organizers. Moreover, the idea of students' engagement has been expressed as another challenge. According to Tercero's (2020) study in the higher education context in the USA, two out of three instructors felt writing should not be taught online because the teachers are unable to engage students in online learning classes. However, because there are many strategies to encourage engagement in such classes, we believe that the online option should not be excluded.

Regarding the feedback element, Jun and Lee (2012) stated that teachers complained about the difficulty of offering online feedback to their students through Moodle. One teacher mentioned that technological issues hindered her teaching in the online environment. Most teachers in the study preferred face-to-face teaching as they believed it gave them more opportunities to interact with students and give them immediate feedback.

Technology in online academic writing classes

As early as 2007, Warschauer opined that information and communication technologies were having a profound effect on all aspects of language use, especially in written communication. He stated that the purposes for which we write, the genres of written communication, and the nature of the audience and the author were all changing at a rapid pace with much of our communication becoming computer-mediated (Warschauer, 2007). As the nature of communication was rapidly changing, so were changes in the global higher education sector. Institutions of higher education were developing blended, online, and other technology-driven approaches to teaching and learning. These developments have meant that we now have technology-enhanced academic writing approaches utilized in many colleges and universities worldwide (Boyle et al., 2019; Hamam & Hysaj, 2021).

Mobile technology (especially the use of smartphones) has become very popular as a teaching tool, especially in the UAE, and it seems it is here to stay. As a result, teachers no longer need to rely merely on the asynchronous teaching model, including in the teaching of academic writing. Instead, they are encouraged to engage in and incorporate blended or hybrid learning into their teaching and technology-enhanced online academic writing.

Research questions

In this chapter, we report on our investigation of UAE-based higher education (HE) teachers' perspectives on the challenges and benefits that resulted from teaching academic writing on line. The main research question developed for the purpose of the current study asks, what are the challenges and benefits encountered in online academic writing classes?

Several sub-questions emerged from the main research question. These questions were the basis of an online questionnaire we circulated to teachers based in university academic writing programs in the UAE:

1. What resources did you use in your online writing classes or when teaching writing online?
2. How was feedback offered to your students during your online academic writing classes?
3. Did you work with the library or any other entity to support your online academic writing classes? Why? Why not?
4. Did you involve peer collaboration in your online academic writing classes? If yes, how? If not, why not?
5. What professional development did you feel you needed to enhance your teaching and online academic writing classes?

6. Did you encounter issues with academic dishonesty and/or plagiarism during your online academic writing classes? If yes, how were these cases handled?
7. Did you encounter technological issues during teaching online academic writing classes?

Research methods

Context

The research was conducted by distributing our questionnaire to writing teachers in seven institutions of higher education in the United Arab Emirates, both public and private. All these institutions use English as a medium of instruction, not only for language classes but also for subject matter content. As per government mandate, all academic writing teachers have a minimum education level of a Masters or Doctoral degree in TESOL and/or Applied Linguistics. In our experience, most if not all institutions are highly technological environments with both teachers and students having a number of devices (i.e., laptops, phones, and iPads) that are fully integrated into classroom practice.

Participants

The questionnaire was sent to a purposive sample of teachers employed at various universities in the UAE. Purposive sampling is a form of non-probability sampling in which researchers rely on their own judgment when choosing members of the population to participate in their surveys. The main goal of purposive sampling is to focus on particular characteristics of a population that are of interest, which will best enable researchers to answer their research questions (Black, 2010). The 12 participants who responded (out of 40 who were invited, a response rate of 30%) were experienced teachers of academic writing. They had all taught academic writing, both in a traditional classroom setting as well as online during the pandemic.

Data collection procedures

We utilized a qualitative approach to collect data through a questionnaire that was developed specifically for the purpose of the study. The questionnaire included seven open-ended questions, paralleling the sub-questions listed above, in order to explore the following technology-based themes: the use of online resources, how feedback was offered, the role of library resources, peer collaboration, professional development, technical issues, and issues of academic dishonesty and plagiarism.

Data analysis procedures

The data were first extracted from the online form used to collect the responses, and the responses to the seven questions were thematically categorized and divided into thematic units and then analyzed using a grounded theory approach. Pseudonyms were used to protect the identities of the participants and their institutions. In presenting our findings, we focused on grouping the challenges and the benefits described by the teachers together to have an overview of the results.

Findings and discussion

In this section we present the findings for each of the seven questionnaire items and relate the responses back to the research questions as well as the secondary sources.

The first question asked participants which LMS was currently in use at their institution. The most frequently identified Learning Management System (LMS) used by five out of the 12 respondents in this study was Blackboard Learn. Other LMS's used were Moodle, Canvas, Google Classrooms, Microsoft Teams, and Edmodo.

Question two inquired as to "What online resources did you use in your online writing classes? Or when teaching academic writing online?" Responses to this question were not consistent and were mainly centered around resources for teaching as well as for assessment. The top response mentioned by teachers in this study was the use of shared drives and/or document features like Google Documents and/or Google Forms, with four teachers mentioning these two resources. Other frequently mentioned teaching resources noted by the teachers were (in order of frequency) Grammarly, the Zoom platform and its features (e.g., breakout groups), various chat features on LMS and WhatsApp, Flipgrid, and web resources such as Read, Write, Think (https://www.readwritethink.org/). IELTS writing practice and Vocabulary Profiler (www.lextutor.ca), as well as the FK Readability Index on Microsoft Word. Other frequently cited assessment resources were Kahoot!, Mentimeter, and Nearpod.

The third question on our survey queried teachers' use of feedback and how it was offered to students in online academic writing classes. Methods of feedback that teachers used included comments in Track Changes and/or in writing, and anti-plagiarism tools like Turnitin or Safeassign reports. The most frequent mechanism for offering feedback in the online environment was the use of voice notes or recordings, with six of the 12 participants mentioning these feedback tools. Daria (one of the teachers who responded) described the situation this way:

> Being in an online context, I experimented with sending my students voice notes, either through our LMS or through WhatsApp. I think this was a popular way for students to get feedback, and I am continuing to use this method even now that we are back in the classroom.

In contrast, Ahmed believed that the feedback element of teaching academic writing online was a cause for stress:

> I believe the pandemic time was stressful for everyone. Teaching academic writing online was a big challenge because I was used to giving feedback face to face. However, when we moved online, I spent a lot of time explaining each comment I made to the students' essays. That was really time-consuming. The biggest success I would say is the shared document where students collaborated and worked together and I was able to monitor that in real time.

The use of peer collaboration was a popular activity for the teachers who participated in our study, with the great majority of teachers (10 out of 12) stating that they regularly encouraged students to engage in peer collaboration and assessment. The most common way of doing so was through the use of break-out rooms in their respective LMS platforms. The small number of teachers (two out of 12) who did not encourage or engage in peer collaborative activities declared that it was not a course requirement.

According to Sally, peer collaboration, especially on group projects, was a key element in the stress she suffered from during her online academic writing classes.

> My writing classes depend on group projects, and sometimes it was challenging to manage the conflict between group members during the online time. The whole group was not always available together; when some came, one or two were absent and so on. Therefore, we depended heavily on emails to finish the task and resolve the conflict. I also felt the students were not motivated to work online because of the pandemic stress and the lack of social life.

An additional question on our survey asked participants to comment on any issues they had with plagiarism and academic dishonesty in their online academic writing courses. In line with the literature, a large majority (11 out of 12) reported issues with plagiarism either from the "copy-paste" culture and/or ghost-written essays, assignments, or projects. The most common means of dealing with this issue was to require students to submit their writing through popular anti-plagiarism software like SafeAssign or Turnitin, as well as through the use of a LockDown Browser Monitor program employed during online assessments. In some instances, when students were found to be plagiarizing, zero grades were awarded, or point deductions were enforced.

Michael noticed more academically dishonest practices among his students once his classes went online.

> In my writing class, students are asked to write on paper. However, to my surprise, my students started plagiarising after moving to online courses. They were first-year students and just wanted to finish the task by copying and

pasting from the internet since they could submit a soft copy. I explained that this was unacceptable and that their work should be authentic. However, it took several attempts until they were convinced and stopped copying. I had to show them several originality reports that detect the copied text and its source, and they were surprised to see this from the teacher's point of view. I wish that students would take a separate course on plagiarism and how to avoid it before joining academic writing classes.

A final question on the survey asked teachers what professional development (PD) they needed to become better at teaching academic writing in an online environment. The top response was that PD would help them acquire increased digital literacy. The second most common answers with seven responses were learning about more online platforms and becoming acquainted with useful tools in peer collaboration, feedback, and online citation and referencing work. Hana shared her views on this issue:

> At the beginning of the pandemic, I felt the need for training. I was overwhelmed by the many things I had to do at the same time, especially in the live online classes. Students complained, and I felt I was very slow. As time passed, and I got used to multi-tasking in the online class, things were easier for me, and I could manage the class properly. However, I guess the biggest challenge for me was the training I needed.

Our research on the benefits and challenges of teaching academic writing online revealed a number of similarities with the literature prior to the COVID-19 pandemic. Several studies reported on the positive side of teaching academic writing online (Iwasaki et al., 2019; Dung, 2020; Jimoyiannis et al., 2018; Jun & Lee, 2012), which revealed positive outcomes to online academic writing classes.
As for the benefits of the experience, Catherine stated,

> At the beginning of the pandemic, I (and my students) looked at the online experience in a positive way in that by keeping safe and studying online it would expose us to a new (more flexible) way of learning. I also welcomed the opportunity to expand my teaching repertoire by learning to teach online. I remember back then that I engaged in many great (and free) online PD opportunities that helped me expand my skills.

Maya identified a different challenge:

> The biggest challenge I faced was asking students to turn on their cameras in the online classes, and in the asynchronous courses, I was unsure of how to motivate students to finish their online work by the deadline.

Daria shared this point:

> My experience during the pandemic was an extremely positive one at the beginning, even though I missed seeing my students in the face-to-face classroom. The online classes went very well and we (students and I) were able to use technology to support our classes. We enjoyed the online activities and the students were very responsive.

Unlike many teachers who experienced challenges during the pandemic, Ayman had only positive things to say about his online experience of teaching academic writing:

> I think my online classes went very well, and I faced no challenges. First, my students were given the freedom to access the material on Moodle any time and from anywhere to study at their own pace. I used Edmodo to manage class discussions, and the students were very active and engaged. For assignments, I used Turnitin for plagiarism detection and gave comments through the same platform. I dare to say that during online classes, everything was positive and went very well.

Previous research refered to the challenges encountered in online academic writing classes, such as the study by Jun and Lee (2012), who encountered issues with feedback and interaction; Sam'ah (2022), who reported issues with internet connectivity; and Rohayati and Rustandi (2021), who found issues related to students' motivation. According to the data, challenges were very similar to the literature pre-pandemic in that teachers reported less interaction with their students, and a drop in motivation on the part of the students as well as technical issues resulting from connectivity, instability of the LMS, etc. For Daria,

> Students from my institution suddenly found themselves at home where not just them but several of their brothers and sisters were simultaneously studying online. This resulted in major Wi-Fi connectivity issues as well as a shortage of available computers. This plus the fact that students often would not turn on their cameras during the lesson created issues with student rapport.

Catherine revealed that

> Even with 30+ years of teaching experience, I felt like a real novice at the beginning of the pandemic. I remember that early on I just wanted to do something simple like circle a word on the screen, but I just couldn't figure out how to do it. One of my students must have figured out what I was trying to do and sent me screenshots through a private message on our LMS. He saved me that day, and I came to the realization that we (teachers and students) were all in this together. I really wish I could remember that student's name!!!

In examining the findings of our study, for us, the most novel and interesting finding is that at the beginning of the research (not surprisingly) many issues were identified by the teachers. However, in hindsight, the great majority of participants look back at the online teaching experience of academic writing as a success. For us, this finding means that the teacher participants were able to find solutions to the issues that arose in their experience of working from home during the pandemic, as well as and subsequently, when teachers gradually shifted to other types of blended and hybrid forms of teaching.

Implications for policy, practice, and future research

If our students are to benefit from online academic writing instruction, online classes must be a joint effort among all involved, including teachers, students, and university authorities. In addition to training sessions in the use of online academic writing programs, teachers and students must have access to cost-effective and powerful internet and Wi-Fi packages, the technological devices needed to succeed, and learning spaces, either residential or otherwise.

A policy also needs to be put in place for ethical technology-mediated academic writing that includes stakeholder awareness of the difference between using appropriate sources and plagiarizing others' works. This policy must also accommodate recent AI advances like ChatGPT, which developed before the data in this chapter were collected. To improve online academic writing teaching practice, increased digital literacy, both self-directed and other-directed, must be prioritized for English language teaching professionals. Especially important is introducing more engaging teaching methods and/or gamified elements for online academic writing courses. In addition to the apps and technology tools used by the participants in this study, teachers need access to new technology tools and increased support. A priority based on the results of this preliminary research is better ways to incorporate peer collaboration in a technology-mediated environment.

Future research related to teaching academic writing online should first investigate the effectiveness or lack thereof of the different modes of instruction (i.e., traditional face-to-face classrooms, blended or hybrid modes of learning, or fully online teaching) in the UAE higher education context. Additional research might also focus on how best to support students in an online academic writing environment. Finally, as the use (or misuse) of AI has arrived on the educational scene in the UAE, more research on how best to incorporate AI in the teaching and learning of online academic writing is urgently needed.

References

Black, K. (2010). *Business statistics: Contemporary decision making* (6th ed.). John Wiley & Sons.

Boyle, J., Ramsay, S., & Struan, A. (2019). The Academic Writing Skills Programme: A model for technology-enhanced, blended delivery of an academic writing programme. *Journal of University Teaching & Learning Practice*, *16*(4). https://doi.org/10.53761/1.16.4.4.

Chong, S. W. (2019). College students' perception of e-feedback: A grounded theory perspective. *Assessment & Evaluation in Higher Education*, *44*(7), 1090–1105.

Dung, D. T. H. (2020). The advantages and disadvantages of virtual learning. *IOSR Journal of Research & Method in Education*, *10*(3), 45–48.

Ganobcsik-Williams, L., Curry, N., & Neculai, C. (2022). Academic writing in times of crisis: Refashioning writing tutor development for online environments. *Journal of Academic Writing*, *12*(1), 10–21.

Hamam, D., & Hysaj, A. (2021, July). Technological pedagogical and content knowledge (TPACK): Higher education teachers' perspectives on the use of TPACK in online academic writing classes. In C. Stephanidis, M. Antona, & S. Ntoa (Eds.). *International Conference on Human-Computer Interaction* (pp. 51–58). Springer.

Hysaj, A., & Hamam, D. (2020). Academic writing skills in the online platform: A success, a failure or something in between? A study on perceptions of higher education students and teachers in the UAE. In H. Mitsuhara, Y. Goda, Y. Ohashi, M. Rodrigo, J. Shen, N. Venkatarayalu, G. Wong, M. Yamada, & C-U. Lei (Eds.), *2020 IEEE International Conference on Teaching, Assessment, and Learning for Engineering (TALE)* (pp. 668–673). IEEE.

Iwasaki, C., Tada, Y., Furukawa, T., Sasaki, K., Yamada, Y., Nakazawa, T., & Ikezawa, T. (2019). Design of e-learning and online tutoring as learning support for academic writing. *Asian Association of Open Universities Journal*, *14*(2), 85–96.

Jimoyiannis, A., Schiza, E. I., & Tsiotakis, P. (2018). Students' self-regulated learning through online academic writing in a course blog. In D. Sampson, D. Ifenthaler, J. M. Spector, & P. Isaías (Eds.), *Digital technologies: Sustainable innovations for improving teaching and learning* (pp. 111–129). Springer.

Jun, H. G., & Lee, H. W. (2012). Student and teacher trial and perceptions of an online ESL academic writing unit. *Procedia-Social and Behavioral Sciences*, *34*, 128–131.

Mouhanna, M. (2016). *English as a medium of instruction in the tertiary education setting of the UAE: The perspectives of content teachers* (Master's dissertation, University of Exeter).

Rahmat, N. H., Sukimin, I. S., Adam, S., Bithiah, S., & Varma, N. F. M. Z. (2022). Reducing cognitive load in learning academic writing online: The case for colours. *International Journal of Academic Research in Business and Social Sciences*, *12*(1), 2138–2149.

Richardson, J. C. (2001). *Examining social presence in online courses in relation to students' perceived learning and satisfaction.* State University of New York at Albany.

Rohayati, D., & Rustandi, A. (2021). Writing argumentative essay in online academic writing class: Students' voice, difficulties, and writing enjoyment. *Jurnal Akrab Juara*, *6*(4), 210–220.

Saeed, M. A., & Al Qunayeer, H. S. (2022). Exploring teacher interactive e-feedback on students' writing through Google Docs: Factors promoting interactivity and potential for learning. *The Language Learning Journal*, *50*(3), 360–377.

Sam'ah, I. U. (2022). *The Indonesian academic writing lecturers' perceptions, issues, and strategies toward teaching writing at a distance* (Doctoral dissertation, Universitas Islam Malang).

Sharma, P., & Barrett, B. (2008). *Blended learning: Using technology in and beyond the language classroom.* Macmillan.

Tercero, T. M. (2020). Self-efficacy and designing and teaching online academic writing courses for multilingual writers (Doctoral dissertation, The University of Arizona).

Tuzi, F. (2004). The impact of e-feedback on the revisions of L2 writers in an academic writing course. *Computers and Composition, 21*(2), 217–235.

Warschauer, M. (2007). Technology and writing. In J. Cummins & C. Davison (Eds.), *International handbook of English language teaching* (pp. 907–918). Springer.

PART IV
Policy

13
LINGUISTIC VISIBILITY IN THE UNIVERSITY OF BAHRAIN'S LINGUISTIC LANDSCAPE

Yasser Ahmed Gomaa

Introduction

Being a linguist does not always entail closely examining reference texts or scholarly papers in a library. In recent years, linguists have been able to gather data by utilizing digital cameras to take pictures of what is known as the linguistic landscape (hereafter LL). It includes notice boards, traffic signs, shop signs, written information in shop windows, advertising posters, and large boards used to display advertisements, as well as flags, banners, graffiti, menus, public transport, shopping centers, T-shirts, tattoos, billboards, and names of buildings in public places.

Public spaces are filled with signage that carries important meanings and context for society. These signs constitute an essential means of communication. They help us develop a mental image of a particular location and set it apart from other locations. Due to their contribution towards modernity and cosmopolitanism, these signs constitute an integral element of the public sphere. As they have become a part of the urban scenery, they form the LL, which Landry and Bourhis (1997) described as "the language of public road signage, advertising billboards, street names, place names, commercial shop signage, and public signage on government buildings [that] combines to form the linguistic landscape of a given territory, region, or urban agglomeration" (p. 25). Accordingly, LL is a public space construction that serves as a symbol. LLs display a range of language and scripts on public signage. Researchers from around the world have examined the "written form" of public spheres languages (Gorter 2006, p. 2), paying particular attention to "multilingual contexts" (Coulmas, 2009, p. 14).

The LL has become a popular research focus in sociolinguistics during the past few years. Many scholars (e.g., Gorter, 2013; Shohamy & Gorter, 2009) argue that the LL is not produced arbitrarily but is the result of interlocking variables

DOI: 10.4324/9781003312444-17

that influence language decisions. These variables include language ideologies, language policies, and communication requirements. That is, "the presence (or absence) of specific language items, displayed in specific languages, in a specific manner, sends direct and indirect messages with regard to the centrality versus the marginality of certain languages in society" (Shohamy, 2006, p. 110).

Accordingly, LLs are considered prominent symbols of the state of languages in multilingual cultures due to their ties to language policy, which is "a body of ideas, laws, regulations, rules and practices intended to achieve the planned language change in the societies, group or system" (Kaplan & Baldauf, 1997, p. xi). Language policy has been defined as "a set of laws or regulations or rules enacted by an authoritative body (like a government) as part of a language plan" (Johnson, 2013, p. 4). Spolsky argues that a speech community language policy has three elements:

> (1) its language practices – the habitual pattern of selecting among the varieties that make up its linguistic repertoire; (2) its language beliefs or ideology – the beliefs about language and language use; and (3) any specific efforts to modify or influence that practice by any kind of language intervention, planning, or management.
>
> *(Spolsky, 2004, p. 5)*

Therefore, language policy is related to the LL and an area that LL studies cover.

Dal Negro (2009) argues that LLs reflect language policy. In addition, Puzey (2012) maintains that LL influences how people perceive language policy. Cenoz and Gorter (2009) assert that LL language policies are strongly tied to language policies governing how languages are used in the media, in education, and in other sectors. Furthermore, Shohamy (2006) indicates that there are various contexts in which language policy is expressed, including languages that are presented in public signage, schools' official language of instruction and exams, the languages that are referred to as a country's official language(s), and the languages used in government buildings. She argues that the legitimacy and superiority of certain languages over others are represented by the LL.

Another element that aids in our understanding of language policy is the distinction between bottom-up and top-down signs. Top-down or official signs are those produced by an authority (such as a government or company), whereas bottom-up or unofficial signs are those produced by individuals and are purported to be the result of personal preferences. Shohamy (2006) asserts that the distinction between the languages displayed on top-down and bottom-up signage in public spaces sheds light on the language policy. Puzey (2012) argues that top-down displays of LL reveal the authorities' preferred language, whereas bottom-up signage demonstrates whether the general populace has adopted and is adhering to this choice. According to Ben-Rafael (2009), given that different signs are produced by various actors for varied audiences, the discrepancy between top-down and bottom-up signage is crucial. In addition, top-down signs "serve official policies" (p. 49). In terms of the context of this study, Article 2 of the Kingdom of Bahrain's constitution states that Arabic is the country's official language.

Issues that motivated the research

Most of the research on LLs has been conducted by looking at the existence of multiple languages that constitute the linguistic repertoire of different urban settings, focusing on store signs, billboards, public signs on government buildings, etc. Gorter (2013) argues that investigating semi-public spaces LL (e.g., universities) is a promising field for future investigation, since little research has been done in such areas.

The LL of university premises is an important component of the LL of any city or country because universities are semi-public spheres. They are homes for many international academic conferences, as well as interactions between academics and students from different cultures. Universities develop local amenities and services to accommodate both native and foreign students. The community's overall awareness of the larger LL can be enhanced by knowing how the university LL is formed and how students from other nations interact and communicate.

At the time of this writing, no research has been done on the Arabian Gulf universities' LLs. Therefore, this chapter aims to provide a perspective on the LL of the University of Bahrain (hereafter referred to as UoB – one of the Arabian Gulf region's higher education institutions), by considering the textual data that is available on its campus signage. The study also examined the UoB students' perceptions of the languages employed on these signs. In addition, it investigated whether the UoB language policy, if it has one, is reflected in its LL. My analysis (1) determined how often certain languages are used on the UoB campus signage, and (2) shed light on how Arabic and English serve as both informational and symbolic systems, in addition to their status in the UoB campus LL.

Many studies have treated LL as a tool to evaluate and understand language situations in certain sociolinguistic contexts (e.g., milieu, topics, participator, and communication modes) The language on signs provides an image of the status of, hierarchy of, functional domains of, and attitudes toward languages in bilingual and multilingual contexts, as well as their spread and use (e.g., Blommaert, 2013). LLs have certain symbolic functions and particular signs' placement in a public area is seldom random. Considering this point, Landry and Bourhis (1997) maintain that "the linguistic landscape may serve important informational and symbolic functions as a marker of relative power and status of the linguistic communities inhabiting the territory" (p. 23). Furthermore, LL studies have centered on the use of English as a globally recognized language and its prominence in the public domain in specific physical settings (e.g., Kroon et al., 2013).

Research questions

This chapter explores the LL of the UoB, Kingdom of Bahrain. It addresses the following research questions:

1. What languages are present in the UoB LL?
2. What position does English hold in relation to other languages displayed on the UoB campus signage?
3. Which signs, top-down or bottom-up, are more common on the UoB campus signage?
4. What are the UoB students' attitudes towards the languages used on signage?
5. What are the UoB students' choices about the order of the languages on signage?

It is anticipated that addressing these questions will improve the study of higher education institutions' LL and lead to further related research.

Research methods

Context

The UoB was founded in 1986. It is the only national public higher education institution in the Kingdom of Bahrain. It provides a variety of degrees and programs, given the philosophy that students' futures do not end at a given academic level but instead continue as they pursue further degrees. Due to its location in an Arab and Islamic nation, UoB focuses on preserving the Arabic and Islamic culture, thus expressing its objective of bridging the past and the present and to meet difficulties head-on in the future.

In 2022, 34,403 students were enrolled at the UoB with 1,908 being international students. At the time of this writing, 1,383 people worked for the institution, 66% of whom were natives of Bahrain and 34% were foreign.

It is noteworthy to mention here that the present study is multifaceted in nature. It is not only an attempt to explain how languages are used in the UoB LL, but also an attempt to demonstrate how such usage is perceived by the intended audience, the sign readers.

Participants

As indicated in the fourth and fifth research questions, I sought to gather information from UoB students, for which I used an online questionnaire. Questionnaire responses were received from 213 UoB students – 52 males (24.4%) and 161 females (75.6%). In terms of their nationalities, 196 were Bahraini (92%), two were Indian (0.9%), three were Saudi (1.4%), four were Jordanian (1.9%), five were Egyptian

(2.3%), and three were Pakistani (1.4%). The respondents' ages ranged from 18 to 23, with an average of 19.78 years.

Data collection procedures

Two methods of data acquisition were utilized. The first was the compilation of a photographic corpus and the second was an online questionnaire.

To answer the first three research questions, a Nikon D5200 digital camera was used to compile a corpus of 409 high-quality photographs of the UoB campus signage, displayed on or outside the UoB buildings. For the purposes of this chapter, a *sign* is defined as any description or identification available in internal UoB campus roads or affixed to or integrated into a building and is intended to direct or attract attention to or announce a place, activity, or institution by means of language. The photographic corpus reflects the general signage at the university. It includes a range of both top-down and bottom-up signage (e.g., building names, guiding information, warning signs, and directory signs).

In addition, to comprehend the respondents' perspectives on language use in the UoB campus signage as well as their perceptions of the actual depiction of the campus LL and policymaking, an online questionnaire was used to gather data from UoB students, the sign readers. Google Forms software was used to create this questionnaire, which consisted of three parts. Part I covered the respondents' demographic background. Part II focused on how UoB students perceived the use of language on campus signage. It aimed at identifying the UoB students' preferences and order of the languages displayed on campus signage. Part III addressed students' standpoints on the significance of languages displayed on campus. I obtained approval from the UoB administration before administering the questionnaire. Then the survey was sent via email to all the UoB students.

Data analysis procedures

The photographs in the corpus were all tallied and processed in Excel. They were then classified by categories. The categorizing process began by dividing the signs into two main groups: monolingual (signs that only utilized one language) and bilingual (those that use two languages). The language(s) displayed on each sign were also identified. In addition, the signs were classified into top-down and bottom-up groups based on their content.

The students' responses to the questionnaire were tallied and percentages were computed. The respondents' open-ended comments were also reviewed, and representative quotes were chosen to illustrate the students' perspectives.

Findings and discussion

Analysis of the corpus data

The first three research questions were addressed by analyzing the photographic corpus. The results indicate that the UoB LL does not reflect high linguistic diversity. Based on the language used, Arabic and English are the only languages presented on the UoB campus signage, which uses Arabic much more frequently than English. This finding is in line with the declaration in Article 2 of the Kingdom of Bahrain's constitution that Arabic is the country's official language. It is used with or without English. There are more signs that display Arabic, both with and without English, than the ones that utilize English alone. Examples of each are shown in Figure 13.1. Of the total of 409 signs in the corpus, 148 where Arabic only, 122 were English only, and 139 were bilingual signs in Arabic and English.

The use of Arabic in signs serves more than just informational and symbolic purposes; it also serves as an important symbol of national identity. Arabic is the embodiment of culture, the lifeblood, and the soul of the Kingdom of Bahrain. It is a major component of the UoB tradition and history. According to Kotze (2010), signage that plays such a role engenders a sense of belonging among the inhabitants of a certain place, just like Arabic provides for the UoB. Alsohaibani maintains that the

> Arabic language, as one of the most spoken languages in the world, is seen by Arabs as a powerful symbol that reflects their national identity and their sense of belonging to past glory, a combatant present and a bright future.
>
> *(Alsohaibani, 2016, p. 19)*

The UoB LL does not include other languages (e.g., French, Japanese, Korean, Turkish). This finding is related to the fourth research question, which addressed the UoB students' attitudes towards the languages used on signs. Some of their comments include the following: (1) "I believe that we should use French as well; however, we shouldn't forget that Arabic comes first, and that the Arabic

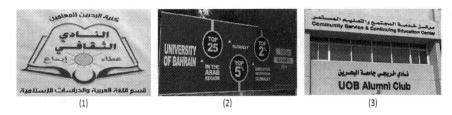

FIGURE 13.1 Examples of UoB campus signs
Note: (1) Example of Arabic UoB campus signage, (2) Example of English UoB campus signage, and (3) Example of Arabic-English UoB campus signage.

language should be on top." (2) "I personally believe the more languages the better." (3) "I do speak Korean, but it wasn't an option!" (4) "Where is Japanese language?" and (5) "There is more languages that students speak that aren't listed above, example: Korean, Japanese, Turkish and these languages are taught in Bahrain either inside university or outside, so please add them."

It is worth noting here that Scollon and Scollon (2003) contend that the languages used on signs may represent social power dynamics in a particular society, "because they are systems of choice, and no choices are neutral in the social world" (p. 7). Accordingly, using Arabic and English in the UoB LL is a deliberate action, which is planned and decided beforehand. It happens on purpose rather than by chance.

The analysis of the corpus also revealed that there is a low number of non-verbal signs on the UoB campus (see Figure 13.2). The use of these non-verbal signs may reflect the efforts of the UoB to solve some of the problems brought on by some people's inability to read Arabic and English. These signs may be used by students, staff, or visitors who cannot read English or Arabic signs as a form of communication across linguistic boundaries.

I attempted to learn more about the policies and processes used to create signs on the UoB campus. It turns out that there are no official written guidelines, norms, or regulations governing the creation of signs displayed on campus. That is, there is no language policy that determines the language used on signs. However, there are ongoing efforts to enhance signage in terms of design, interpretation, and presentation.

As early as 1997, Landry and Bourhis argued that language planning and LL are closely related. The languages used and the order in which they are shown on signs are determined by language rules and regulations related to the target sign-readers' mother tongue and the rules governing minority language use, if any. But in the case of the LL at UoB, since there are no rules or regulations, the practices documented in this chapter generate a de facto policy (i.e., an actual, but unofficially recognized UoB policy).

Accordingly, language policy transpires in signage. As a result, the most prominent languages in a community are frequently listed first on signs, followed by the second-most prominent language. The findings of this study demonstrate that English is being promoted as an official language and as a communication tool. This

FIGURE 13.2 Examples of nonverbal elements in UoB campus signage

finding refers to the value of both Arabic and English in the Bahraini academic domain as well as in the UoB, as indicated by one informant, who observed that "Arabic is an important language, and we need to maintain it. But English is a universal language and everyone enrolled in UoB should be able to read it. Therefore, I think signage should be in both Arabic and English." Another person wrote,

> Sign boards should be in both languages English + Arabic because there are lots of foreigners in Bahrain. But in some cases, we can notice some sign boards with only one single language which is English and that is a real shame for Arab countries! And it might lead those who do not know or understand English to misunderstand the purposes of the sign boards.

Many scholars (e.g., Ben-Rafael et al., 2006; Cenoz & Gorter, 2006; Gomaa, 2017; Landry & Bourhis, 1997) have investigated the differences between top-down and bottom-up language use in signage. In the context of this chapter, *top-down signage* is defined as the official signage that the UoB has placed on its campus, while *bottom-up signage* is the unofficial signage placed by retailers who are authorized to rent a space on the UoB campus for commercial purposes (e.g., retail restaurants across campus, mini market, beauty salon). The results of this study demonstrate that top-down signage, which is both monolingual and bilingual, makes up 94% of all signs, as contrasted with bottom-up signage, which makes up only 6% of all signs. Figures 13.3 and 13.4, respectively, are typical examples of top-down and bottom-up signs found in the corpus.

Analysis of the questionnaire data

Cronbach's alpha was used to determine the reliability of the twelve questionnaire items. It indicated that the degree of stability for the questionnaire responses is 0.705. This alpha value indicates that the respondents were able to provide consistent answers to the survey questions. To put it another way, they have not reacted to it in a careless or arbitrary manner. Responses to the first survey question ("How many

FIGURE 13.3 Examples of top-down UoB campus signage

FIGURE 13.4 Examples of bottom-up UoB campus signage

languages can you read?") revealed that, out of the 213 respondents, 64 (30%) are monolingual readers, 107 (50.2%) are bilingual readers, 35 (16.4%) are trilingual readers, and seven (3.3%) are quadrilingual readers. Also, 199 (93.4%) of the respondents can read Arabic, 186 (87.3%) can read English, 81 (38%) can read Malayalam, 77 (36.2%) can read Hindi, 76 (36%) can read Tamil, 25 (11.7%) can read French, 19 (9%) can read German, nine (4.2%) can read Chinese, and six (2.8%) can read Tagalog.

The second question asked, "Which language(s) do you believe are most frequently used on the UoB campus?" It sought to document how participants perceived the languages used on the campus signage at UoB. The results show that most participants, 97 (45.5%), believe that Arabic-English bilingual signs are the most frequently used, while 62 (29.1%) referred to English-only signs, 45 (21.1%) mentioned Arabic-only signs, and nine (4.2%) referred to Arabic-English-French trilingual signs.

The third and fourth survey questions asked, "Which language(s) do you believe are essential for students to learn on the UoB campus?" and "Which language(s) do you consider to be crucial for students' day-to-day experience on UoB campus?" These items were designed to elicit participants' overall opinions and attitudes on the use of several languages on the UoB campus. The responses to the third question show that 151 (70.9%) of them referred to both Arabic and English, while 20 (9.4%) mentioned English, and 42 (19.7%) mentioned Arabic as being important. Regarding responses to the fourth question, 69 (32%) respondents felt that Arabic was crucial to students' daily life on the UoB campus. Twenty-five (11.7%) respondents noted English, while 119 (64.3%) respondents indicated both Arabic and English. These results demonstrate how important bilingualism is on the UoB campus for both academic settings and day-to-day university activities.

Question 5 asked the students about adding more foreign languages to UoB campus signage: "Would you like the signage on the UoB campus to include any other languages in addition to English?" In response, 132 (62%) indicated that they are satisfied with Arabic and English, while 81 (38%) of the participants called for the need to add Asian languages (e.g., Malayalam, Hindi, and Tamil).

This response may be due to the fact that out of the 1.7 million inhabitants in Bahrain, 43.4% are Asians, who speak Bengali, Hindi, or Malayalam.

Question 6 prompted the participants to rank the languages used on campus signs and to indicate the order they prefer for these languages to appear. As anticipated, the first two choices of 196 (92%) of the participants are in line with the languages commonly used in the Bahraini community (i.e., Arabic and English). A small number of participants, 17 (8%), chose to use three additional languages (i.e., Malayalam, Hindi, and Tamil). Among them, Malayalam and Hindi take the first two places.

Questions 7 to 12 were set up to elicit the participants' viewpoints pertaining to the value of the UoB campus signage languages. The appeal and impact of the Arabic-English bilingual signs on the UoB campus are examined first, followed by a look at how these signs are perceived by the participants, and finally, their overall perceptions of the UoB campus bilingual setting. As shown in Table 13.1, according to the participants' responses to Question 7, 106 respondents (49.8%) agreed that the bilingual signs caught their attention when they first came to campus. When prompted to express their views on whether Arabic should be displayed on the top of the UoB campus signage (question 8), 130 respondents (61%) valued the top position of Arabic. When asked how they felt about campus signage that displayed information solely in English (question 9), 107 respondents (50.4%), indicated that they are not in favor of English only on UoB campus signage.

Questions 7 to 12 (see Table 13.1) aimed to elicit participants' attitudes pertaining to using English on the UoB campus signage. In response to question 10, 107 respondents (80.2%) highlighted the significance of English as it is a medium of instructions at the UoB as well as a vitalness for non-Arabic-speaking UoB students. This demonstrates that English is highly valued and enjoys privilege and status among UoB students. The last two questions (11 and 12) were intended to

TABLE 13.1 Participants' perspectives on the value of languages used on campus

No.	Statement	Agree	%	Neutral	%	Disagree	%
7.	The Arabic-English bilingual signage attracted my attention when I first came to UoB.	106	49.8	76	35.6	31	14.6
8.	It is important to put Arabic on the top of the signage.	130	61	61	28.6	22	10.4
9.	I prefer English-only signage on UoB campus.	44	20.6	62	29	107	50.4
10.	Using English on the signage is important.	171	80.2	33	15.5	9	4.3
11.	Using Arabic on the signage is important.	150	70.4	45	21.1	18	8.5
12.	Using bilingual signage on the UoB campus is good practice.	144	67.3	59	28	10	4.7

gain a picture of the participants' perspectives toward the coexistence of Arabic and English on the UoB campus. The findings reveal that even though 150 respondents (70.4%) emphasized the importance of Arabic, 144 (67.3%) affirm the value of multilingualism.

Implications for policy, practice, and future research

The study reported here investigated language visibility on the UoB campus signage. The findings indicate that the only languages available on the UoB campus signs are Arabic and English, with Arabic being used more frequently than English, which retained the second position and is highly valued by the UoB students. The results also demonstrate that there is a variety of top-down and bottom-up signage on the UoB campus. Top-down signage is more common than bottom-up signage. As for attitudes towards the languages used on the UoB campus signage, many students acknowledged their delight with the use of Arabic and English on signs across the UoB campus. Others argued that languages like Malayalam, Hindi, and Tamil should be added.

Some of the key findings are as follows. First, Arabic is dominant and English has a strong second position and high visibility on the UoB campus LL as a language of communication. Second, the only visible languages on the UoB campus are Arabic and English, and the use of Arabic monolingual signs is far greater than monolingual English signs. However, Arabic-English bilingual signs are visible in the UoB LL and using English on the UoB campus LL is implemented at various levels, even though there is no law defining how it should be utilized in the UoB public sphere. It is clear that "the real language policy of a community is more likely to be found in its practices than in management" (Spolsky, 2004, p. 222).

This study gathered information to better understand a multilingual university community. In addition, the analysis of the UoB campus LL can serve as a starting point for future comparative and diachronic studies of Gulf Arabic higher education institutions from a variety of perspectives. It revealed that the UoB is a semi-public space, which represents a multilingual community composed of an aggregation of students from different countries. Considering this situation, this chapter suggests the need for written rules about the UoB signage. A special committee should be founded to set formal rules that regulate the UoB campus LL (e.g., signs should be written in Arabic with English; other languages should also be adopted based on the number of students). In addition, to globalize the UoB campus and help non-Arabic speaking students succeed on campus, multilingual signs should be provided.

References

Alsohaibani, A. (2016). A critical review on the ideological and symbolic role of the Arabic language in national identity in the Arab world. *International Journal of Humanities Social Sciences and Education (IJHSSE)*, *3*(4), 19–26.

Ben-Rafael, E. (2009). A sociological approach to the study of linguistic landscapes. In E. Shohamy & D. Gorter (Eds.), *Linguistic landscape: Expanding the scenery* (pp. 50–54). Routledge.

Ben-Rafael, E., Shohamy, E., Amara, M. H., & Trumper-Hecht, N. (2006). Linguistic landscape as symbolic construction of the public space: The case of Israel. In D. Gorter (Ed.), *Linguistic landscape: A new approach to multilingualism* (pp. 7–30). Multilingual Matters.

Blommaert, J., (2013). *Ethnography, superdiversity and linguistic landscapes: Chronicles of complexity* (Vol. 18). Multilingual Matters.

Cenoz, J., & Gorter, D (2006). Linguistic landscape and minority languages. *International Journal of Multilingualism*, 3(1), 67–80.

Cenoz, J., & Gorter, D. (2009). Language economy and linguistic landscape. In E. Shohamy & D. Gorter (Eds.), *Linguistic landscape: Expanding the scenery* (pp. 63–77). Routledge.

Coulmas, F. (2009). Linguistic landscaping and the seed of the public sphere. In E. Shohamy & D. Gorter (Eds.), *Linguistic landscape: Expanding the scenery* (pp. 13–24). Routledge.

Dal Negro, S. (2009). Local policy modelling the linguistic landscape. In E. Shohamy & D. Gorter (Eds.), *Linguistic landscape: Expanding the scenery* (pp. 206–218). Routledge.

Gomaa, Y. (2017). Linguistic landscape in the Arabian Gulf: The case of Manama, Kingdom of Bahrain. *Hermes, Cairo University Centre for Languages and Professional Translation*, 2(2). 7–16.

Gorter, D. (2013). Linguistic landscapes in a multilingual world. *Annual Review of Applied Linguistics*, 33, 190–212.

Gorter, D. (2006). Introduction: The study of the linguistic landscape as a new approach to multilingualism. *International Journal of Multilingualism*, 3(1), 1–6. https://doi.org/10.1080/14790710608668382.

Johnson, D. (2013). *Language policy: Research and practice in applied linguistics*. Palgrave Macmillan. https://doi.org/10.1057/9781137316202_1.

Kaplan, R., & Baldauf, R. (1997). *Language planning from practice to theory*. Multilingual Matters.

Kotze, C. (2010). The linguistic landscape of rural South Africa after 1994: A case study of Philippolis (Doctoral dissertation, University of the Free State).

Kroon, S., Blommaert, J., & Jie, D. (2013). Chinese and globalization. *Linguistic Super Diversity in Urban Areas*, 2, 275–295.

Landry, R., & Bourhis, R. (1997). Linguistic landscape and ethnolinguistic vitality: An empirical study. *Journal of Language and Social Psychology*, 16(1), 23–49. https://doi.org/10.1177/0261927X970161002.

Puzey, G. (2012). Two-way traffic: How linguistic landscapes reflect and influence the politics of language. In D. Gorter, H. F. Marten, & L. Mensel (Eds.), *Minority languages in the linguistic landscape* (pp. 127–147). Palgrave Macmillan.

Scollon, R., & Scollon, S. (2003). *Discourses in place: Language in the material world*. Routledge.

Shohamy, E. (2006). *Language policy: Hidden agendas and new approaches*. Routledge.

Shohamy, E., & Gorter, D. (2009). *Linguistic landscape: Expanding the scenery*. Routledge.

Spolsky, B. (2004). *Language policy*. Cambridge University Press.

14
FACTORS INFLUENCING IRANIAN LANGUAGE EDUCATION POLICY

An empirical investigation

Mahdi Dahmardeh and David Nunan

Introduction

There is considerable research into teaching English in Iran from the perspective of the curriculum and the government (e.g., Aghagolzadeh & Davari, 2017; Zarrabi & Brown, 2017; Zarrinabadi & Mahmoudi-Gahrouei, 2018). However, this research reveals "a degree of ambivalence in the attitude of Iranian government towards English" (Dahmardeh, 2009, p. 46). The most commonly used variety is American English. However, the fact that American politicians refer to Iran as an enemy nation supporting terrorists "may not dispose the Iranian government to a particularly positive view of English. Such political issues may have an effect on the experience of students and teachers of ELT [English language teaching]" (Dahmardeh, 2009, p. 46).

Issues that motivated the research

Similar to many countries, when it comes to educational policy in Iran there is a difference between State and government. While the governments tend to change every four years with new presidents getting into office, the State's vision and policy stay the same. There exists almost no research addressing the issue of foreign language teaching in general from the State's perspective. In this chapter, we analyze official documents developed by the Parliament, the Supreme Council of the Cultural Revolution, and the Ministry of Education, in order to determine the attitude of the State towards the role of foreign languages within the curriculum.

Research questions

The following research questions were posed in order to investigate factors influencing Iranian language education policy:

DOI: 10.4324/9781003312444-18

1. Which official organizations influence policies on the teaching of foreign languages in Iran?
2. What is the role of foreign languages in the relevant official documents (i.e., laws, programs, and curriculum) of Iran?
3. What is the stance of the authorities toward the teaching of foreign languages, particularly English, as enshrined in official documents?

In the implications section below, we will also connect these issues to the attitudes of Iranian people, particularly students, towards these languages.

Research methods

Context

Since 1979, when the Islamic Republic came to power, the educational system of Iran has changed several times. As of this writing, schools are either state-supported or private. The former are funded by the government and are free for all pupils between the ages of seven and 18, while private schools require pupils to pay tuition fees.

The educational system in Iran consists of four key stages, as shown in Table 14.1.

The academic year starts in late September and lasts until late June of the following year. All schools, whether state or private, have to follow the national curriculum. They also use the same coursebooks, which are developed and prescribed by the Ministry of Education. These coursebooks are used by all students throughout the country. Some may undergo minor modification, but others are used for years without being updated (Rashidi & Kehtarfard, 2014).

The official language of Iran, Persian (Farsi), is the language of education and the media. While nearly all Iranians speak and communicate in Persian, other minority languages (e.g., Kurdish, Azeri, Arabic, etc.) are also widely used.

Foreign language teaching is very popular in Iran. Language institutes can be found on practically every street corner and there is a growing number of branches in almost every Iranian city (Aghagolzadeh & Davari, 2017). Although there are numerous language institutes, schools are still the main places where students receive foreign language education. They are required by the curriculum to study Arabic and English from Key Stage 3. During the last year of Key Stage 4, they

TABLE 14.1 Key stages of the Iranian Educational System

Key Stage	Label	Duration	Pupils' Ages
1	Pre-school	2 years	5–6
2	Primary School	6 years	7–12
3	Junior Secondary School	3 years	13–15
4	Senior Secondary School	3 years	16–18

may choose to study German, French, English, and Arabic, but nearly all of the students opt for English. Indeed, English is the most popular foreign language among Iranian pupils and their families and there is a remarkable increase in the number of Iranians learning English (Hayati & Mashhadi, 2010).

Data collection procedures

The present study uses a qualitative framework and descriptive approach to investigate the status of foreign languages within the Iranian educational system. For the purpose of this research, we searched through many documents developed by different bodies, including the Ministry of Education, the Supreme Council of the Cultural Revolution, and the Iranian Parliament (see below). All these documents include information and instruction regarding the role of foreign languages and how these languages should be delivered within the Iranian educational system.

Data analysis procedures

We documented all references to foreign languages in the source documents. The first author combed through these materials, seeking and recording any references to foreign languages.

To address the first research question, we identified the official institutions and nature of the source. In order to address the second research question, we identified the role played by each document in shaping foreign language policy. Similarly, we used the references to identify and interpret the stance of the authorities toward the teaching of foreign languages, particularly English, to address the third research question.

Findings and discussion

In addition to the Iranian Ministry of Education, there are other organizations that determine the content and materials included within the country's educational system as well as the type of education that every pupil must receive. In this section, these bodies, along with their instruction on teaching foreign languages, will be described.

Supreme Council of the Cultural Revolution (SCCR)

Established in 1980, the SCCR is the most powerful committee in the country, dealing with a wide range of matters including educational programs. It has members from different parts of the country's ruling bodies including the President, Speaker of the Parliament, Chief Justice, Secretary of the SCCR, and many others. The SCCR's major roles are identified as follows:

Resistance against any foreign influence, cutting dependency on foreign powers, eliminating the undesirable atmosphere in the society that was devoid of revered human values, promoting independent Iranian and Islamic culture in the light of Islamic precepts, all-out development of Islamic culture and ethics, boosting intellectual and psychological health of the individuals, boosting spirituality and faith in the society, nurturing thoughts and scientific development, and gaining self-sufficiency in the majority of social, economic, political, intellectual and cultural fields for an integrated Islamic society
(Supreme Council of the Cultural Revolution, 2011a)

Fundamental Reform Document of Education

In 2011, the SCCR introduced the Fundamental Reform Document of Education (FRDE), which is a strategic document in the county's 20-year vision. Regarding the foreign languages to be taught, the FRDE refers to the "provision of foreign language education within the optional (core-elective) section of the curriculum framework by observing the principle of stabilization and enforcement of the Islamic-Iranian identity" (Supreme Council of the Cultural Revolution, 2011b, p. 32). This is the only reference to the teaching of foreign languages in this document.

Comprehensive scientific plan

In the same year (2011), the SCCR unveiled a Comprehensive Scientific Map (CSM), the country's main plan for long-term sustainable growth in the field of science. It lists 224 scientific projects which must be implemented by the year 2025. Within the humanities, while there are references to a variety of subjects such as economics, theological studies, philosophy, Quranic studies, geography, women's studies, and history, there are none referring to foreign languages (Supreme Council of the Cultural Revolution, 2011c).

However, there are references to foreign languages under the country's 9th Grand Strategy (entitled "Active & Effective Interaction with Other Countries Specially Those in the Region as well as the Islamic Ones in Terms of Science and Technology"). The 10th Grand Strategy ("Reformation and Qualitative & Quantitative Promotion in Arts and Humanities Based on Islamic Education") also names foreign languages. There are four key concepts introduced in the 10th Grand Strategy: (1) modification and reformation in methods and strategies for teaching foreign languages, especially Arabic and English; (2) arrangement and reinforcement of purposeful teaching of foreign languages in order to observe quality improvements; (3) organizing and monitoring institutes of teaching foreign languages as well as diversifying them according to the needs of the country for international engagement in science and technology; and (4) developing and localizing educational programs and teaching materials to teach foreign languages based on Islamic culture.

Supplementary documents of Comprehensive Science Map

Later that year (2011), the SCCR published the "Supplementary Documents of Comprehensive Science Map" (SDCSM). This map is based on studies undertaken by the Ministry of Education regarding the status of education within Iranian society and what must be done to improve the quality of education in the country. According to the document, through the internet a segment of the Iranian society has gained access to, and been influenced by, Western media and popular culture, such as music and videos. Possessing satellite dishes and watching such programs is illegal in Iran. It is thought to subvert the common culture of Iranian society and schools as well as the state media, and is considered to be a great threat to the educational system, in both the short term and the long term (Supreme Council of the Cultural Revolution, 2011c). The authors of the SDCSM argue that families who engage in such illegal practices have provided their children with a home environment that is contrary to the culture of Iranian society (in terms of education and state media). However, beyond the official position of the government or the State, Muslim scholars have various views, ranging from strictly forbidding Western music to allowing it under certain conditions in terms of type of music and the instruments employed.

According to the SDCSM authors, the above-mentioned families steer their children towards their own preferred Western culture and behaviors, such as learning a Western language. Those authors believe that this practice opens the door into an alien culture and shifts the children away from their home culture (Supreme Council of the Cultural Revolution, 2011c).

Interestingly, in another chapter of the map, there is a counter argument supporting teaching foreign languages by explaining about opportunities that are available through language learning (Supreme Council of the Cultural Revolution, 2011c). The authors of the SDCSM further claimed that it is very important to make immediate and substantial changes in the quality of foreign language teaching in schools. They then argued that is it essential to apply suitable policies in English language teaching methods within the educational system. They also recommended helping people to improve their English language speaking skills and suggested that suitable policies must be implemented in this regard.

The parliament

Like many countries around the world, Iran also has a parliament. It consists of 290 members representing 31 provinces. Usually, there are elections in Iran every two to four years. The purpose of these elections is for Iranians to elect the president, members of parliament (MPs), members of the assembly of experts for leadership, and members of the city councils. Since the candidates of parliament are different from those who run for the presidency, the government is separate from the parliament and by law, MPs are not allowed to be members of the government.

When it comes to education, the parliament has its own role to play. The parliament's Commission for Education and Research consists of 23 MPs, who are responsible for considering the affairs related to schools and universities, as well as all related educational matters. Every five years, the parliament considers and approves a development plan to boost investment in education. The development plan sets out the goals and objectives to be achieved by the state over the next five years. The sixth plan (ratified by the parliament in 2017) stated that the government is required to implement the FRDE, the goals of which are important to achieve. Thus, it could be argued that, in terms of foreign languages, the goals in FRDE are also ratified by the parliament even though there is no direct reference to foreign languages in the parliamentary plan.

The national curriculum

Iran's national curriculum was implemented in March, 2013. According to the Secretary of Education, it took about 40 months to prepare the document (Iran Ministry of Education, 2013). Two comments address the foreign language issue: First, Section 7 (Basic Merits) states that students should be able to deploy language skills of one foreign language within the framework of the curriculum's optional section, by observing the principle of Islamic-Iranian identity. Second, in Section 8 (Fields of Education and Learning), there are 11 subsections referring to different subjects. Two of them are The Holy Quran and Arabic, and foreign languages.

The Holy Quran and Arabic

While there is a separate section for foreign languages, even though Arabic is considered a foreign language in Iran, it is presented along with the Holy Quran rather than with other foreign languages. The rationale is that since the Holy Quran is written in Arabic, learning this language would be a great benefit for people to understand messages of this Divine Book. For example, learners will be able to understand the sayings of the 12 infallible Imams (Shia) as well as Islamic culture more generally. Since Persian language and literature are closely related to Arabic (they share similar alphabets), it is thought that learning Arabic would improve pupils' mother tongue (Iran Ministry of Education, 2013).

Foreign languages

According to the National Curriculum (Iran Ministry of Education, 2013), teaching foreign languages will provide valuable opportunities to understand cultural interactions. Foreign language teaching is also a means for transferring scientific achievements in verbal, visual, and written formats for different purposes to different audiences within the framework of the Islamic system.

According to the national curriculum document, social interactions are developed through the influence of communications among nations as well as through technological innovations. Since the development of technology has expanded daily and enables international communication, the rationale behind teaching foreign languages is that it is very important for the students to learn other languages so that they can make constructive and wise relationships with the world.

Developing understanding among nations occurs through social interaction. In recent times, this phenomenon has been greatly facilitated through technology. Having the ability to communicate in global languages such as Arabic and English is crucial for students to develop constructive and meaningful relationships with people who do not speak Farsi.

While the mother tongue enables learners to interact with their families and other Iranians, learning a foreign language allows them to communicate with people in other nations and benefit from those countries' achievements (Iran Ministry of Education, 2013). In addition, fluency in foreign languages will facilitate economic development in areas such as tourism, business, technology, scientific progress, and social-political consciousness.

By the end of the foreign language program, students should be able to communicate effectively in all four language skills. The curriculum stipulates that language programs should familiarize students with the grammatical, lexical, discourse, and sociocultural skills to engage in effective and constructive communication.

The curriculum also stipulates that the goal of teaching foreign languages in Key Stage 3 is teaching the four macro skills for effective communication. When it comes to Key Stage 4, students should achieve a level of proficiency enabling them to comprehend a range of text types in the foreign languages they study. They should also be able to write a short essay and should have the listening and speaking skills to communicate in the foreign language for transactional and interpersonal purposes.

According to the national curriculum (Iran Ministry of Education, 2013), the foreign languages that are to be taught in schools are English, French, German, and/or any other languages that the Supreme Council of Education approves. This document defines general orientations in developing the content (material) and teaching foreign languages as follow:

> Teaching foreign languages must go further beyond world pre-set theories, approaches, and methods and it should act as a platform to strengthen national culture, beliefs, and self-values. Teaching foreign languages is based on a communicative and self-confident approach. In the beginning stages of teaching foreign languages, the content should cover local issues as well as learners' needs (such as health, daily life, the surrounding environment, values, and culture) by employing interesting topics. During the higher levels, the content should move forward towards cultural, economic, scientific and political functions. In the end, based on the teaching contents of

other subjects, students should able to read and comprehend easy texts about technical issues as well as writing essays about technical issues. During Key Stage 4, expanding vocabulary knowledge of professional disciplines would help students to better understand texts and could establish scientific communication.

(Iran Ministry of Education, 2013, p. 38)

The findings of the present study indicate that policy regarding teaching foreign languages within the Iranian educational system is quite complicated. While the Ministry of Education has a major role, it is not the only body responsible for what happens at the school level.

Besides what has been mentioned so far, three important documents published by the SCCR set out the educational goals for Iran. The first is the FRDE, which was produced in 2011. This document addresses the issue of teaching foreign languages from the perspective of social stability and the enforcement of Islamic-Iranian identity. Second, the CSM (also produced in 2011) determines the most important scientific and technological priorities for Iran. Foreign languages are part of the grand strategy of the CSM. Methods and strategies for teaching foreign languages had no clear purpose prior to the publication of the CSM. Reformulating and clarifying the purpose was a major goal of this document.

As mentioned earlier, there are many language institutes in Iran. According to the CSM, all of these centers must be reorganized and diversified to meet the needs of the country for international engagement in science and technology. As with the FRDE, the CSM states that educational programs and materials for teaching foreign languages must be developed according to Islamic culture.

Later in 2011, the SCCR published a third document: the SDCSR. It states that those Iranian families who do not appreciate the culture of the society (including schools) and fail to comply with programs promulgated by state media are a significant threat to the educational system. The CSM further states that families who allow their children to be brought up according to Western cultural practices (such as playing and listening to Western music, which they access through illegal satellite programs) and pay little or no respect to Islam at home are a threat to the fabric of society in general, and to the education system in particular.

There is some ambivalence in the SDCDR about the teaching of Western languages. In one chapter, the practice of allowing children to learn such languages independently outside the classroom is condemned. In another, there is support for the teaching of foreign language as long as it is conducted within the educational system. The document is critical of private language institutes that teach foreign languages using pedagogical materials imported from the West. Materials for teaching English come in for particular criticism for promoting Western cultural values that are at odds with Iranian cultural values. This criticism is not extended to Asian languages or Russian, which are also taught in private language institutes.

Although the main goal of teaching foreign languages is to enable students to communicate, there are many obstacles to achieving this goal. The National University Entrance Exam or *Konkoor* (in Persian) is one such impediment. Most language teachers in Iran teach towards the final examinations (see, e.g., Arani et al., 2012). This phenomenon is common in many parts of the world and is known colloquially as "the assessment tail wagging the curriculum dog"! Teachers and schools (especially the private schools) are judged on how well their students perform in examinations, particularly high stakes tests such as the *Konkoor*. This practice is unfair, as there will always be factors beyond the teachers' control, such as mismatches between the curriculum (which advocates the development of communication skills) and the *Konkoor*, which tests mastery of discrete-point grammar, vocabulary, and reading comprehension. For obvious reasons, both students and teachers will privilege good examination results over the ability to communicate (Khaniya, 1990).

There are other reasons why the policies we have discussed here, along with programs and plans, have not been as successful as expected when it comes to foreign language education in Iran's educational system. Time, or lack of it, is one such critical factor. According to Dahmardeh (2009), pupils in Iran must study English language for many years, "yet the education they receive neither enables the students to attain full competence in using the English language nor helps them to interact with confidence" (p. 46). Similarly, Davari and Aghagolzadeh (2015) claim that, due to the failure of the public education system in teaching the English language, the private sector is flourishing.

However, when it comes to Arabic, the case is even worse. According to some studies most students are not interested in or motivated to learn Arabic (see, e.g., Hakimzadeh et al., 2015; Rezaie, 2012).

This apparent lack of success can be traced back to the curriculum. According to Richards (2001), "One of the basic assumptions of curriculum development is that a sound educational program should be based on an analysis of learners' needs" (p. 51). Some authors assert that Iran's foreign language teaching program is not based on any studies of students' needs or teachers' abilities (see, e.g., Dahmardeh & Kim, 2021). Maftoon et al. (2010) maintain that in Iran "curriculum developers ... have almost certainly neglected to pay attention to students' needs and future demands" (p. 2). Many scholars have accused the Iranian authorities of not doing their best to teach foreign languages effectively within the education system that is provided at schools and the subject has been undervalued for many years (see, e.g., Dahmardeh & Kim, 2021). The reason for this situation may be that the educational system is centralized and does not have enough flexibility to address the diverse needs of students throughout Iran.

Implications for policy, practice, and future research

Iran is substantially different from its neighbors in terms of politics, religion, social values, and so on. It is a country where almost everything is judged from a political perspective. This is particularly true of education. No subject area is more vulnerable to this criticism than foreign language teaching in general. English, which is widely seen as embodying Western cultural values, seems to be incompatible with Iranian/Islamic society.

In response to the first research question, it is clear that there are many independent entities that act as policymakers when it comes to education in Iran. While the educational system seems to be run by the Ministry of Education, this investigation has shown that there are other decision-making bodies that make crucial decisions related to education.

In response to the second research question, this chapter has described the variety of criteria that are included in the documents and policy papers that directly or indirectly deal with the issue of language teaching in Iran. The Supreme Council of the Cultural Revolution, the most powerful political body in Iran, plays a crucial role in shaping the educational system of the country. It might be inferred that this council sees the teaching and learning of foreign languages to be a potential threat to Iranian/Islamic values. According to the SCCR, these languages must be localized (i.e., the foreign values conveyed by those languages must be removed) and delivered via the Iranian educational system. Although the Iranian curriculum has been updated, this was done centrally, and without taking into consideration the diverse needs of students across the country. In addition, the National University Entrance Exam is a major obstacle to students' success in learning foreign languages as it focuses on testing discrete-point morphosyntactic and lexical items rather than the ability to communicate in a foreign language.

In response to the third research question, we found that the official position is to privilege Arabic as a foreign language (even though it is unpopular among Iranian students). In terms of other languages, English is a compulsory subject, while German and French are optional choices for foreign language study.

As noted earlier, English is the most popular foreign language among Iranian pupils and their families and there is a remarkable increase in the number of Iranians learning English (Hayati & Mashhadi, 2010). However, based on the documents analyzed for the purposes of this study, it seems that Iranian policymakers are not very keen to change the situation in favor of people's demands. These include changing the current status of English language teaching at schools towards a more successful approach, and particularly to implement a well-developed system for teaching the language (Rassouli & Osam, 2019). Bearing in mind that seven years of instruction are spent on teaching foreign languages at schools, that amount of time should be sufficient motivation for policymakers to change the system into teaching those languages more communicatively.

References

Aghagolzadeh, F., & Davari, H. (2017). English education in Iran: From ambivalent policies to paradoxical practices. In R. Kirkpatrick (Ed.), *English language education policy in the Middle East and North Africa* (pp. 47–62). Springer.

Arani, A. M., Kakia, M. L., & Karimi, M. V. (2012). Assessment in education in Iran. *SA-eDUC Journal, 9*(2), 101–110.

Dahmardeh, M. (2009). Communicative textbooks: English language textbooks in Iranian secondary school. *Linguistik Online, 40*(4), 45–61. https://doi.org/10.13092/lo.40.431.

Dahmardeh, M., & Kim, S. (2021). An analysis of the representation of cultural content in English coursebooks. *Journal of Applied Research in Higher Education, 13*(5), 1388–1407. https://doi.org/10.1108/JARHE-09-2020-0290.

Davari, H., & Aghagolzadeh, F. (2015). To teach or not to teach? Still an open question for the Iranian education system. In C. Kennedy (Ed.), *English language teaching in the Islamic Republic of Iran: Innovations, trends and challenges* (pp. 5–13). British Council.

Hakimzadeh, R., Motaqizadeh, I., & Sultaninejad, N. (2015). Studying the problems and challenges of teaching Arabic in Iranian schools from the point of view of specialists. *Journal of Critical Study in Humanities Texts and Programmes, 34*(1), 37–59.

Hayati, M., & Mashhadi, A. (2010). Language planning and language-in-education policy in Iran. *Language Problems and Language Planning, 34*(1), 24–42.

Iran Ministry of Education (2013). The Islamic Republic of Iran's National Curriculum. https://mebtedaei.yazdedu.ir/documents/110271/0/%D8%A8%D8%B1%D9%86%D8%A7%D9%85%D9%87%20%D8%AF%D8%B1%D8%B3%DB%8C%20%D9%85%D9%84%DB%8C%2B%20%D8%A7%D8%B3%D9%86%D8%A7%D8%AF.pdf?version=1.0&t=1467084820547.

Khaniya, T. R. (1990). The washback effect of a textbook-based test. *Edinburgh Working Papers in Applied Linguistics. 1*, 48–58. University of Edinburgh.

Maftoon, P., Yazdani, M. M., Golebostan, H., & Beh-Afarin, S. R. (2010). Privatization of English education in Iran: A feasibility study. *The Electronic Journal for English as a Second Language, 13*(4), 1–12.

Rashidi, N., & Kehtarfard, R. (2014). A needs analysis approach to the evaluation of Iranian third-grade high school English textbook. *SAGE Open, 4*(3), 1–9. doi:10.1177/2158244014551709.

Rassouli, A., & Osam, N. (2019). English language education throughout the Islamic Republic reign in Iran: Government policies and people's attitudes. *SAGE Open, 9*(2). https://doi.org/10.1177/2158244019858435.

Rezaie, Y. (2012). The causes of students' disinterest in Arabic language: Methods of motivating students in learning the Arabic language. *Roshd Journal of Quran and Islamic teachings, 82*(1), 32–34.

Richards, J. C. (2001). *Curriculum development in language teaching*. Cambridge University Press.

Supreme Council of the Cultural Revolution. (2011a). Supplementary documents of comprehensive science map. High Council of Cultural Revolution.

Supreme Council of Cultural Revolution. (2011b). Fundamental Reform Document of Education (FRDE) in the Islamic Republic of Iran. https://neqmap.bangkok.unesco.org/resource/fundamental-reform-document-of-education-frde-in-the-islamic-republic-of-iran/.

Supreme Council of Cultural Revolution. (2011c). *Comprehensive Scientific Map (CSM)*. https://sccr.ir/pro/1813.

Zarrabi, F., & Brown, J. R. (2017). English language teaching and learning analysis in Iran. *International Journal of Educational and Pedagogical Sciences*, *9*(10), 3485–3493.

Zarrinabadi, N., & Mahmoudi-Gahrouei, V. (2018). English in contemporary Iran. *Asian Englishes*, *20*(1), 81–94.

15

LANGUAGE PREFERENCES IN THE HASHEMITE KINGDOM OF JORDAN

An exploratory study

Fatima Esseili

Introduction

Issues that motivated the research

In a pioneering report for its time, Harrison et al. (1975) described the language situation in Jordan as "simple" and believed that there was a "homogeneity of the mother tongue" spoken in the Kingdom (p. iv). The report affirmed that Jordanians spoke Arabic to communicate with one another and with other Arabs, that Arabic was "the exclusive medium of instruction" in public schools, and that English was "the only foreign language taught in the school" (p. iv).

While this description might have been true at the time, a great deal has changed over the past four decades, and the linguistic situation in Jordan is far from being simple. English is no longer the only foreign language taught in schools, but it is certainly the most popular. In addition, mixing Arabic and English in daily interaction is getting more and more popular, and Arabic might be losing ground as some of its vital functional allocations are done in English, especially in fields such as science, medicine, business, and tourism. Jordanian youth also use English to communicate with one another, their siblings, and with their parents – a phenomenon that often triggers harsh criticism on social media.

Given the revered status of Arabic among many Jordanians and the sensitive nature of language dynamics in Jordan, investigating Jordanians' language preferences towards Arabic (colloquial and standard), English, and mixing languages is important for many reasons. First, such an inquiry would shed light on the magnitude of the issue – whether Arabic is really losing ground to English, and if so, what can be done. Second, this investigation would help contextualize language interaction better, thus informing the field of applied linguistics in general.

DOI: 10.4324/9781003312444-19

Third, it could also inform language policy in Jordan and the region. Finally, the results of investigating Jordanians' language preferences may enable educators and parents alike to make informed decisions about language choice and language use, both in academic and non-academic settings, especially when considering the socio-economic value of English as a prerequisite language for many jobs.

Research questions

This study explored Jordanians' preference in terms of language use. Primarily, it checked which language(s) Jordanians prefer to use when communicating with certain people and when engaging in certain activities or topics. The language choices investigated are Arabic, both the colloquial and standard varieties, English, and mixing of colloquial Jordanian Arabic and English. While Arabic is the native language, English is used in some schools and universities as a medium of instruction and is taught as a foreign language in other schools.

The research questions addressed in this chapter are:

1. What language do Jordanians prefer to use when communicating with particular people?
2. What language do Jordanians prefer to use when engaging in certain activities or topics?

Research methods

Context

Jordan, or the Hashemite Kingdom of Jordan, is an 89,342 sq. km constitutional monarchy with a parliament, located in the Middle East. It is bordered by Palestine in the west, Syria and Iraq from the north and northeast, and Saudi Arabia from the east and south. The Jordanian Department of Statistics (2022) estimates the population to be at 11,057,000, with many refugees from other Arab countries including Iraq, Syria, Palestine, and Yemen. In fact, it is estimated that the number of Syrian refugees alone is about 675,433 (UNHCR, 2022). While Arabs are the predominant ethnic group, about 2% of the population is made up of Circassians, Kurds, Gypsies, and other minority groups. In terms of religious diversity, 96% of the population are Muslims by birth while Christians constitute about 3.68% of the population (Al-Ab Al-Kildani, 2015).

Several languages and dialects are used in Jordan for different purposes. Jordanian Arabic (JA), or colloquial Arabic, is typically the mother tongue acquired at home, and it is used for daily interaction and communication, local soap operas and TV shows, and radio programs, among other contexts. Jordanian Arabic itself could also be categorized into several dialects. Cleveland (1963) classified colloquial Jordanian into three or four groups of dialects that partially correspond to social, economic, and geographical stratification. Scholars who subsequently examined Jordanian dialects have also categorized them into three to five groups. Saidat (2010), for example, listed four varieties of Jordanian Arabic: Urban, Jordanian Fellahi, Palestinian Fellahi, and the Bedouin dialects. *Fellah* (or *fallah*) is an Arabic word that refers to a peasant, and it is used here to indicate a rural variety. Likewise, Abu Ain's (2016) grouping of dialects followed the classification of the Jordanian population into peasants or Fellahi (Jordanian and Palestinian), urbanities, and Bedouins. Such classifications are often used to formulate opinions or preconceived ideas about speakers of a given dialect (e.g., social class).

In addition to JA, Classical Arabic (CA) and Modern Standard Arabic (MSA) are learned in formal settings and are used for literacy practices. CA is the language of the Holy Quran, and it is used in religious contexts (liturgy and prayers). It is also highly esteemed as a symbol of Arab culture and Islamic religion. MSA, on the other hand, is used for administrative and legal purposes (official transactions and contracts), academic and non-academic publications (including creative writing in Arabic, magazines, etc.), and newspapers, among other uses.

The presence of a codified language in addition to a colloquial variety is commonly known as *diglossia* (Ferguson, 1959). However, other models have been proposed including triglossia, polyglossia, and multiglossia (c.f., Ennaji, 1991; Badawi, 1973; El-Hassan, 1978). Each variety of Arabic has its own function within the society, but it is worth noting that on many occasions code mixing and switching (defined below) do happen, as in many other Arab contexts (Esseili, 2017). Examples include news broadcasts, political speeches, and religious sermons, to name a few.

Besides Arabic, there are other minority languages used in Jordan on different scales and levels, including Circassian, Armenian, Chechen, Turkish, Kurdish, Domari (Abu Ain, 2016), and Syriac. Studies of those languages indicate language maintenance in some cases, such as the languages spoken by Chechens, the Circassians, and the Gypsies. In other cases, such as Armenian and Kurdish (Al-Khatib & Al-Ali, 2010) and Syriac (Dweik & Al-Refa'i, 2015), language loss or language shift has been documented.

In light of American, English, French, German, and Russian interests in the MENA region, these countries' embassies and language and cultural centers' persistence in promoting their respective languages and cultures is only to be expected. Thus, it is not surprising to find Jordanians learning those languages and traveling abroad for education, work, and tourism. English, however, has the lion's share in terms of presence and spread, given that Jordan was under British mandate for 25 years (1921–1946), and given the personal and economic ties between the Jordanian royal family and England.

Finally, English is taught as a first foreign language and is used as a medium of instruction for mathematics and sciences in many private schools and is even used to teach all subjects, except for the Arabic language and religion, in some international private schools. This status, along with the global spread of English, created a phenomenon in Jordan, and the Arabic-speaking world in general, whereby Jordanians mix both Arabic and English when speaking and sometimes when writing. This phenomenon is commonly referred to as *Arabizi*, which, when it comes to writing, is defined as the use of Latinized Arabic to write (Esseili, 2017). Using *Arabizi* occurs when texting, taking notes, and posting on social media.

When it comes to speaking, on the other hand, Arabizi involves code-switching and code-mixing between Arabic and English. *Code-switching* is loosely defined as alternating between two languages or varieties during interaction or adjusting one's speech style or expression according to audience. *Code-mixing*, on the other hand, refers to using one word or phrase from another language. A detailed explanation of the different types of code-switching is beyond the scope of this chapter. However, code-switching and mixing may occur with or without nativizing English words into Arabic, and may or may not be intentional. For example, "fresh" is a word borrowed from English that has become widespread in Jordan to the extent that you see it in advertisements in grocery shops. The word is written in the Arabic alphabet, and its meaning and use are intact. At other times, *nativization* of words happens, whereby the English word undergoes morphological, syntactic, and phonological changes to fit within the structure of Arabic. Examples of this abound: *shayyik* (from *check*), *sayyiv* (from *save*), etc. Mixing the two languages is often overheard in affluent neighborhoods in Amman, in coffeeshops, in prestigious private schools, and in talk shows. At times, mixing or switching may happen intentionally when speakers are aware of their surrounding and are trying to fit in or distance themselves. At other times, this process has become so natural that the speakers are not even aware they are doing it. As seen from this context description, language dynamics in Jordan are far from being simple. This is why it is important to investigate Jordanians' language preferences when they speak with particular people and when they engage certain topics or activities.

Participants

A total of 665 participants completed a 10- to 12-minute questionnaire, with 389 females (58.6%) and 275 males (41.4%) responding. The age distribution ranged from 18 to above 45 years old (M = 1.82, SD = 1.02). Slightly more than half of the participants, however, were between 18–24 years old (55%). Sixteen percent were between 25–34, and 29% were 35 and above. In terms of the participants' education, 62% attended a public high school, while 79.5% attended a public university. In contrast, 34.7% attended a private high school, while 20.4% attended a private university. The rest of the participants (less than 3%) attended UNRWA (United Nations Relief and Works Agency) schools or programs. UNRWA is a United Nations relief and human development agency specifically created for Palestinian refugees, which operates in a few Arab countries including Jordan, Lebanon, and Syria.

In addition, 44% of the participants had a monthly household income of less than JOD 1,000 (US $1,400), compared to 47.2% with household incomes between JOD 1,000–3,000. Only eight percent had an income higher than JOD 3,000 (over US $4,000). Household income was an important variable to consider when investigating the relationship among the preference for English, private education, and income. It is also important to compare the Jordanian context with other Arab countries where the spread of English is related to private education and income, such as in Lebanon (Esseili, 2017).

Data collection procedures

Two forms of the questionnaire were developed, one in English and another in standard Arabic. Thus, respondents had the option to take the questionnaire either in standard Arabic or in English.

The questionnaire consisted of 20 questions and was designed through Qualtrics, which is an online software for data collection and analysis. While I am fluent in both Arabic and English, a professional translator was hired to ensure the questionnaire was correctly written in Arabic. The first phase of the study included piloting the questionnaire with five Jordanians who were asked to take the questionnaire and provide input related to completion time and clarity of questions. Institutional Review Board approval was secured and respondents signed an informed consent form before completing the questionnaire.

The questionnaire consisted of 17 closed-ended questions and three open-ended questions. The 17 questions were categorized into three sections. The first section solicited demographic information including the respondents' gender, age, type of high school and university education, and household income. The second section inquired about the uses or functions of English and Arabic (MSA and Jordanian). The third section investigated preferences and attitudes towards the investigated language varieties. To address the research questions, this chapter will only report on the first and third sections of the questionnaire. As for the three open-ended questions, one question inquired about the reason the participant chose to take the questionnaire in either English or Arabic; another solicited final comments on the topic being investigated; and a third asked the respondents if they would like to be interviewed and requested that they include their name and email address or phone number.

Given Jordan's population of about 11,000,000 people, it was important to get a somewhat statistically representative sample from the general population as well as from people in schools and universities. Thus, it was determined through Qualtrics that an ideal sample size would be 664 participants, which would allow for a 99% confidence level and a 5% margin of error. Even with that point in mind, it was still important to get a wide representation of Jordanian society, rather than just residents of the capital, Amman. It is worth noting that Jordan is divided into 12 governorates, known in Arabic as *Muhafatha*. Each governorate corresponds to a particular geographical and administrative region. Because I have lived in Jordan intermittently since 2009, I already had acquaintances in other governorates that I could recruit initially to disseminate the questionnaire. In addition, to get as much representation as possible, three local research assistants were hired to distribute the questionnaire: One of the assistants worked in a large public university in northeast Jordan (Al-Zarqa Governorate); another was a student in a private university in northern Jordan (Jerash Governorate); and a third was a schoolteacher in Amman (Amman Governorate). The research assistants used Qualtrics-generated links to disseminate the questionnaire. While other governorates (a province or administrative division) in Jordan may not be directly represented in the sample, it may be safe to assume that many residents of Amman hail from different areas in the Kingdom. In addition, one of the research assistants who collected data from the private university was originally from southern Jordan (Maan Governorate) but moved with her family to the capital for work/education purposes. Thus, she was able to distribute the questionnaire to acquaintances in that area.

Finally, data were collected over a period of five months in 2021. A main reason for the long duration was COVID-19 and the way it disrupted the lives of the assistants and me, as well as the overall motivation of people in Jordan and everywhere in the world.

Data analysis procedures

The larger study utilized qualitative (interviews) and quantitative data collection methods to investigate the status of English in Jordan. However, for the purposes of this chapter, I will only report on the quantitative aspect of the study (i.e., the survey research) to offer a snapshot of Jordanians' language preferences when it comes to JA, English, standard Arabic, and mixing languages. Since Qualtrics was used to create and disseminate the questionnaire, it was also used to analyze the data. The data analysis includes descriptive statistics (mean scores, frequencies, percentages, and standard deviations).

The questionnaire responses were checked for missing and incomplete data before the analysis. Initially, a total of 706 participants took the questionnaire. However, 41 participants were excluded from the analysis either because they identified themselves as non-Jordanians or because they mistakenly clicked "do not consent" but still filled out the questionnaire. The sample size, however, may vary across analyses because some participants chose not to provide responses to all the questionnaire items.

Findings and discussion

This section presents findings from the questionnaire, and it answers the two main research questions in turn.

The first research question addressed Jordanian language preferences when communicating with particular people. The respondents were asked to indicate which language they mostly prefer to use when communicating with their grandparents, parents, siblings, friends, teachers or professors, supervisors and co-workers, family doctors, and household helpers. Results are displayed in Table 15.1. Although most participants reported preferring to use JA to interact with their grandparents (97%), parents (90%), siblings (76%), family doctor (65%), friends and household helpers (60%), just 51% of the participants indicated that they use it to communicate with their teachers and professors, and in their work environment (e.g., with their supervisors and co-workers). Moreover, despite the overwhelming preference for JA, about 80% of participants did not think that it should be used as a medium of instruction in schools. Instead, they thought standard Arabic should be used for instruction.

The second most preferred way of communicating was mixing Jordanian Arabic (JA) and English, in what is known as Arabizi. This was the case when speaking to friends (36%), co-workers and supervisors (27%), family doctors and teachers (23%), siblings (19%), and household helpers (16%). English was used by some participants when communicating with household helpers (22%), teachers and professors, and supervisors and co-workers. Finally, standard Arabic was hardly used for daily interaction.

Female participants preferred to mix Jordanian Arabic with English more than males did when speaking with their siblings, friends, and teachers/professors. In addition, Jordanians aged 35 and above, which constituted 29% of the sample, tended to use a mix of English and Arabic when speaking with their family doctors and their household helpers. This result is understandable given the fact many scientific terms are used in English, so it is only natural to use them with doctors when unfamiliar with the Arabic equivalent. Moreover, most household helpers in Jordan hail from countries where Arabic is not spoken. In fact, in a 2015 qualitative study published by the International Labor Organization, the researchers found that one of the major desired characteristics of migrant domestic workers in Jordan is nationality. Jordanians prefer Filipina workers since they are

TABLE 15.1 Jordanians' language preferences by interlocutor

Interlocutor	English	Arabizi	Colloquial JA	Standard Arabic (Al FusHa)	Total
Grandparents	1%	1%	97%	1%	100%
Parents	2%	8%	90%	0%	100%
Siblings	4%	19%	76%	1%	100%
Family Doctor	8%	23%	65%	4%	100%
Friends	3%	36%	60%	1%	100%
Teacher/Professor	19%	23%	51%	7%	100%
Supervisor/Co-workers	18%	27%	51%	5%	100%
Household Helpers	22%	16%	60%	2%	100%

viewed as "more sophisticated...look more presentable and...have superior English language skills" (International Labor Organization, 2015, pp. 6–7). Other nationalities of interest included Bangladeshi, Kenyan, and Sri Lankan. A recruitment agency manager was quoted saying that "employers prefer English skills to Arabic unless the domestic worker needs to care for an older person" (p. 7). In short, a household helper's nationality and language proficiency are more important than the kind of chores they are able to perform – a situation which resembles that in Lebanon (Esseili, 2017).

In contrast to the first age group, Jordanians aged 25–34 (16%) tended to mix JA and English in their work environment, while Jordanians aged 18–24 (55%) mixed the two languages when interacting with their siblings, friends, and teachers and professors. Finally, participants who attended private schools were more likely to mix languages and use JA and English in their work environment, as well as with their household helpers, teachers, and professors than were respondents who attended public schools.

The second research question examined the language that participants mostly prefer to use when engaged in certain topics or activities. Table 15.2 reveals again

TABLE 15.2 Percentages of participants' language preference use by activity/topic

Activity/Topic	Colloquial JA	Standard Arabic	Arabizi	English
To talk about a literary topic	55%	27%	8%	11%
To talk about politics	73%	14%	9%	4%
To tell jokes	88%	1%	9%	3%
To express anger	80%	1%	10%	9%
To read newspapers	51%	29%	10%	10%
To write an email	15%	11%	10%	64%
To talk about taboo topics	68%	10%	12%	11%
To insult someone	76%	3%	12%	10%
To read a book for fun	42%	26%	13%	19%
To complete a job application	24%	16%	14%	46%
To greet someone	67%	8%	17%	8%
To talk about intimate topics	63%	4%	18%	15%
To write a text/instant message	51%	9%	21%	21%
To watch movies	26%	4%	21%	49%
To surf the internet	27%	14%	23%	37%
To write a tweet and/or update Facebook status	41%	12%	23%	24%
To listen to songs	45%	3%	26%	26%
To order in a restaurant or a coffee shop	56%	2%	28%	13%
To talk about a scientific topic	33%	13%	29%	25%

that colloquial JA is preferred in most of the listed activities and topics, particularly when discussing politics, telling jokes, insulting others, and expressing anger – a finding that is similar to the Lebanese context (Esseili, 2011).

It is surprising to see that 51% of the respondents preferred JA to read newspapers since except for some news reports that use a mix of standard Arabic and JA, there are no newspapers published solely in a dialect. The selection could have been made in a haste without looking at the difference between JA and standard Arabic, or it could be that they would like to see a newspaper published in JA. The latter explanation does not seem plausible since a majority of the participants (63%) think that standard Arabic should be the medium of instruction. Similarly, very few books are published in JA, so the fact that 42% selected preferring it for reading books is also questionable. Standard Arabic seems to be mostly preferred when discussing literary topics (27%), reading the newspaper (29%), and reading books (26%). Since standard Arabic is the language of published written works, this finding is expected.

The results show that English is preferred when writing emails (64%), completing a job application (46%), surfing the internet (37%), and when watching movies (49%). This finding highlights the instrumental importance of English as a language of business communication and entertainment. For instance, Hollywood movies are extremely popular in Jordan and the rest of Arab countries.

When it comes to gender and age differences, females were more likely to use English or Arabizi than males to talk about taboo and intimate topics; insult, greet, and express anger; and listen to songs, watch movies, read books, and surf the internet. In addition, compared to the other two age groups investigated in the study, participants aged 18–24 were more likely to use Arabizi to talk about literature, to insult and to greet others, to surf the internet, and to tweet or update their Facebook status. They are more likely to use English to complete job applications, listen to songs, watch movies, and read books for fun.

Finally, a relationship exists between participants who attended private schools and universities and had higher household incomes with their language preference for English when engaged in the aforementioned activities and topics. Those who graduated from a private school were more likely to use English when discussing taboo, intimate, scientific, literary, and political topics. In addition, participants with an income over JOD 2,000 and who graduated from a private school were more likely to use English to talk about scientific topics, to complete job applications, to write a text/instant message, to read books for fun, to tweet, and to surf the internet.

Although standard Arabic did not seem to have a place in daily communication with different interlocutors or to engage in various topics and activities, most participants thought that it is an important indicator of Arab identity (81%). Standard Arabic is also viewed as a means to communicate with other Arabs (68%) and to perform religious duties or ceremonies (77%), and it is their way of getting to know about their Arab heritage and culture (80%). In addition, 57% of the participants indicated that it should be the language of instruction of subjects like mathematics and science. Slightly less than half (48%) associated it with formality and prestige.

When it came to taking the questionnaire in either Arabic or English, most participants (74%) chose to take the questionnaire in Arabic while only 26% chose English. This finding is not surprising, especially when considering Jordanians' values and cultural and religious loyalty to Arabic. However, it is interesting when comparing it to a similar study that took place in Lebanon where the opposite was true. Out of 274 Lebanese participants, 76.3% took the questionnaire in English, 21.5% took it in Arabic, and only 2.2% took the French version (Esseili, 2011). When asked to comment on why they selected English or Arabic to take the questionnaire, Jordanian participants' responses were mostly written in Arabic.

Their responses could be grouped into five categories. The first category constituted comments about the fact that Arabic is their native language and the language of daily interaction, and therefore, it makes sense to use it. The second group commented on being Arabs and how Arabic is a source of pride. The third group believed that since Arabic is the language of Islam or the Qu'ran, it should be the language used. The fourth group thought that taking the questionnaire in Arabic would save them time since they are more fluent in Arabic than English; and many commented on their lack of adequate proficiency in English. Finally, there were a few comments on how Arabic is losing ground to English and that is why it was important to use it to take the questionnaire. Here are some example comments that were translated into English: "Arabic is my language and the language of my religion, and I am proud of it"; "I am Arab, and I refuse to use English unless absolutely necessary"; "to protect Arabic from going extinct"; "Because Arabic is being used less with time and this is something that annoys me."

In contrast, participants who took the survey in English indicated that they did so because (1) English was either easier for them or they were more comfortable with it; or (2) they just clicked on the English version automatically; or (3) they were unaware that an Arabic version was available. This last choice seems curious, given that the consent form clearly indicated that the questionnaire was available in two languages and the links were clearly labeled.

Implications for policy, practice, and future research

This study serves as an initial investigation of language preferences of Jordanians when it comes to the use of colloquial JA, standard Arabic, English, and mixing JA and English in spoken and written communication.

Findings revealed that the status of Arabic, both in its standard and colloquial forms, is strong in the Jordanian context. More than 85% of the participants expressed pride in their native language and considered it as a symbol of national, Arab, and Muslim identity. Not a single participant expressed a negative attitude towards Arabic. This study revealed that some of these factors include strong ties to Jordanian traditions and culture, loyalty to Arab identity, and firm religious beliefs. It is worth investigating additional factors or reasons that make Jordanians proud of Arabic and of using it. Other Arab contexts struggling to strengthen the status of Arabic could learn valuable lessons from Jordan.

In addition, the fact that 63% of participants wanted the language of instruction to shift to Arabic is worth investigating, and it should inform policymakers regarding imposing a foreign language to teach mathematics and sciences (as well as other subjects in private schools). English does have an instrumental function in Jordanian society, but that function should be clearly established in the curriculum. To elaborate, in the participants' open-ended responses to the question, "Why did you chose to take the questionnaire in Arabic rather than English", many participants indicated that they did not believe their English was good enough to enable them to understand questions and to answer them with ease. Therefore, educators could focus on building confidence in foreign language skills and on motivating students to learn the language for instrumental purposes. Future research could also focus on ways to improve foreign language education in Jordan. While this chapter did not directly address education, it was obvious from the participants' responses that it is an area worth investigating.

Regarding mixing languages, half of the participants (54%) indicated that they mixed English and Arabic because they did not know the Arabic equivalent of a particular word they wanted to use. Such words are generally related to computers, technology, business, and medicine, among other fields. Although an Arabic equivalent may have been created to all such words (e.g., e-mail, internet, etc.) that have been mostly nativized, it is easier for interlocutors to use the English word rather than the Arabic one since the latter often occurs in standard Arabic and may sound too formal for oral communication. To inform language policy and curriculum developers, future studies could investigate both vocabulary items that do not have Arabic equivalent and those that are nativized. Nativized words should be officially accepted as borrowed words into the Arabic language and treated as such.

Findings also revealed that mixing languages was neither about appearing to be modern and "cool" (65%) nor was it about showing prestige (65%) or trying to fit in within a social group (58%). In fact, 69% of the participants indicated that one of the possible reasons for mixing languages could be due to lack of proficiency in either Arabic or English. Self-reports on proficiency in the two languages, standardized national exam results, and standardized language proficiency test scores (e.g., TOEFL) could all be utilized in future studies. Although these reports have several limitations, they could still be carefully used to improve learners' performance and to inform various stakeholders, including teachers and parents. When drawing appropriate inferences from such reports, it is important to consider the particularities of the Jordanian context and Jordanian users of English.

A final related finding was that mixing languages was popular among Jordanian youth more than among the adult participants, and this pattern may be concerning in the long run. First, given the spread of Arabizi and the mixing of and switching between languages, will Jordanians be able to maintain full bilingualism in Arabic and English in the long run? Second, results also revealed that participants aged 35 and above (who constitute about 30% of the total sample) were less likely to mix languages than those aged 18 to 24, with only 11.8% mixing languages most of the time. Given this finding, would administering the same questionnaire in the future yield a different result in terms of the strong status of Arabic? In other words, such a finding may potentially result in a future generation that is not as attached to Arabic as were the older participants in this study. Thus, it is important to engage in future research in this area and to raise awareness regarding possible future threat to Arabic.

Acknowledgments

This study was partially funded by a grant from Zayed University, Dubai.

References

Abu Ain, N. (2016). A sociolinguistic study in Saham, Northern Jordan (Doctoral dissertation, University of Essex). http://repository.essex.ac.uk/id/eprint/19387.
Al-Ab Al-Kildani, H. (2015, July 8) Nisbat al-ordoniyeen al-masihiyeen al-muqimeen 3.68% [Father Hinna Al-Kildani: The percentage of Jordanian Christians is 3.68%]. *Abouna*. http://www.abouna.org/holylands/الأب-د-حنا-كلداني-نسبة-المسيحيين-الأردنيين-المقيمين-368-انفوجرافيك.
Al-Khatib, M. A., & Al-Ali, M. N. (2010). Language and cultural shift among the Kurds of Jordan. *SKY Journal of Linguistics*, *23*(1), 7–36.
Badawi, E. M. (1973). *Mustawayaat al-Arabiyya al-Mu 'aasira*. Dar Al-Ma'aarif.
Cleveland, R. (1963). A classification for the Arabic dialects of Jordan. *Bulletin of the American Schools of Oriental Research*, *171*(1), 56–63.
Department of Statistics. (2022). http://dosweb.dos.gov.jo/DataBank/Population_Estimares/PopulationEstimates.pdf.
Dweik, B. S., & Al-Refa'i, T. J. (2015). Language shift among the Assyrians of Jordan: A sociolinguistic study. *Journal of Language, Linguistics and Literature*, *1*(4), 101–111.
El-Hassan, S. A. (1978). Variation in the educated spoken Arabic of Jordan with special reference to aspect in the verb phrase (Doctoral dissertation). University of Leeds, England.
Ennaji, M. (1991). Aspects of multilingualism in the Maghreb. *International Journal of the Sociology of Language*, *87*, 7–25.
Esseili. F. (2017). A sociolinguistic profile of English in Lebanon. *World Englishes*, *36*(4). 684–704.
Esseili, F. (2011). English in Lebanon: Implications for national identity and language policy (Unpublished PhD dissertation). Purdue University.
Ferguson, C. (1959). Diglossia. In P. Giglioli (Ed.), *Language and social context* (pp. 232–251). Penguin Books.
Harrison, W., Prator, C., & Tucker, R. (1975). *English-language policy survey of Jordan: A case study in language planning*. The Center for Applied Linguistics.
International Labor Organization. (2015). Employers' perspectives towards domestic workers in Jordan: A qualitative study on attitudes, working condition and the employment relationship. ILO Regional Office for Arab States.
Saidat, A. M. (2010). Language attitude: The case of Jordan. *International Journal of Academic Research*, *2*(6), 235–243.
UNHR. (2022). Total registered Syrian refugees. https://data.unhcr.org/en/situations/syria/location/36.

16

FACTORS CONTRIBUTING TO GAZA PRE-SERVICE TEACHERS' POOR PROFICIENCY IN ENGLISH LANGUAGE

Enas Abdullah Rajab Hammad

Introduction

Issues that motivated the research

English is one of the most widely used languages in the world. According to Crystal (2012), English has been utilized as a mother tongue in many countries, and some countries (e.g., India) use English as an official language. Over 100 countries consider it as the chief foreign language to be taught in schools. More (2019) and Shiyab (2017) also state that English is the language of the world's sports, commerce, technology, media telecommunications, fashion, and glamor.

Due to the global importance of English as a foreign language, many educators are interested in the issues affecting English language learning. In this regard, Renandya (2013) refers to many factors that may impact the success and failure of foreign language learning, such as teachers, teaching materials, learners, and educational environments. First, the teacher factor is related to teacher's personality, language competence, and teaching practices, as teachers can affect the quality of learning process (Liu, 2012).

A second factor is the learner's intelligence, language aptitude, language learning strategies, personality, motivation, attitudes, and language anxiety. An intelligent and motivated student learns more effectively than others with less intelligence and motivation (Arihant Experts, 2021). The learner's personality (including shyness, withdrawal, outgoing nature, and anxiety) also can affect foreign language (FL) learning (Law & Eckes, 2010). Besides, students' attitudes (beliefs, feelings, and intention with respect to FL learning) and motivation (the drive to engage in a particular activity in learning FL) can influence the outcomes of learning (Lalleman, 1996).

DOI: 10.4324/9781003312444-20

A third factor is connected with the teaching materials (i.e., commercial materials, teacher-prepared materials, and authentic print or audio materials) that can provide much of the language input students practice in the classroom (McGrath, 2013). In fact, language materials play a significant role in facilitating language acquisition (Tomlinson, 2011).

A final factor is the learning environment. A friendly, supportive, and non-threatening classroom may enhance students' motivation to learn a language (Liu, 2009). Overcrowded classrooms and atmosphere conditions (high temperature and humidity) may have negative effects on the learning of English as a foreign or second language (EFL/ESL) students' language performance (Arihant Experts, 2021).

Though students' English proficiency is affected by many factors, to date, I have found no researcher examining the conditions influencing Palestinian students' English proficiency. It is noteworthy that some studies (e.g., Assaf, 2015; Hammad, 2016, 2021, 2023; Sha'at, 2017) referred to such students' lack of competence in English language skills. For example, Assaf (2015) described Palestinian university students' problems with English listening, such as their lack of background information and lexical competence. Hammad (2016) also indicated that Palestinian university students' English writing performance was poor. Furthermore, Hammad (2021, 2023) revealed that Gaza university students' proficiency in English reading comprehension was low. Moreover, Sha'at (2017) concluded that the oral proficiency of Al-Azhar University English majors was unsatisfactory.

Additionally, through eight years of experience as an English language teacher trainer in Gaza public and private schools and 16 years of experience as an instructor of English language teaching courses at two universities in the Gaza Strip, I have found that most Palestinian university students do not have the linguistic competence required for communicating in English effectively. However, to the best of my knowledge, no previous studies have examined the reasons behind such weaknesses. Consequently, the study discussed in this chapter explored the factors contributing to the poor proficiency level of pre-service English teachers in Gaza.

Research questions addressed

The study addressed two research questions:

1. How do pre-service teachers in Gaza view the factors contributing to their poor English proficiency?
2. What are the factors contributing to pre-service teachers' poor English proficiency as perceived by the EFL university teachers?

It was essential to define the key terms used in this study, the first of which is *proficiency*: the learner's overall knowledge of the target language, including linguistic, sociolinguistic, and communicative competence (Carrasquillo, 1994). In the present study *proficiency* also refers to the students' appropriate use of English listening, speaking, reading, and writing. That use is based on the students' knowledge of the language domains: phonetics, phonology, morphology, syntax, and semantics.

Pre-service teachers are the students who are enrolled in teacher-training programs and who have no prior teaching experience. The participants in this study were selected from the students in English language instruction programs at Gaza universities.

In this chapter, *factors* refers to facts, situations, or conditions that affect a result (Cambridge English Dictionary, 2022). The study aimed to explore some situations and conditions that contributed to the poor proficiency level of pre-service English teachers in Gaza.

Research methods

Context

English is taught as the main foreign language in Palestinian schools and universities. It is an obligatory subject at both public and private schools, starting from the first grade. Furthermore, academic plans in all Palestinian universities and colleges state that English is a compulsory subject.

There are three types of universities in the Gaza Strip: governmental universities funded by the Palestinian government, public universities funded by non-governmental institutions, and private institutions owned by individuals. The Palestinian Ministry of Education imposes certain entry restrictions on most universities, i.e., completion of year 12 of secondary school with a minimum average grade of 65 %. Faculties of Education in most Gaza universities provide English language instruction programs, which aim to prepare new qualified teachers of English language.

Participants

The sample consisted of 20 fourth-year English language instruction majors (pre-service teachers) selected from three universities. The selection of the fourth-year students was based on the fact that the trainees had studied most of the English courses. It is worth mentioning that while Al-Aqsa University (a governmental university) included more than half of the Gaza fourth-year English language instruction majors (357 male and female students) in the academic year 2021–2022, the rest of Gaza's universities (seven universities) included only 270 English instruction majors. Consequently, I selected 12 male and female participant trainees from Al-Aqsa University and eight participants from two other universities (a public university and a private university). Furthermore, I considered the students' average grades (high achievers, 85%–100%; intermediate achievers, 70%–84%; and low achievers, 69% and below) when selecting the interviewees.

Additionally, I invited six university English teachers to participate in the study. Four teachers were selected from Al-Aqsa University and one teacher from each of the other two universities. These instructors were teaching different English language courses to Gaza pre-service teachers.

Data collection procedures

First, I conducted focus group semi-structured interviews with the 20 pre-service English teachers, with four students in each group. I then interviewed the six English language instructors individually. All participants used their mother tongue in the interviews so as to express their viewpoints clearly. Each interview lasted 40 minutes and was audio-recorded. I subsequently translated the interviewees' comments into English.

Data analysis procedures

To analyze the interview data, I employed the steps described by Lodico, Spaulding, and Voegtle (2006). The interviews were transcribed, coded, and organized into several categories which arose from the data. The following categories emerged from the 20 students' interviews: teachers' use of teacher-centered approaches in English classes, lack of teachers' feedback on students' compositions, teachers' use of reading aloud for comprehension strategy and neglect of silent reading strategy in reading classes, teachers' overuse of the first language (L1) in English literature and reading classes, teachers' neglect of the highest levels of cognitive development in Blooms Taxonomy (analysis, synthesis, and evaluation) in their evaluations, students' lack of opportunities to practice language learning strategies, students' lack of practice opportunities for listening to English audiocassettes, and teachers' bad personality qualities. There were also categories derived from the six teachers' discussions: their own lack of knowledge about the strategies of teaching and learning English, students' lack of linguistic intelligence and aptitude, novice teachers' lack of plans and guidelines for delivering English language courses, and large class sizes. To determine the credibility of the interview data categories, another researcher reviewed and coded the material, and we greed on 90% of the codings.

It is essential to say that I employed two qualitative procedures in this study: semi-structured interviews with the instructors and focus group semi-structured interviews with the pre-service teachers. Hitchcock and Hughes (1995) note that semi-structured interviews can give researchers opportunities to probe, discuss, and expand the interviewees' responses. Based on some relevant references (e.g., Liu, 2009, 2012; Renandya, 2013), I wrote the interview questions (see Appendices A and B) and introduced them to a jury of experts teaching English language courses at Gaza universities. I considered their comments prior to finalizing the instruments' items.

Findings and discussion

The first research question was "How do pre-service teachers in Gaza view the factors contributing to their poor English proficiency?" The interview data indicated that though some students were intrinsically motivated to learn English, they did not achieve high levels of proficiency due to their problems with the English language teachers. The most common issue raised by the trainees was that the teaching styles of their English language teachers were uninteresting and dull, since the teachers used to dominate the lessons, and the students were not allowed to actively participate in the learning process or practice the language productively. The following quotes illustrate this theme.

> Participant 15 (intermediate proficiency): "I often feel bored with the teaching styles of my teachers, specifically English literature teachers. Most of them used to read the materials, including plays, novels, poems, and books aloud without any kind of discussion. What is required from us as students is to listen attentively to them, write their explanations, and memorize theses commentaries for final exams. We rarely practice English speaking in classes."
>
> Participant 1 (high proficiency): "In writing classes, I can remember that the teacher explained the rules of writing a paragraph and an essay like the unity of a paragraph, topic sentences, body sentences, parts of an essay, but she rarely asked us to write an essay. She asked us to write only one essay in 'Writing Two'."

Related to the EFL teachers' writing classes, a majority of the students complained that they were never provided with any kind of feedback on their compositions. For example Participant 18 (low proficiency) said, "My English writing teacher did not give me any correction or comments on any scripts. How then can I recognize my errors or problematic areas in my writing, like grammatical and lexical errors?"

In addition, more than half of the trainees reported that the teachers utilized reading aloud rather than silent reading for developing comprehension strategies in English reading classes. This procedure might have impeded the students' use of English reading strategies. These include metacognitive strategies (e.g., determining the purpose of a task, previewing a passage, changing their reading speed to suit the difficulty of contents, checking their comprehension of textual information, and evaluating their reading strategies) and top-down strategies (such as drawing inferences, predicting, and guessing implicit information from a text). Here is an illustrative comment:

> Participant 3 (high proficiency): "Do not ask me about English reading subskills. What happens is that the teacher reads a passage aloud, translates every sentence into Arabic, and then we discuss the answers of the questions

following the text. At the end of the course, we keep all texts with questions associated with them by heart, as we will be tested in one or more of such reading tasks."

As mentioned in the last excerpt some students felt that a few teachers tended to use the mother tongue excessively for illustrating textual information. It is also obvious that the students were used to employing rote-learning for getting high scores in their English exams. It seems that when assessing the students' proficiency, the teachers considered the lowest level of cognitive development in Bloom's Taxonomy (knowledge, simple recognition, and recall of information) rather than the highest levels of cognitive development (analysis, synthesis, and evaluation).

Over-reliance on memorization techniques also might have prevented the students from practicing other crucial language learning strategies (metacognitive, social, and/or affective strategies) that could enhance their English performance. For instance, Participant 1 (high proficiency) said, "I do not have time to practice the learning strategies you just mentioned. I devote much of my time to recall of information for final exams."

As for the teachers' strategies in English listening classes, some students reported that they rarely practiced listening to native English speakers. According to them, some teachers did not use any audiocassettes in English listening classes, and the students did not have adequate time to practice listening to authentic materials in English at home (television, movies, weather forecasts, and radio programs), due to dedicating substantial time to recalling study materials for exams.

Participant 4 (low proficiency): "I finished the listening courses last year. I did not like them at all. What happened was that the teacher never brought audiocassettes with him. Instead, we read the audio material from the book and answered the questions associated with it. We practiced reading rather than listening in English listening classes!"

Participant 5 (intermediate proficiency): "I cannot understand recorded speech of native English speakers because I am not familiar with native speakers' accents. I rarely watch English films or shows because I used to spend time on studying the learning materials for final tests."

Some other students complained that although some teachers employed tape-recorders in English listening classes, their listening proficiency had not improved due to their lack of familiarity with native English speakers' accents:

Participant 11 (intermediate proficiency): "I was a first-year student when I had my listening courses. My listening teacher asked us to listen to the cassette twice and answer the questions written in the book. Frankly speaking, I could not comprehend anything at that time because the accents seemed to be strange."

In addition, some students criticized some teachers because they felt the instructors lacked the linguistic proficiency necessary for teaching English to university students:

> Participant 2 (intermediate proficiency): "Some teachers have problems with English pronunciation. In order to learn the correct pronunciation of English words I usually look up my dictionary. I wonder why they did not do the same—checking their dictionaries! It happened that a student corrected a pronunciation error committed by one of our instructors. The teacher immediately got angry and threatened the student to fail."
>
> Participant 13 (high proficiency): "As you know, in learning English we should focus on Standard British English and American English. Why then do some teachers use other accents like the Indian accent? When we objected that we could not understand their accents, because they were not Standard, they became furious and said, 'You do not understand anything.' They think that we are stupid!"

Furthermore, the interviews revealed that some teachers were dictatorial and unfriendly. Such personality qualities could increase the students' anxiety, anger, and frustration, which might have a role in impeding the students' linguistic development:

> Participant 10 (intermediate proficiency): "During my university study some lecturers bullied me many times because I provided incorrect answers for their questions in English classes. As a result of that I stopped participating in English classes. They are grinning all the time."
>
> Participant 2 (high proficiency): "I feel angry with some teachers. They do not take our opinions into consideration, and they do not listen to us. If we show our objections, they threaten to fail us."

To sum up, the students' interview data showed that the university English teacher factors were viewed by Gaza pre-service teachers as the most important issues contributing to their poor English proficiency. Such factors were related to teachers' practices in English classes. These included their teacher-centered approach, the lack of feedback on students' compositions, reading aloud for comprehension strategy development, neglecting silent reading in reading classes, overuse of the L1 in English literature and reading classes, neglecting the highest levels of cognitive development in Bloom's Taxonomy in their evaluations, and the lack of practice opportunities for listening to audiocassettes in English classes.

The second research question was, "What are the factors contributing to pre-service teachers' poor English proficiency as perceived by the EFL university teachers?" Individual semi-structured interviews were carried out to answer this question. Most interviewees reported that one main factor contributing to the students' lack of competence in English was that some students did not have adequate aptitude, knowledge, intelligence, and/or the capacity required for majoring in a foreign language:

> Participant T1 (male, 15 years of experience): "Unfortunately, the departments of English in most Gaza universities do not conduct entrance exams. Consequently, we as instructors encounter problems with some unqualified students, who do not have appropriate degrees of linguistic intelligence, aptitude, tendency, knowledge, and capacity needed to specialize in English language major."
>
> Participant T3 (female, 16 years of experience): "Many students majored in English because it can open doors to many career opportunities, such as teaching English at Gaza private and public schools, giving private English classes, working in a translation center, working in translation from home, etc., apart from whether they had the linguistic intelligence required for that or not."

A second factor was related to the teachers themselves. Some teachers stated that they faced obstacles when they taught the English skills courses. Such troubles included the teachers' lack of knowledge about the strategies of English language teaching and learning.

> Participant T5 (female, two years of experience): "I am specialized in English literature, and I know nothing about the methods of teaching and learning language skills, such as reading, listening, writing, and speaking. I need to know about English language sub-skills I should teach and how I should teach them."
>
> Participant T2 (male, 25 years of experience): "You ask me about Bloom's Taxonomy and test objectives! I have never heard of such things. I think that most instructors majoring in English literature do not have adequate knowledge about these issues."

Moreover, two of the instructors felt that overcrowded classes might have affected the students' efficiency in learning English, because students were not provided with ample opportunities to practice English language productively. Besides, the writing teachers expressed their inability to assess students' compositions regularly due to such large class sizes:

> Participant T3 (female, 16 years of experience): "How can students in a class of 60 practice a foreign language communicatively?"
>
> Participant T5 (female, two years of experience): "I know that I should check the students' written works, but how can I score 60–200 essay assignments a week? Of course, I cannot. I wish I could limit the number of students in each class into a maximum of 30."

One of the novice English teachers noted that new teachers at the university were not supplied with any guidelines or plans that could assist them in delivering English language courses:

> Participant T4 (female, two years of experience): "As a new English teacher, I do not have any teaching materials, plans, or even guidelines for teaching my courses in the university. I think that a committee of experienced instructors should determine the teaching materials of English courses and plans for teaching such courses."

In brief, the teachers' interviews revealed their views on the conditions affecting Gaza pre-service teachers' English proficiency. From their perspectives, such conditions were connected with the students (their lack of linguistic intelligence and aptitude), the learning environment (large class sizes), and the teachers themselves (their lack of knowledge about the strategies of teaching and learning English language and novice university teachers' lack of plans and guidelines for delivering English language courses).

Implications for policy, practice, and future research

In this study, I concluded that many teacher trainees had not achieved high levels of proficiency due to their problems with their English language teachers, among other factors. The results showed that the pre-service teachers felt their English teachers at Gaza universities utilized the traditional teacher-centered approach where all class activities were focused on the teachers rather than the students. In this regard, Cornelius-White and Harbaugh (2010) note that a student-centered approach focuses on the student and the learning process, which is innovative when compared to the conventional teacher-centered method. Student-centered learning also employs many active techniques, such as inquiry and cooperative learning. Indeed, Gaza EFL university teachers need to replace the teacher-centered method with a more student-centered approach so that the students can actively participate in the learning process and use English communicatively.

Related to the teachers' practices in English classes, the analyses of the interview data revealed that some teachers did not give the students any kind of feedback on their writing assignments. In line with this result, Hammad (2016) reported that some Gaza university EFL instructors did not provide corrective feedback on the students' compositions. According to Hyland and Hyland (2006), teacher feedback is essential for enhancing second language skills, including writing. Thus, Gaza EFL university instructors are strongly advised to give the students comments on their writing. As a result, the students would be able to recognize their language errors and improve their writing performance.

Furthermore, I found that some English teachers utilized reading aloud rather than silent reading for developing the students' comprehension in English reading classes. This choice might impede the students' use of English reading strategies, such as the metacognitive strategies noted above and top-down strategies (skimming, scanning, drawing inferences, predicting, and guessing implicit information from a text). In this respect, Doghonadze (2017) states that teachers should conduct silent reading accompanied by reading comprehension questions from time to time. For Gaza pre-service teachers to be strategic readers, their English teachers need to give them time to read texts silently and do exercises focusing on reading strategies.

Another result was related to English listening. My findings showed that some teachers rarely utilized recordings of native speakers in the English listening classes. Moreover, some students complained about their inability to comprehend native speakers' accents. One main reason for the students' poor listening comprehension might be students' lack of practice listening to recorded materials of native speakers' voices. In fact, Gaza teacher-trainees need to become familiar with native English speakers' accents, which could be accomplished through watching English movies and videos. Additionally, Gaza university teachers should use authentic listening materials in the English listening classes and urge the students to practice listening to authentic audio-materials at home.

Additionally, the interview data indicated that some students employed rote learning for getting high scores in their English exams. It seems that the teachers considered the lowest level of cognitive development in Bloom's Taxonomy (knowledge, simple recognition, and recall of information) rather than the highest levels of cognitive development (analysis, synthesis, and evaluation) when assessing the students' English proficiency. Gaza EFL university teachers are strongly recommended to use all the levels of Bloom's Taxonomy, specifically the higher levels (i.e., analysis, synthesis, and evaluation) in their evaluations.

Another view expressed by the pre-service teachers in this study was that a few instructors used the mother tongue excessively for illustrating information in English literature and reading classes. Agudo (2012) notes that L1 overuse in second language classes is harmful and unbeneficial, and the L1 should be employed under limited conditions for certain purposes, such as illustrating grammatical rules and explaining abstract words. Therefore, Gaza university teachers should minimize their use of the L1 in classes and urge students to use English communicatively.

In addition, my results indicated that some teachers lacked the linguistic proficiency and pedagogical knowledge necessary for teaching English to university-level students like these teacher trainees. The student interviews also revealed that some teachers were dictatorial and unfriendly. Such personality qualities might increase the students' anxiety, anger, and frustration, which might have hindered their linguistic development. Liu (2012) states that the teacher's personality, linguistic performance, and teaching practices are central to learners' motivation, and that active autonomous teachers can positively affect their students' behaviors and performances. Liu (2009) also claims that the learning environment can impact

English language acquisition. A friendly, supportive, and non-threating classroom may enhance language learners' motivation. Thus, I recommended that Gaza EFL university teachers work on developing their teaching performance as well as their language competence Moreover, expert teachers should provide novice university EFL teachers with plans and guidelines that can assist them in delivering lessons using various English language materials.

A final result of the present study was that both teachers and students complained about large class sizes at their universities. Both groups felt the students were not given any opportunities to practice English language productively, and teachers were not able to assess the students' spoken and written performances due to such overcrowded classes. Arihant Experts (2021) claim that classroom size (overcrowded classrooms) may have negative effects on students' proficiency in English. Additionally, Solheim and Opheim (2019) state that reducing class size can improve academic achievement. Thus, it is advisable for the academic affairs departments at Gaza universities to reduce the number of students in a class to enhance the quality of language teaching and learning.

References

Agudo, J. (2012). One classroom, two languages in contact: Teaching and learning in two languages. In J. Agudo (Ed.), *Teaching and learning English through bilingual education* (pp. 35–60). Cambridge Scholars Publishing.

Arihant Experts. (2021). *English language & pedagogy: CTET & TETs*. Arihant Publications.

Assaf, A. (2015). The difficulties encountered by EFL learners in listening comprehension as perceived by ELC student at the Arab American University, Jenin (Unpublished M. A. Dissertation). Annajah University, Palestine.

Carrasquillo, A. L. (1994). *Teaching English as a second language: A resource guide*. Garland Publishing Inc.

Cornelius-White, J., & Harbaugh, A. (2010). *Learner-centered instruction: Building relationships for student success*. Sage.

Crystal, D. (2012). *English as a global language*. Cambridge University Press.

Doghonadze, N. (2017). Types of reading. In N. Doghonadze (Ed.), *Teaching EFL reading and writing in Georgia*. (pp. 19–24). Cambridge Scholars Publishing.

Cambridge English Dictionary. (2022). Factor. Cambridge University Press. https://dictionary.cambridge.org/dictionary/english/factor.

Hammad, A. E. (2016). Palestinian university students' problems with EFL essay writing in an instructional setting. In H. Abouabdelkader & A. Ahmed (Eds.), *Teaching EFL writing in the 21st century Arab world: Realities and challenges* (pp. 99–124). Macmillan.

Hammad, A. E. (2021). Palestinian EFL university students' problems with the reading sections of the TOEFL Internet-based Test and the Revised TOEFL Paper-delivered Test. *Arab World English Journal*, *12*(3), 51–65.

Hammad, A. E. (2023). Al-Aqsa University students' use of metacognitive reading strategies in relation to their English reading comprehension competence. *An-Najah University Journal for Research (Humanities)*, *37*(2).

Hitchcock, G., & Hughes, D. (1995). *Research and the teacher: A qualitative introduction to school-based research*. Routledge.

Hyland, K., & Hyland F. (2006). Contexts and issues in feedback on L2 writing: An introduction. In K. Hyland & F. Hyland (Eds.), *Feedback in second language writing: Contexts and issues* (pp. 1–18). Cambridge University Press.

Lalleman, J. (1996). The state of the art in second language acquisition research. In P. Jordens & J. Lalleman (Eds.), *Investigating second language acquisition: Studies on language acquisition* (pp. 3–70). Mouton de Gruyter.

Law, B., & Eckes, M. (2010). *The more-than-just-surviving handbook: ELL for every classroom teacher*. Portage & Main Press.

Liu, M. (2009). *Reticence and anxiety in oral English lessons*. Peter Lang.

Liu, L. (2012). The factors facilitating learner's motivation of English learning. In H. Kim (Eds). *Advances in technology and management* (pp. 545–552). Springer.

Lodico, M., Spaulding, D., & Voegtle, K. (2006). *Methods in educational research: From theory to practice*. John Wiley & Sons.

McGrath, I., (2013). *Teaching materials and the roles of EFL/ESL teachers: Practice and theory*. Bloomsburg.

More, L. (2019). *Communicative language teaching*. Lulu Publications.

Renandya, W. (2013). Essential factors affecting EFL learning outcomes. *English Teaching*, 68(4), 23–41.

Sha'at, M. (2017). The oral proficiency of English majors at Al-Azhar University-Gaza. *Journal of the University of Palestine Research & Studies*, 7(3), 1–26.

Shiyab, S. M. (2017). *Translation concepts and critical issues*. Garant Publishers.

Solheim, O., & Opheim, V. (2019). Beyond class size reduction: Towards more flexible ways of implementing a reduced pupil-teacher ratio. *International Journal of Educational Research*, 96, 146–153.

Tomlinson, B. (2011). Introduction: Principles and procedures of materials development. In B. Tomlinson (Ed.), *Materials development in language teaching* (pp. 1–34). Cambridge University Press.

Appendix A: The students' interview

1. Why did you join the *English Language Teaching* program?

    a   Do you like the study of English language?
    b   Do you study English language to get a career?
    c   Do you study English language to help you travel abroad?

2. Do you admire your teachers (language competence, teaching practices, and personal qualities)? Why/Why not?
3. Do you practice English pronunciation in language labs? Why/Why not?
4. Do you practice English language skills effectively during your study at your university? How?
5. Is the learning environment supportive (i.e., classroom size, temperature, humidity)? How?
6. Do you find the study of English language difficult or easy? Why?
7. Are the materials you study suitable (authentic or graded, difficult or relevant to your proficiency level, focusing on all language skills)? How?

Appendix B: The teachers' interview

What are factors that may contribute to the success and failure of Gaza pre-service teachers in English language?

a   Are they provided with helping learning environments? How?
b   Are they hard workers?
c   Do they have the linguistic intelligence and aptitude required for majoring in a foreign language?
d   What problems do you encounter when teaching English courses to pre-service teachers?

INDEX

Abdel Latif, M. M. M. 76–88
Abdelslem, H. 73, 75
Abduh, M. 77, 86, 87
Abdulaal, M. A. A. 133, 142
Abidoye, B. 49, 62
Abu Ain, N. 199, 208
Activity Theory 115–119, 123
Aghagolzadeh, F. 185, 186, 193, 195
Agudo, J. 218, 219
Aimah, S. 134, 142
Akar, B. 24, 25, 34
Akbaş, E. 135, 142
Al Qunayeer, H. S. 160, 169
Al-Rubai'ey, F. 8, 91–102
Al-Ab Al-Kildani, H. 198, 208
Al-Ali, M. N. 199, 208
Alalou, A. 50, 60, 61, 62
Al-Busaidi, K. A. K. 93, 101
Al-Gahtani, S. 99, 102
Algouzi, S. 77, 86, 87
Al-Issa, A. 92, 94, 96, 101
Al-Khatib, M. A. 199, 208
Allami, H. 134, 143
Allen, P. 20, 75
Allington, R. L. 25, 35
Al-Refa'i, T. J. 199, 208
Alsohaibani, A. 178, 183
Alsup, J. 115, 125
Al-Surmi, M. 144–57
Amara, M. H. 184
Anwardeen, N. H. 134, 142
Arani, A. M. 193, 1965

Aridi, R. 2, 23–35
Arihant Experts 219
Aslanabadi, M. 132, 142
Assaf, A. 210, 219
Assassi, T. 11, 12, 131–43
assessing speaking 34, 36–37, 39–45

Badawi, E. M. 199, 208
Bailey, K. M. 1, 3, 19, 20, 34, 81, 87
Baldauf, R. 174, 184
Bal-Gezegin, B. 134, 142
Bandura, A. 104, 113
Bardovi-Harlig, K. 99, 101
Barkhuizen, G. 114, 115, 125
Barrett, B. 160, 169
Baş, M. 134, 142
Beebe, L. M. 92, 94, 101
Beh-Afarin, S. R. 195
Beijaard, D. 114, 125
Bekkari, H. 50, 62
Bell, D. C. 145, 156
Bell, J. H. 145, 156
Ben-Rafael, E. 174, 180, 184
Bentahar, A. 49–63
Benyelles, R. 143
Berry, A. 115, 125, 126
Bielinska-Kwapisz, A. 146, 156
Bigozzi, L. 24, 34
Bithiah, L. 170
Black, K. 163, 168
Blasiman, R. W. 157
blended learning 5, 159, 169

Index   223

Blommaert, J. 175, 184
Blum-Kulka, R. W. 91, 93, 94, 101
Borg, S. 4, 19, 45, 46, 77, 86, 88
Bouchemet, T. 142
Boudersa, N. 135, 142
Boukhari, O. 50, 62
Bourhis, R. 173, 175, 179, 180, 184
Bowen, J. 1, 19
Boyle, J. 162, 169
Breuch, L. A. M. K. 146, 156
Brown, J. R. 185, 196
Brown, P. 93, 98, 102
Bruner, J. 18, 19
Burneikaité, N. 134, 142

Camiré, M. 63
Carino, P. 145, 156
Carrasquillo, A. L. 210, 219
Carter-Tod, S. 148, 150, 152, 153, 156
Casal, J. E. 134, 143
Cenoz, J. 174, 180, 184
ChatGPT 14, 159, 168
Chaudron, C. 6, 19
Cheng, L. 36, 46
Choi, J. 10, 20
Chong, S. W. 160, 169
Chow, J. Y. 63
Christian, D. 34
Clark, V. L. P. 39, 46
Cleveland, R. 198, 208
Cohen, A. 8, 19, 91, 102
communicative language teaching 5, 7, 20,
    64, 75, 78, 87, 121, 220
communicative orientation 5, 20, 64–66, 75
Çomoğlu, İ. 114, 123, 125, 126
Cook, L. S. 127
Coombe, C. 13, 158–170
Corbin, J. M. 41, 46
Cordova, V. H. 126
Cornelius-White, J. 217, 219
Coulmas, F. 173, 184
Couper, M. P. 35
COVID-19 2–4, 12, 19, 23–24, 49–51, 54,
    60–63, 146, 202
Creswell, J. W. 39, 46, 52, 62
Crookes, G. 72, 75
Cross, G. 115, 116, 126
Crusan, D. 42, 46
Crystal, D. 209, 219
Cullen, R. 76, 87
culture 9, 15, 18,91, 94–99, 101–105,
    107–113, 118, 120, 165, 174–176, 178,
    188–189, 190, 192, 199, 205–206

curricular reform 37
curriculum development 24, 193, 195
Curry, N. 169
Curtis, A. 36, 46

Dahmardeh, M. 15, 185–196
Dal Negro, S. 174, 184
Damerow, R. 19
Dang, T. K. A. 115, 116, 126
Danielewicz, J. 114, 126
Darvin, R. 98, 101, 102
Davari, H. 185, 186, 193, 195
Davies, M. J. 38, 45, 46, 73, 75
De Costa, P. 124, 126
Deci, E. L. 104, 113
Deng, F. 76, 87
dialect 1, 16, 38, 198–199, 205, 208
Dikilitaş, K. 114, 123, 125, 126
Dinitz, S. 147, 155, 156
discourse completion task 93
Doghonadze, N. 218, 219
Dörnyei, Z. 66, 75, 99, 101, 104, 113
Dubeck, M. M. 27, 34
Dung, D. T. H. 160, 166, 169
Duruk, E. 133, 134, 142
Dweik, B. S. 199, 208
Dzanic, N. D. 112, 113

early grade reading assessment (EGRA)
    27, 34
Eberharter, K. 46
Eccles, J. 104, 113
Eckes, M. 209, 220
Eckstein, G. 145, 156
el Houche, K. 6, 64–75
El-Hassan, S. A. 199, 208
Elledge, S. R. 145, 156
Elmeski, M. 49–63
Elsheikh, A. 103–113
Elsheikh, E. 114, 126
Enders, D. 145, 156
engagement 1, 4–5, 7, 10, 19, 32, 39,
    41–43, 50–52, 54, 58, 60–62, 86, 115,
    117, 124, 126, 133–134, 137–140, 161,
    188, 192
Engelsen, K. S. 36, 46
Engeström, Y. 115, 116, 123, 126
English 2, 3, 5–19, 23–28, 31–37, 39, 42,
    45, 47–48, 50, 52–53, 56–60, 62, 75,
    71, 74–82, 85–87, 92–101, 103–115,
    118–121, 124–127, 131–136, 138,
    141–148, 154–156, 158, 163, 168–170,
    175–176, 178–183, 185–189, 191–221

English as a foreign language (EFL) 3,6, 9–10, 17, 20, 36–37, 40–42, 45, 47, 49–53, 57–58, 60–62, 64–65, 70, 74–77, 87–88, 92–94, 96–99, 101–104, 106–109, 112–113, 115, 117–120, 125, 127,134, 209–210, 213, 215, 217–220
Ennaji, M. 199, 208
Erling, E. J. 34
Esseili, F. 16, 197–208
Ezzi, N. A. A. 77, 87

Faigley, L. F. 144, 156
Farjami, H. 135, 142
Farrell, T. S. 76, 86, 87
Feak, C. B. 135, 143
feedback 12–13, 17, 40, 47, 101, 118, 122–123, 144–147, 152, 154–155, 159–167, 169–170, 212–213, 215, 217, 220
Felix, J. 62
Félix-Brasdefer, J. C. 92, 102
Ferguson, C. 199, 208
Field, A. 40, 46
Finley, S. 35
flipped learning 60, 62
Flowerdew, J. 12, 19, 131, 141, 142
foreign language teaching 15, 185–186, 189–190,193–194
formulaic language 133, 142
Fotos, S. 76, 87
Freire, P. 124, 126
French 2, 24, 26, 66, 178, 181, 187, 191, 194, 199, 206
Fröhlich, M. 6, 20, 66, 75
Fry, P. G. 127
Fulcher, G. 38, 45, 46
Furukawa, T. 169

Gabriel, J. T. 142
Ganobcsik-Williams, L. 161, 169
Gardner, R. C. 103, 110, 113
Gearon, M. 115, 116, 126
Gebril, A. 46
Golebostan, H. 195
Gomaa, Y. 14, 15, 173–184
González, A. J. R. 126
Gorter, D. 173, 174, 175, 180, 184
Grabe, W. 144, 156
grammar instruction 7, 76–87
grammar pedagogy 87
grammar teaching beliefs 77, 79, 88
Gray, R. 146, 156
Gregersen, T. 20

Grove, A. 27, 34
Gulf universities 175

Haim, O. 36–48
Hakimzadeh, R. 193, 195
Hall, J. K. 97, 99, 102
Hamam, D. 13, 158–170
Hammad, A. E. 17, 209–121
Harbaugh, A. 217, 219
Harding, S. 36, 37, 38, 39, 44, 45, 46
Harrison, W. 197, 208
Hassim, M. 49–63
Hayati, M. 187, 194, 195
Hinkel, E. 144, 156
Hitchcock, G. 212, 219
Hofstede, G. 103, 104, 109, 113
House, J. 101
Hoyt, J. 146, 156
Hughes, D. 212, 219
Human Rights Watch 23, 35
hybrid learning 4, 24, 50, 60, 63, 159, 162
Hyland, F. 217, 221
Hyland, K. 11, 20, 131, 132, 133, 134, 137, 142, 217, 220
Hysaj, A. 161, 162, 169

Ibrahim, A. H. 76–88
Ifadah, M. 142
Ikezawa, T. 169
Ilieva, R. 124, 126
Inbar-Lourie, O. 38, 45, 46
interaction 6, 8, 15, 20, 44, 50–51, 53–54, 58–61, 64–71, 79, 97–101, 115–116, 118, 141–142, 145, 161, 167, 169, 175, 188, 190–191, 197–198, 200, 203, 206
interactional resources 11, 133
interactive resources 135, 139
investment 102, 104, 192
Ishihara, N. 92, 100, 102
Iwasaki, C. 160, 166, 169

Jackson, A. Y. 127
Jalbout, M. 23, 35
Jamiai, A. 50, 62
Jebbour, M. 50, 61, 62
Jenkins, J. 98, 100, 102
Jie, D. 184
Jimoyiannis, A. 160, 166, 169
Johnson, D. 174, 184
Johnson, K. E. 116, 126
Johnson, R. B. 39, 47
Jun, H. G. 160, 161, 166, 167, 169

Kakia, M. L. 195
Kalajahi, S. A. 142
Kaplan, R. 174, 184
Kapto, G. 62
Karimi, M. V. 195
Kassab, S. 2, 23–35
Kasper, G. 8, 20, 91, 92, 101, 102
Kathpalia, S. S. 145, 157
Kee, Y. H. 63
Kehtarfard, R. 186, 195
Khalili, A. 132, 142
Khaniya, T. R. 193, 195
Kim, H. Y. 92, 102
Kim, S. 193, 195
Koh, K. T. 63
Koo, S. L. 145, 157
Kotze, C. 178, 184
Kozma, E. 2, 23–35
Kremmel, B. 38, 39, 46
Krippendorff, K. 30, 35
Kroon, S. 175, 184
Kuo, I. C. V. 76, 87

L2 writing 147, 220
Lalleman, J. 209, 220
Landry, W. S. 173, 175, 179, 180, 184
Lang, W. S. 59, 62
language assessment literacy (LAL) 3, 4, 36–47
language learning 2, 10, 20, 34, 38, 81, 87, 100, 102–108, 113, 117–118, 121, 126, 169, 189, 209–210, 214
language policy 87, 136, 174–175, 179, 183–184, 187, 198, 207=208
language preference 197–198, 200, 202–206
language program 20, 191
language visibility 183
Lantolf, J. P. 100, 102
Law, B. 209, 220
learner identity 8, 91–92, 102
learner-centered approach 67–68, 70, 86, 219
learning loss 27, 32, 34
Lee, H. W. 160, 161, 166, 167, 169
Lee, J. J. 134, 143
Lee, Y. J. 115, 116, 126
Leijten, J. T. 157
Lessler, J. T. 35
Levi, T. 36–48, 38, 45, 46
Levinson, S. C. 93, 98, 102
Li, Y. 135, 143
Lim, P. C. P. 76, 86, 87

Lin, Y. 76, 87
linguistic landscape 14–15, 173, 175, 184
Liu, L. 209, 210, 212, 218, 220
Liviero, S. 76, 87
Locke, E. 104, 113
Lodico, M. 212, 220
López-Gopar, M. E. 125, 126
Luyee, E. O. 142

MacIntyre, P. 20
Mackiewicz, J. 144, 157
Maftoon, P. 193, 195
Malik, F. A. 134, 143
Malone, M. E. 38, 46
Manasreh, M. 144–157
Marandi, S. 134, 143
Markee, M. 72, 75
Martin, E. 35
Martin, J. 35
Martin-Martin, P. 135, 143
Masgoret, A. 104, 113
Mashhadi, A. 187, 194, 195
McBride, K. 2, 23–35
McBride-Chang, C. 30, 35
McGrath, I. 210, 220
McIlwain, M. J. 35
Menard-Warwick, J. 115, 126
Mercer, S. 2, 20
Merhi, M. 2, 23–35
Merriam, S. B. 80, 87, 117, 119, 126
metadiscourse 11, 20, 131, 133–138, 142, 143
metadiscourse markers 132–137, 139–143
Millard, D. J. 76, 87
Mirshamsi, A. 134, 143
Mirzaei, A. 92, 102
Moore, C. 127
More, L. 209, 220
Motaqizadeh, I. 195
Motha, S. 127
motivation 3, 9–11, 17, 50, 94, 99, 103–105, 107–113, 144, 146–147, 157, 161, 167, 194, 202, 209–210, 218, 220
Mouhanna, M. 158, 169
Moussu, L. 144, 152, 157
Mulyadi, D. 142
Murray, B. A. 35
Murray, G. 35
Murray, M. A. 28

Nassaji, H. 76, 87
National Institute of Child Health and Human Development 35
National Reading Panel 25, 33, 35

Neculai, C. 169
Nelson, J. 147, 157
Niiler, L. 144, 157
Nordlof, J. 144, 157
Norton, B. 92, 94, 97, 98, 100, 101, 102, 104, 112, 113, 126
Nunan, D. 1–20, 144, 157, 185–196

Olsen, B. 114, 123, 125, 126
online teaching o 4–5, 13–14, 50–52, 60, 158, 160, 168
Opheim, V. 219, 220
Osam, N. 194, 195
Osman, G. D. 146, 157
Ounis, A. 65, 75
Ounis, T. 65, 75
Oyanedel, J. C. 77, 86, 88

Palmquist, M. 146, 157
Parhizkar, R. 92, 102
Park, G. 127
Patterson, L. 62
peer collaboration 13, 159, 162–163, 165–1266, 168
Pejic, A. 112, 113
Pennycook, A. 125, 126
Pfrenger, W. 144, 157
Phipps, S. 77, 86, 88
Pill, J. 36, 38, 46
Pinto, G. 34
plagiarism 13–14, 140, 159, 163–168
Plakans, L. 46
Plano Clark, V. L. 52, 62
Powers, J. 147, 157
pragmatic choices 7–8, 90, 92, 94, 96–98, 100–101
pragmatic transfer 8, 20, 91–92, 94–95, 99–102
Prator, C. 208
pre-service teachers 17, 210–212, 215, 217, 221
Presser, S. 32, 35
Pressley, M. 25, 35
professional development 4–5, 13, 32, 54, 56, 61, 66, 113, 125–126, 160, 162–163, 166
proficiency 3–5, 7, 9, 11, 17–18, 36–37, 48, 51, 53–58, 65, 82, 85–86, 92, 99, 102, 106, 131, 156, 191, 204, 206–207, 209–211, 213–215, 217–220
Puzey, G. 174, 184

Racine, S. J. 146, 156
Rahmat, N. H. 161, 169
Ramsay, S. 169
Rashidi, N. 186, 195
Rassouli, A. 194, 195
Ravindran, A. 126
Razkane, H. 51, 62
reading instruction 30, 35, 62
Reeves, J. 127
refusal 93–98, 100–102
Ren, H. 135, 143
Renandya, W. 209, 212, 220
resilience 8, 50–51, 107
Rezaie, Y. 193
Richards, J. C. 10, 20, 193, 195
Richardson, J. C. 14, 160, 169
Richardson, L. 14, 20
Roever, C. 99, 102
Rohayati, D. 161, 167, 169
Roth, W. M. 115, 116, 126
Rothgeb, J. M. 35
Rustandi, A. 161, 167, 169
Ryan, R. M. 104, 113

Saeeaw, S. 135, 143
Saeed, M. A. 160, 169
Saidat, A. M. 199, 208
Salem, L. 145, 146, 157
Sam'ah, I. U. 161, 167, 169
Sanchez, H. 77, 86, 88
Santos, M. B. 131, 143
Santos, M. B. D. 135, 143
Sasaki, K. 169
Sato, M. 77, 86, 88
Savić, M. 92, 102
Sayeh, A. Y. 50, 51, 62
Scarino, A. 38, 47
Schiza, E. I. 169
Scollon, R. 179, 184
Scollon, S. 179, 184
self-efficacy 9, 62, 103–105, 107–108, 110, 112–113, 170
Severino, C. 144, 157
Sha'at, M. 210, 220
Sharma, P. 159, 169
Shiyab, S. M. 209, 220
Shohamy, E. 46, 173, 174, 184
Shrestha, R. 2, 23–35
Shulman, L. S. 112, 113
Singer, E. 35
Smagorinsky, P. 115, 123, 127
Smith, K. 36, 46
Solheim, O. 219, 220
Spada, N. 6, 20, 75
Spanoudis, G. 47

Spaulding, D. 212, 220
speech act 7–8, 19, 91, 93–94, 98, 102
Spolsky, B. 174, 183, 184
Strauss, A. L. 41, 46, 108, 113
Struan, A. 169
students' perceptions 145, 147
Sughrua, W. M. 126
Sukimin, I. S. 169
Sultaninejad, N. 195
Supreme Council of the Cultural Revolution 16, 187–189, 194
Swales, J. M. 135, 143

Tada, Y, 169
Taguchi, N. 100, 102
Taguchi, T. 66, 75
Takahashi, T. 101
Talbot, K. 20
Tangkiengsirisin, S. 135, 143
Tarchi, C. 34
Taylor, L. 38, 47
teacher identity 11, 113, 115–116, 118–120, 123–127
teacher training 2, 24, 26, 28, 32, 34, 211
teacher uptake 26, 32
teacher-centered approach 6, 17, 67–68, 84–86, 212, 215, 217
teachers' beliefs 42, 44–48, 50, 59, 70, 72, 74–88, 95, 101, 104, 114, 117, 119, 122, 158
teaching speaking 41–48
Tercero, T. M. 161, 170
Thomas, J. 8, 20, 91, 92, 101, 102
Thompson, I. 144, 157
Thornbury, S. 7, 20
Tisdell, E. J. 117, 119, 126
Tomlinson, B. 20, 87, 210, 220
Tou, N. X. 61, 63
Trent, J. 127
Trumper-Hecht, N. 184
Tsagari, D. 37, 38, 47
Tse, P. 131, 132, 142
Tsiotakis, P. 169

Tucker, R. 208
tutor(s), tutorial(s) 12–13, 142, 144–156
Tuzi, F. 160, 170

Uliss-Weltz, R. 101
Uludag, P. 144–157
UNESCO 4, 49–50, 63, 195
UNHR 208
UNICEF 24, 35, 49, 63
United Nations Development Program 61, 105, 113
Uştuk, Ö, 114–127

Vagnoli, L. 34
Valente, E. 34
Van Waes, L. 146, 157
Van Weijen, D. 157
Varghese, M. 115, 125, 127
Varma, N. F. M. Z. 169
Vera, G. R. 126
Voegtle, K. 212, 220
Vogt, K. 36, 42, 47
Vogt, W. P. 39, 47

Wang, C. 35
Warschauer, M. 162, 170
Wigfield, A. 104, 113
Williams, J. 144, 157
Winder, R. 145, 148, 151, 152, 157
Winter, J. 157
World Bank 23, 25, 50, 61, 63
writing centers 145–149, 152, 154–155

Yahia, E. 103–113
Yamada, Y. 169
Yazan, B. 114–27
Yazdani, M. M. 195
Yin, R. K. 94, 102

Zakaria, M. K. 134, 143
Zarrabi, F. 185, 196
Zarrinabadi, N. 185, 196

Printed in the United States
by Baker & Taylor Publisher Services